A House for all Peoples

A House for all Peoples

ETHNIC POLITICS IN

CHICAGO 1890-1936

John M. Allswang

The University Press of Kentucky

Standard Book Number: 8131–1226–5

Library of Congress Catalog Card Number: 76–119810

Copyright © 1971 by The University Press of Kentucky

A statewide cooperative scholarly publishing agency
serving Berea College, Centre College of Kentucky,
Eastern Kentucky University, Kentucky State College,
Morehead State University, Murray State University,
University of Kentucky, University of Louisville,
and Western Kentucky University.

Editorial and Sales Offices: Lexington, Kentucky 40506

for
my father,
of blessed memory,
and my mother

Contents

Preface

In this book I am trying to investigate the relationship between ethnic pluralism and American politics in an era of political and social change. The study has been worked out over a lengthy period of time, in several stages. Where I originally sought to inquire into a limited area of political analysis and a small number of elections, I have found myself being pushed into a steadily expanding period of time and a wide variety of interrelated sociopolitical and intellectual problems. During the course of this intellectual voyage my conception of the problem has changed considerably; new questions have supplanted older ones. Similarly, new methods and tools have been required to deal adequately with the complexities of the problem.

The analysis of political behavior seems particularly suited to quantitative analytical techniques. The methodological discussion in the Appendix will explain how I have endeavored to build quantitative models for description and analysis. Hopefully a reasonable balance has been struck between the number and the word, with the strengths and weaknesses of each being duly recognized. Certainly the myriad forces involved in mass political behavior in a democratic society require all the analytical devices and insights the historian can bring to them.

Throughout my work I have had the sage counsel of Prof. Samuel P. Hays of the University of Pittsburgh; he has shared with me his shrewd critical insights into specific problems and into historical inquiry generally, and I am most grateful to him. I have also been greatly assisted by the substantive and methodological work of a generation of social scientists, a debt inadequately expressed in the impersonality of footnotes.

I am grateful also to Profs. Richard Jensen of Washington University and Robert Zemsky of the University of Pennsylvania for their effective presentation of insights into the handling of quantitative techniques in history at the 1968 summer program of the Inter-University Consortium for Political Research at Ann Arbor. Despite these and other debts, remembered and forgotten, the responsibility for the substance and method of the study is of course my own.

I would like to thank the following institutions for the facilities and assistance made available to me: the Chicago Historical Society, the Newberry library, the American Jewish Archives, the Midwest Interlibrary Center, the University of Chicago libraries, the Roosevelt University library, the Northern Michigan University library, the library of the National Opinion Research Center, and the Johnson Publishing Company. The Board of Election Commissioners of the City of Chicago, and particularly its warehouse staff, were especially hospitable to my burdensome needs on a number of occasions. And the Department of Economics of California State College–Los Angeles generously made available for my use its Underwood-Olivetti Programma desktop computer.

My wife, Suzanne, has devoted hundreds of hours to this study, in recording countless election returns, calculating endless percentages, helping with the preparation of graphs and tables, proofreading, and relocating data which I was sure was lost forever. Additionally, she has rendered those intangible assistances which are so essential to sanity amidst scholarship; without her this book would not have been completed. My daughter, Eden, contributed her smile.

Part One

Ethnic Politics
1890–1936

I. *Ethnic Groups & Their Politics*

This book comprises a study of the political behavior of the ethnic groups of a major American city from 1890 to 1936. More specifically, it centers on the role of those groups in the rise to unprecedented power of the Democratic party in Chicago. Thus emphasis will be placed on the period from the end of World War I to the first Roosevelt election.

The central questions will be: what was the role of ethnic groups in Chicago's politics, and to what extent was the changing political balance of power attributable to their political behavior? I shall first be concerned with describing ethnic political behavior, and then with uncovering the reasons behind it.

In the course of the inquiry, a number of ancillary questions will also arise. How do ethnic groups make their way into the American political system and into American society generally? What is the key to party and leadership success in the politics of a pluralistic society? What kinds of issues mean the most to American voters? Are local, state, and national politics one, or separate? What are the dynamics of political relationships and are they one-way or reciprocal? Do American political parties have discoverable ideologies or self-conceptions?

A number of methodological questions will also arise. How are political relationships to be understood? How easily determined is the apparently simple question: to which party does a group of people belong? What are the best tools for analyzing political history? Which among a group of variables is most important in the only partly rational phenomenon called political behavior?

The role of urban ethnic groups in bringing about the revival of the national Democratic party by the early 1930s has been appreciated by many historians. Only since they have begun to employ new methods, however, have the origins and extent of this role begun really to be understood. Samuel Lubell, in his pace-setting *The Future of American Politics,* studied the political behavior of American counties and cities and used their demographic variations to explain political development. He pointed to the 1928 election as the great turning point in the revival of the Democratic party.[1] Historians have followed his lead and have examined this development more intensively.[2]

The tools of social science have been central to this more careful understanding of the role of groups in the American political process. These tools have been important in two ways. First, they can be employed in historical analysis, providing more complete and more definite information than was previously available. The use of quantification was a first step, and one that is still being taken.[3] More sophisticated, not necessarily quantitative, social science concepts are now also available and pertinent to political history.[4] And second, historians have been directed toward new foci of investigation—leaving behind traditional and stereotyped foci and moving on to consideration of perhaps more meaningful interrelationships among men and groups of men.[5]

This study attempts to analyze political development through a combination of quantitative and qualitative techniques. Its statistics and methodology are elementary and technically simple, which well suits the

[1] Samuel Lubell, *The Future of American Politics,* 2d ed. (Garden City, N.Y., 1956).

[2] E.g., J. Joseph Huthmacher, *Massachusetts People and Politics, 1919–1933* (Cambridge, Mass., 1959); David Burner, *The Politics of Provincialism* (New York, 1968).

[3] See William C. Aydelotte, "Quantification in History," *American Historical Review* 71 (April 1966): 803–25; and response by Samuel P. Hays and Lee Benson, American Historical Association *Newsletter* 4 (June 1966): 8–16.

[4] On voting, see Bernard Berelson and others, *Voting: A Study of Opinion Formation in a Presidential Campaign* (Chicago, 1954); Angus Campbell and others, *The Voter Decides* (Evanston, Ill., 1954); Paul Lazarsfeld and others, *The People's Choice,* 2d ed. (New York, 1948). An outstanding example of the kinds of conceptual tools afforded is Robert K. Merton, *Social Theory and Social Structure,* rev. ed. (Glencoe, Ill., 1957). On the relevance of these concepts and methods to historiography, see Edward N. Saveth, ed., *American History and the Social Sciences* (New York, 1964).

[5] See Samuel P. Hays, "History as Human Behavior," *Iowa Journal of History* 58 (July 1960): 193–206, and "New Approaches to American Political History, 1880–1920," Paper presented to the meetings of the American Historical Association, Dec. 1961.

complexities of political relationships. Conceptually, the method is somewhat more ambitious, since it employs theories of social science which
have remained largely unapplied. It assumes that the historian is fortu-
nate in his straddling of the humanities and the social sciences, being able
to take from each that which best suits his particular area of analysis. If
this appeals to neither determined methodologists nor implacable tradi-
tionalists, it nonetheless seems ideal for studying the sometimes rational,
sometimes irrational, and always complex dynamics of historical development.

An ethnic group is a group of people held together by a common
culture, which can be national, racial, religious, or simply historic. Here
we shall be dealing with seven ethnic groups whose cultural tie is
basically national: Czechoslovakian-Americans, Polish-Americans, Lith-
uanian-Americans, Yugoslavian-Americans, Italian-Americans, German-
Americans, and Swedish-Americans; one whose cultural tie is basically
racial: Negroes; and one whose cultural tie is religious, with elements
of race and nationality: Jews. On occasion other ethnic groups will be
referred to, for example, the white Anglo-Saxon Protestant American,
whose cultural tie, as the label suggests, is mixed. The ethnicity of each
of these groups is pretty clearly defined. Although there were internal
divisions within them, the forces of integration were almost always
greater than those of disintegration.

The ethnic group is important in politics only if its members make
political decisions as members of the group—that is, when the ethnic
group is a reference group. One has many membership groups; those that
he uses for decision are reference groups.[6] Almost all of an individual's
social decisions are made in a frame of reference produced by the groups
to which he consciously or unconsciously belongs. Different situations
will produce a response in the same individual from various of his
reference groups, depending upon which of the memberships is evoked by
the situation. A further valuable distinction can be made between positive
and negative reference groups.[7] In the former, one is motivated toward
the norms of the group. In the latter, one positively forms counternorms

[6] Robert K. Merton, "Continuities in the Theory of Reference Groups and
Social Structure," in *Social Theory and Social Structure*, p. 307.
[7] Ibid., pp. 282–83, 300–301.

in an effort, again conscious or unconscious, to reject the group (e.g., a German-American who positively decides opposite to what he sees as the German-American reaction to a situation). The reason for the latter is often a desire to feel part of a group to which one does not really belong. An "Uncle Tom" practices negative reference group behavior. In either case, of course, the individual is operating in such a manner that this is his reference group.

These concepts are important in dealing with ethnic political behavior because the ethnic group is a most important reference group, particularly for the first generation, but also, in reduced force, for succeeding ones. Obviously, the ethnic voter need not always vote as a member of his ethnic reference group. He might also vote as a member of the working class, or of the white race, or something else; the situation will tend to dictate this. But there are sufficient reasons to conclude that ethnicity provided the strongest consistent frame of reference for the ethnic voters of Chicago in the first third of the twentieth century. In any event, reference groups strongly influence political behavior. They tend to establish what have been called "political roles"; a German-American, for example, would tend strongly to vote Republican because "Germans have always voted Republican," and so on.[8] This kind of force is as strong as the ethnic tie itself and tends not to be overcome until the political role itself is somehow changed. That is, if a German votes Republican because he feels that "Germans vote Republican," he is not likely to switch to the Democrats unless he is somehow persuaded that the German group is switching. If the ethnic tie has kept him in one line of behavior, he will not tend to vary his behavior unless this variation is reinforced by the ethnic tie. All of this again assumes that the ethnic reference group is primary, and this was generally the case in the period under study. There were times when the variables of a given political situation served to minimize ethnicity in favor of some other reference group, mainly socioeconomic. But such instances were rare. For the immigrant, nothing was so close to him as his immigrant group: his strangeness from the rest of American society was a function of his being a Pole, or German, or whatever. His security came through his group; his communication was through its language; his very survival, even his path to "Americani-

[8] See Lee Benson, "Voting Behavior," in *American History and the Social Sciences*, ed. Edward N. Saveth (New York, 1964), p. 301.

zation," were through his ethnic group.[9] As one contemporary historian of the immigrants put it: "What sort of an American could be made out of one able in any circumstances—worst of all under repressive compulsion, to turn his back upon the tongue, the traditions, and the associations of his fathers."[10] It is quite clear that few immigrants indeed came to America because of a desire to forsake their ancestral culture; this was simply not an important reason for leaving the Old World. And these same forces seem to apply to the non-national (Jewish and Negro) ethnic groups as well.

While the individual ethnic group is most important, it is also possible for the several ethnic groups together to form a single reference group—that of non-Native-Americans (a majority numerically, but psychologically a minority group). It took a particular congeries of circumstances to overcome the forces separating the various groups, but this did come to pass on occasion. For instance, in the 1931 mayoralty campaign, Mayor William Hale Thompson took an essentially nativist position against his rival, Anton Cermak. This resulted in a virtually united ethnic stand against him and the formation, briefly, of what could be considered a reference group of ethnic minorities, from which Cermak profited. A similar phenomenon obtained in the 1928 presidential election. Charles E. Merriam pointed out at the time that if the several ethnic groups were able more often to work together, they would be able to dominate Chicago politics.[11] This they seldom did, but the fact that they came closer and closer to doing so during the 1920s explains the rise of the Democratic party.

There were many things dividing the various ethnic groups, however, and this explains the slowness of their coming to political power proportionate to their numbers. One of these factors was religion. The ethnics of Chicago represented a wide variety of religious beliefs. The Scandinavians were overwhelmingly Lutheran, while the Poles, Italians, Slovaks, and Lithuanians were Roman Catholic. The Germans were fairly evenly

[9] This has been noted by earlier and more recent students of the immigrants: Robert Park, *Old World Traits Transplanted* (Chicago, 1925); John P. Gavit, *Americans by Choice* (New York, 1922); Oscar Handlin, *The Uprooted* (New York, 1951).

[10] Gavit, *Americans by Choice,* p. 38.

[11] Charles E. Merriam, *Chicago: A More Intimate View of Urban Politics* (New York, 1929), p. 137.

divided between Catholics and Protestants, and the Czechs between Catholics, Freethinkers, and nonreligious. Among the Yugoslavs, the Croats and Slovenes were Roman Catholic, and the Serbs were Eastern Orthodox. The Negroes were divided among a variety of Protestant sects and denominations, and the Jews professed varying philosophies of Judaism. Clearly these divisions could lead to intragroup as well as intergroup division.

There was a good deal of interethnic negative stereotyping (i.e., prejudice) on religious as well as cultural grounds. In part this was carried over from the Old Country, as in Polish anti-Semitism, which was common in Chicago.[12] It also found a particularly New World expression in rivalries within the Catholic Church. Both Italians and Poles, for example, complained about Irish control of the churches to which they contributed money, wherein they prayed, and where their children were sent to school. They wanted parishes that were ethnic as well as Catholic, and intergroup conflict resulted.[13] Protestant religious missions to Catholic and Jewish immigrant neighborhoods were sources of further division and resentment.[14]

Religious conflict also divided ethnic groups internally. Part of the lingering disharmony between Czechs and Slovaks stemmed from their religious differences. And within the Jewish community, there arose long-term conflict between the religiously liberal, assimilationist, Older Immigrant German Jews, on the one hand, and the religiously orthodox, particularist, newer immigrant eastern European Jews on the other.[15]

[12] *Narod Polski,* Aug. 6, 1919, and Aug. 18, 1920, quoted in Works Projects Administration, *Chicago Foreign Language Press Survey.* (This survey, which consists of 77 reels of microfilm translations of Chicago foreign language newspapers from the 1880s to the 1930s, was done as a WPA project during the New Deal. It contains much otherwise lost information; hereafter cited as WPA. *Dziennik Zwiazkowy,* May 27, 1919, and June 27, 1919, WPA; Louis Wirth, *The Ghetto* (Chicago, 1928), p. 229.

[13] Francis J. Brown, "Italian-Americans," in *One America,* ed. Francis J. Brown and Joseph S. Roucek (New York, 1946), p. 226; *Przebudzenie,* Oct. 29, 1931, and Nov. 27, 1937, WPA.

[14] See Rev. John Stuart Canning, "An Adventure among the Jews," *Missionary Review of the World* 52 (July 1929): 539–42; Rev. Paul Fox, "Among the Poles of Chicago," *Missionary Review of the World* 48 (Aug. 1925): 610–11. The missionaries had little understanding of the peoples with whom they were dealing, nor had they much respect for their institutions. However well intentioned their efforts, they were bound to be resented.

[15] Bessie L. Pierce, *A History of Chicago,* 3 vols. (New York, 1937–1957),

There were other reasons for interethnic and intraethnic division as well. Shifting loci of population resulted in one ethnic group moving in on another, and conflict; this reached its most sanguinary level when the adolescents of the respective groups engaged in real warfare to establish claims to a "territory."[16] Varying rates of assimilation into American society and of economic advance also produced suspicion and animosity between groups. This was particularly evident among the Poles, who were one of the slowest groups to assimilate, and the group most outspokenly prejudiced against others.[17]

There was considerable anti-Negro prejudice among the white ethnic groups, and it was reciprocated by Chicago's Negroes, who often resented the gains made by "non-American" immigrants at the expense of the still-oppressed Afro-American.[18] Chicago experienced a race riot in 1919, triggered when a Negro boy swam across the invisible line that separated the implicit white and colored parts of a south side beach. Ultimately thirty-eight people died in the riot, and much of its impetus came from the social, economic, and residential conflict between Afro-American and newer immigrant.[19]

Thus there were centrifugal as well as centripetal forces at work within each ethnic group, and there was little natural intersympathy among the several groups. But the forces which reinforced group integrity were much greater than those which operated against it. It has frequently been noted that many American nationality groups really developed their sense of nationality only after arriving in the United States. The Sicilian and the Tuscan, for example, had little in common in Italy and could

---

2:23–24; 3:38–42. Maintenance of separate clubs, hospitals, and other institutions demonstrated the extent of this division by the early twentieth century. And the rise of Zionism among the eastern European Jews furthered the conflict. See Philip P. Bregstone, *Chicago and Its Jews* (Chicago, 1933), pp. 88–90.

[16] Harvey W. Zorbaugh, *The Gold Coast and the Slum* (Chicago, 1929), p. 160.

[17] Park, *Old World Traits*, p. 219; *Narod Polski*, Aug. 6, 1919, and June 8, 1921, WPA. Such intergroup rivalries, and some intragroup ones, point to the applicability to ethnic group history of the concept of relative deprivation.

[18] E.g., Chicago *Defender*, Sept. 27, 1924, p. 12. See also St. Clair Drake and Horace R. Cayton, *Black Metropolis* (New York, 1945), ch. 16.

[19] Chicago Commission on Race Relations, *The Negro in Chicago: A Study of Race Relations and a Race Riot* (Chicago, 1922), pp. 1, 3, and 1–51 passim; Drake and Cayton, *Black Metropolis*, pp. 65–69; *The World's Work* 45 (Dec. 1922): 131–34.

hardly even understand one another; but in America they found that they had, relatively speaking, a great deal in common, and they became Italians. Czechs and Slovaks were better able to find common ground in Pittsburgh than at home, and thus from afar played an important role in the founding of Czechoslovakia. Irish-American nationalism flourished in the United States, and the American Irish played an equally important role in the quest for independence of their homeland. The sense of "Scandinavian"—denoting a common culture for Swede, Norwegian and Dane—likewise flourished in the United States. And these are but a few indications of the strength of the ethnic tie in America, and of the fact that the American experience reinforced ethnicity.

Moreover, the forces arguing for interethnic cooperation also became more and more powerful as time went by and as the ethnic conflict of interest with the Native-American became more evident. The political issues which most interested the ethnics, for example, found them largely together in opposition to the Native-Americans. Their quest for political power relative to their numbers required that they work together to succeed. Political leaders arose who understood this, and built upon it. Only in this way could ethnic groups assert themselves in Chicago politics.

In dealing with the political behavior of ethnic groups, it is important to understand how the individual ethnic voter arrived at his conception of a given political situation. That is, we must inquire into the channels of communication through which he was informed and his opinions influenced. By and large these channels reinforced ethnicity, because they consisted of ethnic group influentials and the ethnic press.

The ethnic press (foreign language except in the case of the Negroes) was important in a number of ways. There has been little dispute among scholars about its influence on the immigrant: it provided the breadth and depth of his information and interpreted America to him.[20] Even where the editorial views of the paper were not accepted by the mass of readers, and this did happen, the readers were nonetheless affected because the ethnic journal was often their only source of contact with the world. Devotion to the mother tongue contributed to this loyalty. As Robert Park, the first major student of the ethnic press, put it:

[20] Oscar Handlin, "The Immigrant and American Politics," in *Foreign Influences in American Life,* ed. D. F. Bowers (Princeton, N.J., 1944), p. 88.

"Mother tongue is the natural basis of human association and organization."[21] Or, as an immigrant woman said to a social worker during the anti-foreign language hysteria of the First World War, "Why, Miss McDowell, to take my language away from me is to snatch the cradle I was born in from under me."[22] Even those immigrants who had learned English (or those whose first language was English, as with the Negroes) continued to read the ethnic press because they had emotional ties to the language and/or because this was the best source of news about the group.[23] This combination of linguistic and cultural ties resulted in a closer feeling of mutuality between the ethnic press and its readership than was the case with the metropolitan press.[24]

Whether or not the foreign language press contributed to or detracted from the Americanization of the immigrant is moot. Assimilation did require the ability to speak English, and since the foreign language press reinforced use of the mother tongue it could be seen as retarding assimilation.[25] But in fact the ethnic press generally urged the immigrant to learn English and become a citizen, and devoted much of its space to the American news that helped the immigrant come to terms with America.[26] A survey of readers of the Yiddish press in New York in 1920 found that

[21] Robert E. Park, *The Immigrant Press and Its Control* (New York, 1922), p. 5.

[22] Manuscript essay, "The Foreign Born," Mary McDowell Papers, The Chicago Historical Society.

[23] Mordecai Soltes, *The Yiddish Press: An Americanizing Agency* (New York, 1924), pp. 39–40. Also, on the popularity and influence of the ethnic press: Mary McDowell, "The Foreign Press and Its Influence on Foreign Populations," Mary McDowell Papers; Drake and Cayton, *Black Metropolis,* pp. 410–11; Reuel G. Hemdahl, "The Swedes in Illinois Politics: An Immigrant Group in an American Political Setting" (Ph.D. diss., Northwestern University, 1932), p. 448; Giovanni Schiavo, *The Italians in Chicago* (Chicago, 1928), p. 104; *Denni Hlasatel,* April 9, 1918, WPA; Alex Gottfried, *Boss Cermak of Chicago: A Study of Political Leadership* (Seattle, Wash., 1962), pp. 41–42. A contrary view is expressed in Gustave R. Serino, "Italians in the Political Life of Boston" (Ph.D. diss., Harvard University, 1950), pp. 191–93.

[24] *The Interpreter* (Foreign Language Information Service), 3:5 (May 1924), pp. 3–8.

[25] See Stanley Lieberson, *Ethnic Patterns in American Cities* (New York, 1963), pp. 8, 16; Handlin, "The Immigrant and American Politics," p. 88.

[26] *The Bulletin* (Foreign Language Information Service), 1:8 (Nov. 1922), pp. 3–10; Joseph S. Roucek, "The Foreign Language and Negro Press," in *One America,* ed. Francis J. Brown and Joseph S. Roucek (New York, 1946), p. 371.

over 86 percent were either citizens or had taken out their first papers.[27] This did not indicate an antiassimilationist effect from reading the Yiddish press.

The period 1890–1936 was really the high point of the ethnic press, especially for the Newer Immigrants. The 1920s saw the great majority of them emerging from alien to citizen status and participating in American politics in unprecedented fashion; the ethnic press played a central role in this process.[28] One thousand and fifty-two foreign language newspapers were published in the United States in 1920, in thirty-one languages, with between nine and ten million readers.[29] The political world of the ethnic in this decade was very much defined by the interests and coverage of his native-language newspaper.

There was tremendous variety in the newspapers themselves, in terms of professionalism, coverage, disinterestedness, and honesty. Many of these papers were very marginal, and the mortality rate was high.[30] They were often personal, reflecting the interests and views of their owners; and they could be bought or otherwise influenced.[31] Their political sophistication varied considerably. The Older Immigrant papers, by the 1920s, had already undergone a lengthy process of attrition, and those remaining were fairly sophisticated, issue-oriented, and impersonal—in short, business newspapers. Among the Newer Immigrant papers there was much more variety; some were quite good and some very poor, with the majority somewhere in between. For all ethnic groups, however, the papers that succeeded were those which were the most ethnocentric, which put the group and its interests first at all times. To lose sight of the group and its goals was disastrous to an ethnic newspaper, while to think and act always in terms of the group was the path to success. Most Chicago ethnic newspapers clearly understood this.

[27] Soltes, *The Yiddish Press,* p. 47.

[28] E.g., Edmund G. Olszyk, *The Polish Press in America* (Milwaukee, Wis., 1940), p. 76.

[29] *The Bulletin,* 1:3 (May 1922), p. 8.

[30] Ibid.

[31] One of the most famous instances involved the American Association of Foreign Language Newspapers, 1908–1918, under Louis L. Hammerling, which apparently put economic pressure on foreign language papers as a "service for the national Republican Party" (Park, *The Immigrant Press,* ch. 16). There was also an alleged effort by the Wilson administration to pressure foreign language papers in the 1918 campaign (Chicago *Tribune,* Nov. 1, 1918, p. 6).

Whether the ethnic press led or followed its readers is also moot. Probably it did neither, or both; by anticipating correctly it could lead; if it anticipated wrongly, it followed or left course. Its influence was greater when it was able to feel its way ahead of its readers, and in that way it led. But the ethnic press, like the metropolitan press, could not lead people where they saw no advantage in going. It did play a stronger leadership role in terms of interethnic cooperation. Well before the ethnics themselves were cooperating, the ethnic newspapers had got together in matters of mutual interest—in anti-Prohibition activity, for example. There were feelings of mutuality among the papers of the several groups, and the same people sometimes wrote for papers of more than one group. In this sense of commonalty with other ethnic groups, the ethnic press did play a leadership role in a most significant ethnic development.

The flow of information and of influence is not necessarily through the printed word. Indeed, particularly in the realm of politics, participation and influence involve interpersonal interaction to a considerable extent, and this interpersonal flow of influence is often more powerful than that obtained in the relative isolation of reading.[32] Personal influence has been seen as moving through a "two-step flow of communication," wherein the mass of any group are influenced by vocal intercourse with a relative few "influentials," who, in turn, have obtained their opinions from the media or elsewhere.[33] That is, the majority of people are less influenced by what they read in the papers about rival political candidates or parties, than by the spoken opinions of other people whose views they respect. It is important for our purposes to understand that the influentials for an ethnic group member would tend to be other members of his own group: "For leadership in political discussion people mainly turn to others like themselves."[34] "Social distance" intervened between the ethnic voter and a nongroup political worker, for example, while there was no such separation with a member of his own group who was reputed to be "in the know" in a given area of interest.[35]

[32] M. Rosenberg, "Dimensions of Political Apathy," in *Political Behavior: A Reader in Theory and Research,* ed. H. Eulau and others (Glencoe, Ill., 1956), p. 161.

[33] Elihu Katz and Paul Lazarsfeld, *Personal Influence: The Part Played by People in the Flow of Mass Communications* (Glencoe, Ill., 1955), chs. 14, 15.

[34] Berelson and others, *Voting,* pp. 109, 168–70.

[35] Ibid.; and Zorbaugh, *Gold Coast and Slum,* pp. 216–17.

Robert K. Merton's concept of "local" and "cosmopolitan" influentials is somewhat difficult to apply in the ethnic political context.[36] The same people and organizations tended to be active in all political spheres among the immigrants of Chicago. Where purely local ethnic influentials probably distinguished themselves was at the ward and precinct level, for minor but important offices and jobs about which there unfortunately is little information; this would conform with Merton's conclusion that local influentials relied more on personal contact, and cosmopolitan influentials on organizations.[37] This particular concept, which is very helpful in determining patterns of influence, cannot be helpful here, both because of the nature of ethnic interpersonal relations and because of the lack of documentation about interaction at the person-to-person level.

These concepts do reinforce the importance of the ethnic group per se and help explain why I will devote considerable attention to the political preferences and beliefs of leaders and leadership organizations among the several groups. This is not, however, to minimize the importance of the ethnic press. Indeed, the "two-step flow" hypothesis can be bent to allow the ethnic press to fill the role of influential. That is, the very personal ethnic press, upon which many ethnics for language reasons had to rely, served often as the "influential" to its highly related readers, interpreting to them the metropolitan press and American life in general.

[36] Merton, "Patterns of Influence: Local and Cosmopolitan Influentials," in *Social Theory and Social Structure,* pp. 387–420.
[37] Ibid., pp. 397–98.

II. *Chicago's Ethnics & Their Politics to 1917*

Chicago, like other great American cities, is a city of immigrants. And like other American cities by the onset of the twentieth century, it was no longer Anglo-Saxon. Chicago's ethnic groups arrived at varying points in time, and from different cultures, but their reasons for coming were generally the same: a better life. As a later writer put it, Chicago was "never a city of brotherly love . . . Chicago was born out of lust for furs and land." And it was, "like Carthage, founded by cheating the natives out of the land."[1]

The first permanent settler in Chicago was a West Indian Negro, Jean Baptiste Point de Sable, who resided there from 1779 to 1796. After he left, more than a century passed before many more Negroes arrived. But other groups did come in the interim. In the 1830s, when Chicago was becoming a city, and its population was climbing from the dozens into the hundreds, and then into the thousands, its citizens were largely Anglo-Saxon, French-Canadian, and half-breed Indian. Even then it was cosmopolitan. "Long John" Wentworth, an early journalist and politician, said of the 1830s: "We had people from almost every clime, and almost every opinion. We had Jews and Christians, Protestants and Catholics and Infidels. . . . Nearly every language was represented. Some people had seen much of the world and some very little. Some were quite learned and some were ignorant."[2]

Of the ethnic groups that would be important in Chicago's history, the first to arrive in large numbers were the Irish, in the early 1840s. In Chicago, as elsewhere, they were immediately active in politics.[3] Shortly thereafter, the Scandinavians began to trickle in. David Johnson, a Norwegian, came to Chicago in 1834 to run the press of John Wentworth's Chicago *Democrat,* the city's first newspaper.[4] In the late 1840s and then the 1850s, the Scandinavians continued to arrive; there were an estimated 1,000 Swedish families there by 1850. Chicago rapidly became the center of things Swedish in the United States.[5] The Germans, too, began to arrive about this time, in a stream that grew steadily larger. They were numerous enough to form their own societies in the mid-1850s and to support their own press in the 1860s.[6] German Jews also came. In 1847 Chicago's first synagogue was founded, and Chicago's Jews were numerous enough to organize their own company for the Civil War.[7]

These are the groups generally referred to as the "older" or "earlier" immigrants, as distinguished from the "newer" or "recent" immigrants from southern and eastern Europe in the late nineteenth and early twentieth centuries. With these early groups Chicago grew from a hamlet of forty or fifty people in 1830, to a city of over 4,000 in 1837, and a bustling young metropolis of 30,000 by 1850. In 1850 its population was over 50 percent foreign stock (foreign-born or native-born of foreign or mixed parentage), and that figure would increase as the century wore on.[8] On the eve of the Civil War, 20 percent of the city's population had been born in Germany, 18 percent in Ireland, and over 2 percent in the Scandinavian countries.[9] In Chicago, as elsewhere, the immigrants were not always welcomed by Native-Americans (native-born white of native-born white parentage). The Catholicism of the Irish, and the liberalism of the German "Forty-Eighters," as well as the drinking habits of both, led to a rise of Know-Nothingism in the mid-1850s; the nativists swept the city elections in 1855.[10] Their crusade soon died out, but its sentiments and resentments lived on.

[1] Edgar L. Masters, *The Tale of Chicago* (New York, 1933), pp. 13, 65.

[2] Quoted in Lloyd Lewis and Henry J. Smith, *Chicago: The History of Its Reputation* (New York, 1929), p. 31.

[3] Bessie L. Pierce, *A History of Chicago*, 3 vols. (New York, 1937–1957), 1:179.

[4] O. M. Norlie, *History of the Norwegians in America*, pp. 153–54, WPA.

[5] Pierce, *A History of Chicago*, 1:185; Hemdahl, "The Swedes in Illinois Politics: An Immigrant Group in an American Political Setting" (Ph.D. diss., Northwestern University, 1932), p. 152 n; Gustave E. Johnson, "The Swedes of Chicago" (Ph.D. diss., University of Chicago, 1940), p. 74.

[6] Masters, *Tale of Chicago*, pp. 134, 157.

[7] Pierce, *A History of Chicago*, 1:184; Lewis and Smith, *Chicago*, p. 142; Louis Wirth, *The Ghetto* (Chicago, 1928), p. 165.

[8] Pierce, *A History of Chicago*, 1:179.

[9] Ibid., 2:482.   [10] Lewis and Smith, *Chicago*, pp. 71–73.

TABLE II:1   *Time of Arrival and Peak Year of Immigration of Immigrants in the United States in 1930 (Percentage of those coming by 1930)*

Country of origin	Arrived by 1900	Arrived 1900–1914	Arrived 1914–1920	Peak year of immigration
Germany	61	16	23	1882
Sweden	55	29	16	1882
Russia*	22	61	17	1913
Czechoslovakia	31	54	15	1921
Poland	19	66	15	1921
Lithuania	18	74	8	(n.a.)
Italy	18	56	26	1907
Yugoslavia	9	72	19	(n.a.)

Source: F. J. Brown, "Meaning and Status of Minorities," in *One America*, ed. F. J. Brown and J. S. Roucek (New York, 1945), pp. 9, 636.

*Primarily Jews.

These same groups continued to dominate immigration into America and Chicago until near the end of the century. Although they continued to come after that time, their numbers paled beside those of the Italians, Poles, Czechs, Lithuanians, Yugoslavs, Yiddish-speaking Jews, and others from southern and eastern Europe. These groups arrived in ever-increasing numbers from the 1880s to the onset of the First World War, and then from the war's end to the coming of immigration restriction in the 1920s. Table II:1 indicates the relative times of arrival of most of the ethnic groups which are included in this study.

It was in this late period, too, that Negroes began to pour into Chicago, particularly during the Great War, when employment opportunities were unusually bright.[11]

In 1890, when Chicago first reached a population of one million, 78 percent of its population was of foreign stock, and 20 percent was Native-American. Tables II:2 and II:3 give the numbers of foreign born

[11] Roi Ottley, *The Lonely Warrior: Life and Times of Robert S. Abbot* (Chicago, 1955), p. 9.

TABLE II:2 *Ethnic Groups in Chicago, 1900 (Chicago population = 1,698,575)*

Group	Foreign born	Second generation[*]	Total ethnic group percentage of city population
Austrians	11,815	19,369	1.7
Bohemians	36,362	76,480	6.6
Danes	10,166	16,563	1.6
Germans	170,738	416,755	34.5
Hungarians	4,946	6,966	0.7
Irish	73,912	215,385	17.0
Italians	16,008	26,810	2.5
Norwegians	22,011	41,055	3.7
Poles[†]	59,713	109,711	10.0
Russians	24,178	38,589	3.7
Swedes	48,836	100,176	8.8
Negroes	30,150[§]	—	1.8
White Ethnics	585,254	727,341	77.3

Source: *Twelfth Census of the U.S., 1900.*

[*]Includes native-born children with both parents born in same foreign country, and with one parent born in a foreign country and the other native-born; does not include children of two foreign-born parents born in different countries. The figures for White Ethnics include all foreign-born and all native-born with one or both parents born in foreign countries.

[†]Includes immigrants—and children thereof—who declared "Polish" as nationality, though coming from Austria, Germany, Russia, or unknown country.

[§]Total Chicago Negro population.

TABLE II:3   *Ethnic Groups in Chicago, 1930 (Chicago population = 3,376,438)*

Group	Foreign born	Second generation[*]	Total ethnic group percentage of city population
Czechoslovakians	48,814	73,725	3.6
Danes	12,502	16,193	0.8
Germans	111,366	266,609	11.2
Hungarians	15,337	15,090	0.9
Italians	73,960	107,901	5.4
Lithuanians	31,430	32,488	1.9
Norwegians	21,740	30,968	1.6
Poles	149,622	251,694	11.9
Russians	78,462	91,274	5.0
Swedes	65,735	75,178	4.2
Yugoslavians	16,183	16,108	1.0
Jews	325,000[†]	———	9.6
Native-Americans[§]	943,301	———	27.9
Negroes	233,903[Δ]	———	6.9
White Ethnics	842,057	1,332,373	64.3

Source: *Fifteenth Census of the U.S., 1930,* and *Census of Religious Bodies, 1926.*

[*]Includes native-born of foreign or mixed parentage.

[†]All Jews, regardless of country of origin.

[§]Native-born white of native-born white parentage; figure is for all Native-Americans in Chicago.

[Δ]All Negroes.

and second generation of the major ethnic groups in Chicago in 1900 and 1930 and their percentage of the city's population.

The balance among the ethnic groups changed over time. In 1900, for example, the Germans comprised over 34 percent of the city's population, the Irish 17 percent, and the Scandinavians over 14 percent. By 1930 the Germans comprised only 11 percent and the Scandinavians 7; while the Poles, Italians, and Negroes, who were respectively 10, 2.5, and less than 2 percent in 1900, had risen by 1930 to 12, over 5, and 7 percent of the city's population.

By the end of the First World War, Chicago was the third most "foreign" city in America, after New York and Boston. Seventy-two percent of its people were foreign stock in 1920, and this would decline only to 64 percent by 1930. Add to the immigrant groups the rising number of Negroes, and it is clear that the number of Native-Americans was slight indeed (about 24 percent in 1920, 28 percent in 1930; some of whom were third generation and still quite "ethnic"). Chicago was also distinguished by the variety of immigrant groups in its population; more than perhaps any other American city, Chicago had sizable colonies of many different groups. It was the largest Scandinavian, Polish, Czech, Serbo-Croat, and Lithuanian city in the nation; the second largest German, Greek, Slovak, Jewish, and Negro city; and the third largest Italian.[12]

The ethnics of Chicago moved steadily, though not precipitously, to citizenship and participation in the political process. There was some intergroup and intragroup variation in this aspect of Americanization, but the potential fruits of participation in the political system were obvious to group leaders.[13] As Table II:4 indicates, once the ethnics became citizens

[12] Paul F. Cressey, "The Succession of Cultural Groups in Chicago" (Ph.D. diss., University of Chicago, 1930), p. 209.

[13] Harold F. Gosnell estimated that the naturalization process took about ten years ("The Chicago Black Belt as a Political Battleground," *American Journal of Sociology* 39 [Nov. 1933]: 331). A study of the length of time between arrival in the United States and filing of first papers, however, indicates a somewhat longer period: Irish—9.6 years; Russians—9.6 years; Danes—10.2 years; Scots—10.6 years; Swedes—13.1 years; Germans—11.9 years; Italians—11.4 years; English—11.7 years (John P. Gavit, *Americans by Choice* [New York, 1922], pp. 241, 245). This would indicate that although there were differences between newer and older immigrant groups in terms of time taken for cultural assimila-

TABLE II:4 *Nonvoting in Chicago Mayoral Election, 1923*

Group	Percentage of Chicago voting population	Percentage of nonvoters
Native Americans	25.0	25.0
Negroes	6.0	6.6*
Native White of foreign parentage	39.0	25.0
Naturalized foreign born:	30.0	37.0
Irish	3.0	2.3
German/Austrian	7.0	7.0
Scandinavian	4.0	5.7
Russian	3.0	5.2
Polish	3.2	5.4
Italian	1.3	5.0
Czech, Slav, Hungarian[†]	2.9	4.5

Source: C. E. Merriam and H. F. Gosnell, *Non-Voting: Causes and Methods of Control* (Chicago, 1924), p. 6. Based on a sample of 6,000.

*The Negro figure is not very reliable.

[†]The writers' definition of "Slav" is not clear.

they all tended to vote at roughly the same level of participation. The many immigrants who had never voted before coming to America learned the advantages of doing so here. There is no great difference in likelihood to vote on the part of newer immigrant group citizens as opposed to those of the more established groups; the second generation of immigrant families were the most likely to vote of all groups of voters. This table is based on one election only, however, and in fact rates of nonvoting varied considerably from election to election. The majority of ethnics were neither unduly optimistic nor unduly apathetic about the

---

tion, the same phenomenon did not prevail in terms of their awareness of the advantages of citizenship.

potentials of voting; when there seemed reason to do so, they voted, and when not, they stayed home. These levels of participation could be important.

Although differences in time taken for naturalization and in rate of voting among citizens of the various groups were not large, the differences in time of arrival are very important for analytic purposes. Indeed, in considering the voting of immigrant groups before the First World War it is necessary to remember also the proportion of members of these groups who were naturalized and thus able to vote. One could, for example, find an area whose population was perhaps 60 percent Polish in the 1890s, in which the majority of voters was non-Polish, because the Poles were such recent comers. This is an important qualification for all prewar voting studies of immigrant groups.

Table II:1 showed the time of arrival and peak year of immigration for major immigrant groups in the United States. There is no reason to believe that Chicago's immigrants varied from the norm. If to these dates of arrival we add a conservative minimum average time for naturalization of ten years,[14] it becomes obvious that several of the groups were voting in small numbers before the War. For example, 81 percent of the Poles, 82 percent of the Lithuanians and Italians, 91 percent of the Yugoslavs, 78 percent of the Russians, and 69 percent of the Czechoslovakians arrived only after 1900, some of them well after. Those who arrived at the beginning of the century would be starting to vote only in its second decade. And accepting the logical conclusion that most of these latecomers arrived during the peak years of immigration (ca. 1905–1913), it is equally obvious that many, perhaps the majority, were not voting until during or after the First World War.

In 1920, for example, over 70 percent of Chicago's foreign-born Irish, Swedes, Germans, and Norwegians were naturalized; but only 57 percent of the Czechs, 34 percent of the Poles, 35 percent of the Italians, 45 percent of the Russians, and 25 percent of the Lithuanians were naturalized.[15] As that decade progressed, these differentials lessened considerably.

[14] Ibid.
[15] Gosnell Materials (unclassified), Charles E. Merriam Papers, University of Chicago.

These figures cannot be ignored in studying ethnic political behavior before the War, and explain the variant methodology and more general approach I shall employ for these early years. Indeed, the simple facts of time of arrival and naturalization preclude any definitive conclusions about the political loyalties of the newer immigrants before the 1920s— there were simply too few of them voting. Newer immigrant political coalitions could be formed only in the 1920s, and thus I shall concentrate on that period.

Data on 1890–1917, then, can only suggest the way in which the ethnics of the time seemed to be leaning politically and the political proclivities of the *areas* in which these groups settled. These suggestions are significant, however. They tell us about the milieu of political origination of the several ethnic groups which influenced their earliest political frames of reference and helped establish the political inertial forces which would lead them to one party or another.

Chicago's voting behavior in the period of large-scale new immigration was a mixed one: the Republicans were more successful nationally and the Democrats locally. Cook County, which consisted of Chicago and its suburbs, was politically the least stable county in Illinois, partially because of the fluctuating loyalties of its ethnic groups. New immigrants tend to favor the party in power, since it is the organization most able to minister to their needs. The county tended to be more Republican than the rest of the st^te when the Republicans were winning, and more Democratic when the Democrats were winning.[16] Chart II:1 pictures national and state voting for Illinois, Chicago, and the mean of seven Chicago ethnic groups, 1890–1916.[17]

Of the twenty-five elections studied for 1890–1916, the Democrats won ten, the Republicans nine, the two parties shared the victory in three,

[16] Milton J. Bluestein, "Voting Tradition and Socio-Economic Factors in the 1936 Presidential Election in Illinois" (M.A. thesis, University of Chicago, 1950), pp. 60–61.

[17] The "ethnic mean" used here consists of the mean voting percentage of the mean voting percentages of each of the seven ethnic groups studied in this chapter. Thus each group, regardless of its actual size or the size of the sample studied, has equal weight in the ethnic mean. A complete description of the sample can be found in the Appendix.

and other parties won three.[18] In presidential elections, the Democrats carried the city only once, in 1892, while the Republicans carried it five times, and Progressive Theodore Roosevelt had a plurality in 1912. The Republican presidential victories were quite strong in 1896, 1908, and especially 1904, but in 1900 and 1916 they were narrow. In two of the Republican presidential years—1900 and 1908—the governorship went to the Democrats; and in the Progressive-dominated election of 1912, the Democratic gubernatorial candidate, rather than the Progressive, had a plurality in the city.

In off-year elections, the office of state treasurer tended to foreshadow the presidential and gubernatorial outcome two years later. The office went Democratic in 1890, Republican in 1894, narrowly Democratic in 1898 (reflecting the 1900 Republican-Democratic division of presidency and governorship), Republican in 1902 and 1906, and Democratic in 1910. The first popular vote for United States senator, in 1914, went to the Democrat by a plurality. Overall, there was a consistent relationship between state and national voting.

The Democrats were more successful at the local level (see Chart II:2). Of eleven mayoralties held during this period (it was a two-year office until 1907, when it became four-year), the Democrats won seven times and the Republicans four. However, of the seven Democratic victories, six were won by the Carter H. Harrisons, father and son (each of whom won the office five times in his career), so that the party element in this dominance may be less than first appears. For example, elections for county sheriff, which were held every four years (in the fall, to be followed by a mayoralty the next spring), were more evenly divided: four Democratic victories and three Republican.

Chicago, then, was rather bipartisan in the years before America's entry into the First World War. The new eastern and southern European immigrants, who entered the city and its political life during this period, did not enter a one-party situation and were subject to the conflicting pulls of two relatively strong and relatively successful major parties. The fact that the Democrats controlled the city political organization so much of the time, however, was important; it gave them the advantage of being

---

[18] In order not to confuse the reader with an unassimilable quantity of charts and graphs, only some of the relevant data is included in the graphs here given. For full data on all contests referred to in this chapter, see the Appendix.

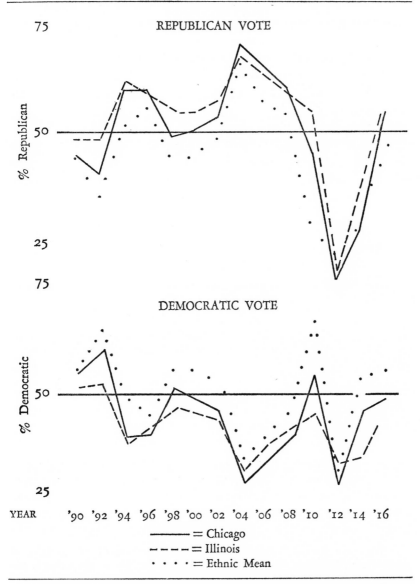

Chart II:1

Chicago, Illinois, and Ethnic Mean National and State Voting,
1890–1916*

REPUBLICAN VOTE

75

50

% Republican

25

75

DEMOCRATIC VOTE

% Democratic

50

25

YEAR   '90 '92 '94 '96 '98 '00 '02 '04 '06 '08 '10 '12 '14 '16

———— = Chicago
– – – – = Illinois
· · · · = Ethnic Mean

* Calculated on basis of Democratic and Republican percentages of two-party vote, except for 1912 (four-party) and 1914 (three-party). For definition of "ethnic mean" see note 17. For complete data, sample description, and contests included, see the Appendix.

Chart II:2

*Chicago and Ethnic Mean Democratic Voting for National/
State and Local Offices, 1890–1916*[1]

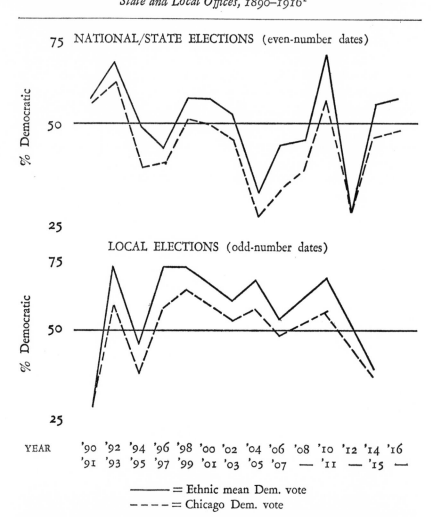

75 NATIONAL/STATE ELECTIONS (even-number dates)

% Democratic

50

25

LOCAL ELECTIONS (odd-number dates)

75

% Democratic

50

25

YEAR   '90 '92 '94 '96 '98 '00 '02 '04 '06 '08 '10 '12 '14 '16
        '91 '93 '95 '97 '99 '01 '03 '05 '07 — '11 — '15 —

———— = Ethnic mean Dem. vote
– – – – = Chicago Dem. vote

[1] For definition of "ethnic mean" see note 17. Calculated on basis of Democratic percentage of two-party vote, except for 1891, 1897, 1912, and 1914—Democratic percentage of total vote. For complete data, sample description, and contests included, see the Appendix.

in a stronger position vis-à-vis groups whose major needs were best responded to at the local level. This can be seen clearly in Chart II:2.

Third parties exerted considerable effect in the progressive period. In 1912, Theodore Roosevelt had a plurality in the city, with 38 percent of the total vote, while Eugene Debs received 13 percent, to 31 percent for Wilson and 18 for Taft. In the gubernatorial race of the same year, the Democratic candidate had a plurality (40 percent), while the Republican and Progressive candidates had 24 percent each, and the Socialist 12 percent. For state's attorney, the Democrat had a narrow plurality (at 29 percent), with the Socialist running second (26 percent), and then the Republican and the Progressive. That there was some sort of revolt is clear, but it lacked any clear direction.

The Progressive vote continued significant in 1914 (24 percent), when the Democratic candidate for United States senator won with a plurality of 47 percent. By 1916 the Progressives had ceased to be a factor in Chicago politics, allowing the Republican presidential and gubernatorial candidates to win with slim majorities; but another strong Socialist vote for state's attorney resulted in another Democratic plurality.

Thus at both the national and state levels it is quite apparent that most Progressive and even Socialist votes came from Republican voters, and that were it not for this revolt within the Republican party, the Republicans would have dominated Chicago voting in the second decade of the century as they had in the first. The Democratic victories at the state and national level were almost by default in these years; the Democrats did not assert themselves at these levels in anything like the fashion they did in local politics.

Chart II:1 clearly shows that both Chicago and Illinois followed the national pattern to Republicanism in 1894–1896, remaining rather consistently on that side of the ledger through the Taft election of 1908.[19]

[19] Although the primary concern in this monograph is ethnic political behavior, and not elections as such, I shall nonetheless consider the idea of "critical" elections or periods of voting change, as first enunciated by V. O. Key, Jr. ("A Theory of Critical Elections," *Journal of Politics* 17 [Feb. 1955]: 3–19), and reiterated by many others, including Duncan MacRae and James A. Meldrum ("Critical Elections in Illinois, 1888–1958," *American Political Science Review* 54 [Sept. 1960]: 669–83).

Key's definition of a "critical election" was one wherein the electorate was "unusually deeply concerned, in which the extent of electoral involvement is

Nineteen ten and the Progressive-dominated elections of 1912–1914 broke this Republican hegemony, but Democratic percentages did not benefit. But the 1916 presidential returns seemed to indicate that the Republicans were overcoming their insurgency problems without having lost serious ground to the Democrats. As the country went to war, the Republican party seemed likely to maintain in Chicago and Illinois the dominance it had held since the depression of the 1890s. The proof of this remained to the postwar years.

Charts II:1 and II:2 compare Illinois' and Chicago's voting with the mean vote of the seven ethnic groups studied in this chapter. Overall the ethnic mean seems to respond to the same forces and move in the same direction as the city and state vote. The ethnic mean was consistently more Democratic, however, and while it, too, went Republican in 1894–1896, this was less permanent than for city, state, and national voting patterns. Ethnic groups on the whole did not, therefore, exhibit any crucial political change as a result. But neither did the ethnic mean show firm allegiance to either party. Indeed, for the seven presidential elections through 1916, the ethnic mean majority was as often Republican as Democratic (and Progressive, by plurality, in 1912). The critical elections of 1894–1896, that led to a generation of Republican hegemony, took place without major ethnic influence one way or the other. And this is quite congruent with our data on time of arrival and naturalization for the immigrants: the ethnics were simply not a major political factor in the 1890s.

Equally interesting is the fact that, while the Illinois Democratic vote increase from 1914 to 1916 was about ten percentage points, that of

relatively quite high, and in which the decisive results of the voting reveal a sharp alteration of the pre-existing cleavage within the electorate. Moreover . . . the realignment made manifest in the voting in such elections seems to persist for several succeeding elections" (ibid., p. 4).

Using this definition, or an expanded idea of a critical period rather than a single election, Key and others have concluded that 1894 and 1928 were major critical elections and important turning points in American voting behavior. Some scholars are beginning to apply Key's model to other areas, in an effort to see if it is universally applicable throughout the United States, and at least one has raised serious question to Key's findings (John L. Shover, "Was 1928 a Critical Election in California?" *Pacific Northwest Quarterly* 58 [Oct. 1967]: 196–204). The present study includes an ethnically oriented test of the model, on somewhat different quantitative measures, for Chicago.

Chicago and the ethnic mean was almost nil. Chicago Progressive voters were returning to the Republican party; for Chicago and its ethnic groups as a whole 1916 was not a critical election since it led to no new coalition.[20]

What was true for the city and the ethnic mean, however, was not necessarily true for each individual group. Indeed, individual group variations can be most significant for understanding voting patterns. Chart II:3 portrays local and national/state Democratic voting for each of the seven groups.[21]

In their voting for national and state offices there is a clear separation between older immigrant group and Negro areas, on the one hand, and newer immigrant ones on the other. Only the Negro areas were always Republican; no group was always Democratic. Moreover, these ethnic area graphs reiterate my earlier conclusions about ethnic groups not contributing to the lasting political changes of 1894–1896. Each group did show a clear Democratic dropoff in 1894–1896, but only the Swedish and German areas can be considered as demonstrating any crucial change.

One of the most striking things suggested by these graphs is the strength of Theodore Roosevelt, who had majorities among all groups in 1904 and pluralities among the three most Republican ones in 1912. Thus again, the basic Republicanism of the Progressive party is made clear, although the graphs also show that Roosevelt was supported by many Democratic voters as well. The newer immigrants responded only to the man, however, as is made clear by their return after 1912 to their previous political stance. If we look only at presidential elections—disregarding the 1910 state treasurer race which saw all but Negroes voting

[20] Cf. Shover's suggestion that 1916 created a greater change in California politics than did 1928 ("Was 1928 a Critical Election in California?" p. 203). I would suggest that a better picture of criticality can be drawn by looking at ethnic groups rather than cities, counties, etc., because what can be a very critical election for some groups can be unimportant for others; reference group theory clearly points toward this kind of orientation.

[21] On the voting traditions of these groups, see Andrew J. Townsend, "The Germans of Chicago" (Ph.D. diss., University of Chicago, 1927); Hemdahl, "The Swedes in Illinois Politics"; Johnson, "The Swedes of Chicago"; Alex Gottfried, *Boss Cermak of Chicago: A Study of Political Leadership* (Seattle, Wash., 1962); Serino, "Italians in the Political Life of Boston"; Lawrence J. Fuchs, *The Political Behavior of American Jews* (Glencoe, Ill., 1956); Philip P. Bregstone, *Chicago and Its Jews* (Chicago, 1933); Chicago *Defender*, Oct. 30, 1920, p. 12.

Chart II:3
*Ethnic Group Democratic Voting for National/State and Local
Offices, 1890–1916[1]*

75   GERMAN-AREA DEMOCRATIC VOTING

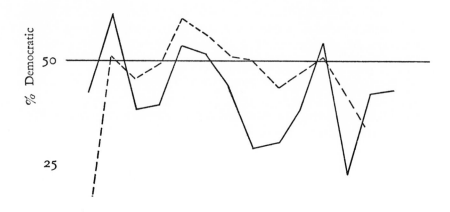

75

SWEDISH-AREA DEMOCRATIC VOTING

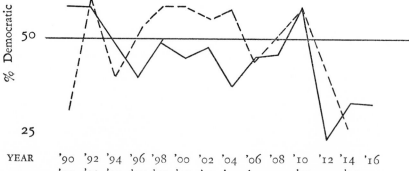

YEAR   '90 '92 '94 '96 '98 '00 '02 '04 '06 '08 '10 '12 '14 '16
        '91 '93 '95 '97 '99 '01 '03 '05 '07 — '11 — '15 —

———— = National/State voting (even-number dates)
– – – – = Local voting (odd-number dates)

[1] See note 1 to Chart II:2.

Chart II:3 (*continued*)

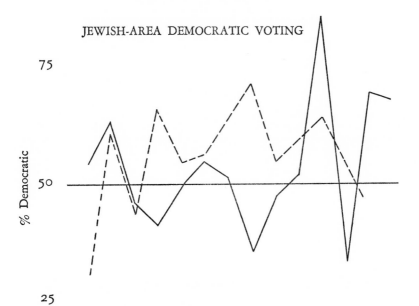

JEWISH-AREA DEMOCRATIC VOTING

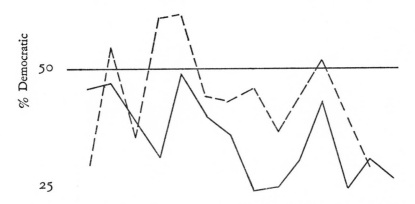

NEGRO-AREA DEMOCRATIC VOTING

YEAR '90 '92 '94 '96 '98 '00 '02 '04 '06 '08 '10 '12 '14 '16
      '91 '93 '95 '97 '99 '01 '03 '05 '07 — '11 — '15 —

Chart II:3   (*continued*)

ITALIAN-AREA DEMOCRATIC VOTING

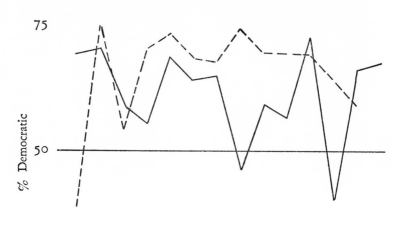

POLISH-AREA DEMOCRATIC VOTING

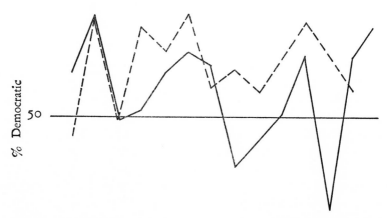

YEAR	'90 '92 '94 '96 '98 '00 '02 '04 '06 '08 '10 '12 '14 '16
25	'91 '93 '95 '97 '99 '01 '03 '05 '07 — '11 — '15 —

Chart II:3   (*continued*)

BOHEMIAN-AREA DEMOCRATIC VOTING

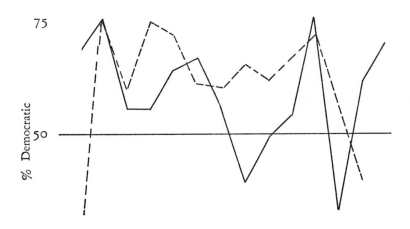

75

% Democratic

50

25

| YEAR | '90 '92 '94 '96 '98 '00 '02 '04 '06 '08 '10 '12 '14 '16 |
| | '91 '93 '95 '97 '99 '01 '03 '05 '07 — '11 — '15 — |

Democratic—the Democratic dropoff to Roosevelt becomes somewhat less dramatic. The impermanence of progressivism as a national political movement is clear; and it certainly was not built upon large-scale support from lower-class urban ethnic groups.[22]

The graphs show clearly that Bohemian, Polish, and Italian immigrants were settling in areas which tended to be Democratic in national and state elections, whereas the opposite was true for settlers in German, Swedish, and Negro areas. The Jewish ghetto exhibited the most mixed tradition. What effect these phenomena would have on the building of permanent political loyalties when the majority of each group would be voting would be demonstrated only after the Great War.

[22] A somewhat contrary view to this generalization can be found in J. Joseph Huthmacher, "Urban Liberalism and the Age of Reform," *Mississippi Valley Historical Review* 49 (Sept. 1962): 231–41.

Most ethnic groups were overall on the same side of the political ledger in local voting as in national and state, following the ethnic mean, which stayed consistently more Democratic than the Chicago vote. The German, Swedish, and Negro areas showed an interesting similarity in voting at all levels; Democratic voting tended to rise and fall at the same time locally and nationally. This suggests that these groups were more party-oriented than the newer immigrants. Voting patterns among the latter groups were more volatile, suggesting that their voting was influenced by personalities, and perhaps issues, rather than comprising a long-term party commitment.[23]

The graphs also point to the popularity of the Carter H. Harrisons, father and son; their popularity was considerable with all ethnic groups (for example, the low Democratic vote in 1891, when the senior Harrison ran as an independent; and the Democratic majorities among all seven groups in 1911, when the junior Harrison reentered local politics for the last time). More significant for the future, however, was the general popularity of William Hale Thompson in his first mayoral race in 1915. He carried not only the traditionally Republican ethnic groups but also the Jews and Bohemians, and had considerable support among the remaining two groups as well. On the whole, Thompson received one of the largest ethnic votes for mayor of the period; his career as mayor was starting strong.

As the United States entered the First World War, Chicago's political future was unclear, reflecting the developing nature of ethnic group political loyalties. Large numbers of recent immigrants and Negroes, as well as some latecoming members of older immigrant groups, were only beginning to vote at the time of the War, and many not until the start of the 1920s. Thus we must be wary in generalizing about voting traditions

---

[23] One explanation for the relatively high local Democratic voting among Swedes—which might apply to other groups as well—was that the most important Swedish-American political organization, the John Ericsson Republican League of Illinois, while very active and always Republican in state and national politics, had a policy of nonparticipation in local politics (Hemdahl, "The Swedes in Illinois Politics," p. 220). The relative independence of Jewish voting may well reflect the Jews' being less reliant on political organizations for relief, etc., because of unusually well-developed intragroup charitable organization.

in the period 1890–1917. The next decade would in good part provide the milieu for cohesion and coalition, when firm mass group loyalties would be established for the first time.

This phenomenon is further emphasized by the nature of party organization in Chicago at this time. By and large the parties were not well integrated on a citywide basis. Rather, Chicago politics was characterized by personal and group factions within parties, which tended to dominate given regions of the city. Citywide organization among either the Democrats or Republicans was short-lived when it did occur. The Democrats had the Harrison, Edward Dunne, Roger Sullivan, and other groupings, each with its own areas of support. The Republicans had Lorimer-Thompson, Charles Deneen, and several other factions. Thus voter loyalties—including those of ethnic groups—were often more Harrison, or Deneen, or Lorimer loyalties than truly partisan ones.[24] This helps explain variant voting among two or more wards dominated by the same ethnic group. Whether any of these factions could be built into truly citywide party organizations, which could be effective at local, state, and national voting levels, was a question for the 1920s to answer.

It remained to be seen if the Republicans, who would emerge from the War as the dominant national party, would also be able to build a united local organization with committed ethnic support. Likewise, the possibility existed that the Democrats could, in a period of national adversity, build a local organization strong enough to prevail among the ethnics locally even while their party was out of power at the national and state level. The latter is eventually what did happen in Chicago, as the Republicans remained divided and the Democrats united; but this was not easy to foretell in 1917.

The Democrats had a good chance to hold the support of the new immigrant groups, if they were able to meet the needs of their increased numbers in the 1920s. But could this really be done if the Democratic party was out of power nationally and/or continued to be dominated by nonurban groups and values? The Democratic hold on these groups was seriously strained, and in some cases broken, in the ensuing decade; the tenuousness of newer immigrant Democratic loyalty became apparent

[24] E.g., Charles N. Glaab and A. Theodore Brown, *A History of Urban America* (New York, 1967), pp. 208–209.

immediately after the War. Likewise the strong ethnic support in the election of Thompson as a Republican mayor in 1915 did not augur well for the Democrats.

The Republicans, for their part, seemed to be in a pretty good position with older immigrants and Negroes, and to some extent the Jews, in 1917. And developments in national politics during the War would of course help them. But the similarities between these groups and the newer immigrants—in values, aspirations, and behavior—were greater than the differences. Could the members of a factionalized Republican party maintain their loyalties as the wartime issues receded in importance?

Thus the period 1890–1917 raises more questions than it answers, in terms of the political loyalties and interests of Chicago's ethnic groups. The next fifteen years would provide answers to these questions that would hold for at least another generation.

III. *Ethnic Voting Behavior, 1918–1936*

This chapter will begin the study of postwar political behavior with an intensive look at the voting behavior of nine ethnic groups. For the decade of the 1920s a number of problems attendant upon the earlier period are no longer present: far higher proportions of the newer immigrants were citizens and able to vote; methodological problems are fewer, permitting analysis at the precinct level; thus the ethnicity of political areas is clearer and one can more confidently generalize about the voting behavior of individual groups. The nine groups included are Poles, Czechoslovaks, Yugoslavs, Lithuanians, Italians, Germans, Swedes, Jews, and Negroes. And for all but the Lithuanians and Yugoslavs comparisons can be made to 1890–1916. Native-American voting patterns will serve as another basis for comparison.

Overall, the period saw considerable voting change. In 1932, as in 1920, there were races for president, senator, and governor. These races for the nine ethnic groups comprised twenty-seven contests for each election. In 1920, only three of the twenty-seven resulted in Democratic majorities; in 1932, twenty-three of the twenty-seven did so.[1] Since the pattern of 1932 would continue thereafter, it is clear that the period saw some important voting developments.

The trend at the local level was less pronounced, since the ethnic groups were traditionally more Democratic in local races than in national. Six of the nine voted Democratic in 1919, and seven of the nine in 1931. These patterns are portrayed in Charts III:1 and III:2. Chart III:1 shows the Democratic presidential vote, 1892–1932, for the mean of the ethnic groups, and for Chicago as a whole. Chart III:2 shows the mean ethnic Democratic vote for the national/state offices (every two years) and the mayoral vote, 1890–1936.

These charts provide a more complete look at the developments of the decade, and the generation preceding it, than the synopsis above. The mixed ethnic tradition in presidential elections before the First World War was supplemented by one of unparalleled Republicanism in the first two elections of the 1920s. The 1924–1928 change comprises the largest interstitial jump of the whole period and, for the first time, was not followed by a Republican majority in the next presidential election (indeed, the Democratic majority would continue through the 1930s and beyond). Thus, while the ethnics could be confidently labeled neither Democratic nor Republican in presidential voting before the 1920s, from 1928 on they were clearly Democratic. In Chart III:2, where we consider off-year national (United States senator) and state (state treasurer—in the years there was no senatorial election) elections as well as the presidential, a similar pattern emerges, but with even more variation. There is a general—though not universal—tendency for a higher ethnic Democratic vote in off-year elections, especially from 1910 on. This is

[1] Insofar as we shall spend a good deal of time considering the "criticality" of 1928 and suceeding elections, we should here consider the problem of "deviant" or unusual elections. Recent studies of the 1928 election and its role as a turning point have tended to qualify if not dismiss the importance of the 1928 vote because of this question of "deviance" (e.g., Jerome M. Clubb and Howard W. Allen, "The Cities and the Election of 1928: Partisan Realignment," *American Historical Review* 74 [April 1969]: 1205–20, esp. pp. 1207–1209; John L. Shover, "Was 1928 a Critical Election in California?" *Pacific Northwest Quarterly* 58 [Oct. 1967]: 196–204, esp. p. 198). These suggestions do not seem reasonable, however, at least for the period from the First World War through the Depression. Perhaps no election is truly ordinary, and all have some measure of deviance. The 1928 election is no exception here (Clubb and Allen, "The Cities and the Election of 1928"), nor, as a basis of comparison, are 1920 or 1924 (Shover, "Was 1928 a Critical Election in California?"). The presidential election of 1916 took place in a fervor of war-fears and the vote for Wilson was an unusual (because infrequent in terms of situation) phenomenon. The 1918 vote came hard on the heels of a successful war effort, with unusually great sympathy for the administration that had pursued that effort. Indeed, the pro-administration feelings of 1918 were very similar to the antiadministration feelings of 1920—after the tragedy of Versailles had been played out. And the unusualness of that election was matched by that of 1924 when a major third party was again in the running. One could go on and on, the point being that we have to take elections as they come; each has some measure of "deviance," at least in this period of American history. Perhaps that is in the very nature of the electoral process; varying rates of "deviance" do not seem meaningfully measurable, and the concept is probably more obstructive than anything else.

Chart III:1

Chicago and Ethnic Mean Democratic Presidential Vote, 1892–1936[1]

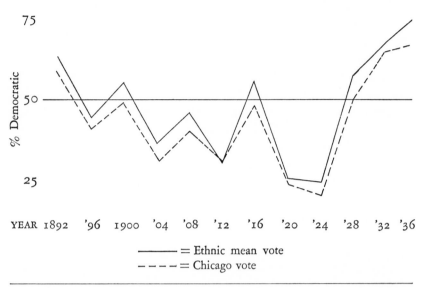

```
YEAR 1892   '96   1900   '04   '08   '12   '16   '20   '24   '28   '32  '36
```

————— = Ethnic mean vote

– – – – = Chicago vote

[1] Ethnic mean vote = mean of the means of each of the groups involved (7, 1892–1916; 9, 1920–1936); see Appendix. Calculated on basis of Democratic percentage of two-party (1912, 1924: three-party) vote.

perpetuated, although in diminished form, in the 1920s. There is a major break in the cycle in 1928, when the Democratic presidential vote is actually higher (by one percentage point) than the senatorial vote of 1926; from this point it moves on to unprecedented highs. Thus in off-year elections as well as presidential ones,[2] there is a rather mixed tradition up to 1928, but a clearly Democratic one thereafter.

[2] This will perhaps meet the reasonable qualification raised by some scholars about the unreliability of using data for presidential elections only (e.g., Clubb and Allen, "The Cities and the Election of 1928," pp. 1209–12). It is arguable whether presidential elections should be compared only to other presidential elections, or to off-year ones as well. In seeking the clearest possible indications of ethnic voting behavior, and its contribution to political coalitions, I have tried here to use both measures.

In local voting, on the other hand, the ethnic mean is generally Democratic from the mid-1890s. It does go Republican in the mayoralties of 1915 and 1927 (two of William Hale Thompson's campaigns), and only very narrowly Democratic in 1919 (also a Thompson campaign, as was 1931). There does not appear to be any direct relationship between voting for local office on the one hand, and for state and national on the other.

All of this is based on the mean vote of the means for the nine groups. Table III:1 gives the Democratic vote of each of the nine groups for the major national/state and local elections of 1918–1932; and Chart III:3 pictures the vote for 1890–1936 for those seven groups for which data are available for this whole period.

The nine ethnic groups can reasonably be divided into four categories to facilitate the study of their voting: older immigrants (Germans and Swedes); newer immigrants (Poles, Czechoslovaks, Lithuanians, Yugoslavs, Italians); Jews; and Negroes. Despite variations in voting within the first two categories, they have some real unity: time of immigration into the United States, degree of assimilation into the American value system, religion (in large part), general socioeconomic status, and general political sophistication and behavior.

The newer immigrants tended to be more Democratic than the other ethnics and the Native-Americans. All five groups were strongly Democratic in the senatorial election of 1918 (over 60 percent); by 1920, they were still somewhat more Democratic than the older immigrants, but only the Lithuanians gave a Democratic majority for any of the three major contests. Comparing the senatorial vote of 1918 with the presidential vote of 1920, the Czechs, Italians, and Yugoslavs all decreased their Democratic support by about forty percentage points. The Poles dropped by thirty-one points and the still-Democratic Lithuanians by twenty-four. The Republican vote for senator and governor in 1920 was smaller than that for president, but among none of the groups was the variation for the three offices more than seven points, a relatively narrow range.

Between these two elections was the 1919 mayoralty. All five newer immigrant groups were Democratic in that election, with percentages ranging from fifty-two to seventy-six (mean = 63 percent). Between the national elections of 1920 and 1924, in the 1923 mayoralty, all five were again Democratic, and a little more so than in 1919 (mean = 73 per-

Chart III:2

Ethnic Mean Democratic Vote for National/State and Local Elections, 1890–1936[1]

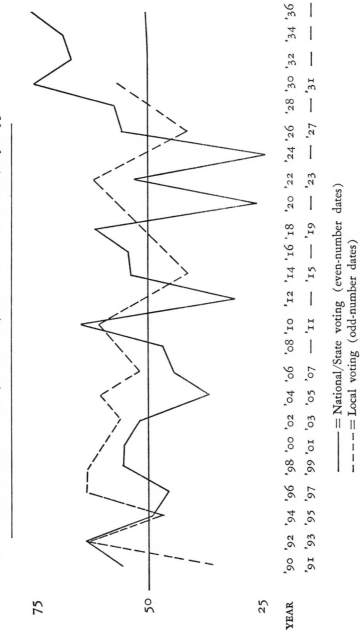

75

50

25

YEAR   '90 '92 '94 '96 '98 '00 '02 '04 '06 '08 '10 '12 '14 '16 '18 '20 '22 '24 '26 '28 '30 '32 '34 '36

        '91 '93 '95 '97 '99 '01 '03 '05 '07 — '11 — '15 — '19 — '23 — '27 — '31 — —

——— = National/State voting (even-number dates)

- - - - = Local voting (odd-number dates)

[1] Calculated on basis of Democratic percentage of two-party vote, except for 1891, 1897, 1912, and 1924—Democratic percentage of total vote. For complete data, sample description, and contests included, see Appendix.

TABLE III:1   *Democratic Vote of Nine Ethnic Groups and Native-Americans in Chicago Elections, 1918-1932 (Percentage Democratic)* *

Year and office	Czechoslovaks	Poles	Lithuanians	Yugoslavs	Italians	Germans	Swedes	Jews	Negroes	Native-Americans
1918:										
Senator	84	71	77	61	71	54	44	60	35	46
Congressman	79	64	76	51	65	46	32	45	28	—
Sheriff	86	66	75	57	65	47	36	54	30	—
1919:										
Mayor	73	55	76	52	61	51	35	40	22	42
1920:										
President	43	39	53	22	31	18	17	15	11	20
Senator	44	41	54	23	28	23	22	20	12	23
Governor	49	46	57	25	36	31	34	31	19	45
1923:										
Mayor	76	76	82	52	80	45	42	57	53	43
1924:										
President	40	35	48	20	31	14	15	19	10	16
Senator	59	49	58	36	39	37	33	39	20	35
Governor	51	42	54	28	35	30	37	41	19	50
1927:										
Mayor	59	54	57	36	42	37	38	39	7	55
1928:										
President	73	71	77	54	63	58	34	60	23	40
Senator	82	75	77	58	62	64	41	64	21	43
Governor	70	66	71	49	52	52	34	53	19	40
1930:										
Senator	89	85	85	74	68	85	73	83	24	68
Congressman	82	78	61	70	59	72	52	70	19	—
Pres.-Cnty. Bd.	85	81	67	73	63	75	54	77	20	56
1931:										
Mayor	84	70	62	64	47	58	53	61	16	61
1932:										
President	83	80	84	67	64	69	51	77	21	43
Senator	81	76	80	62	59	65	42	73	19	39
Governor	81	75	78	59	57	67	53	83	20	63

*Percentage Democratic of the two-party vote except for 1924—of the three-party vote.

Chart III:3

Ethnic Group Democratic Voting for National/ State and Local Offices,
1890–1936[1]

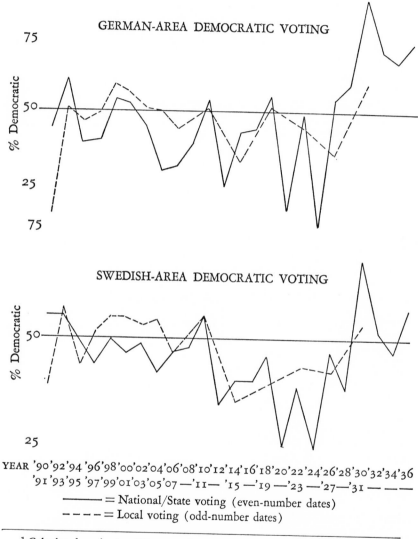

GERMAN-AREA DEMOCRATIC VOTING

SWEDISH-AREA DEMOCRATIC VOTING

YEAR ’90’92’94’96’98’00’02’04’06’08’10’12’14’16’18’20’22’24’26’28’30’32’34’36
’91’93’95 ’97’99’01’03’05’07 —’11— ’15 —’19 —’23 —’27—’31 — — —

————— = National/State voting (even-number dates)
– – – – = Local voting (odd-number dates)

[1] Calculated on basis of Democratic percentage of two-party vote, except for
1891, 1897, 1912–1914, and 1928—Democratic percentage of total vote. For
complete data, sample description, and contests included, see Appendix.

Chart III:3   (*continued*)

ITALIAN-AREA DEMOCRATIC VOTING

POLISH-AREA DEMOCRATIC VOTING

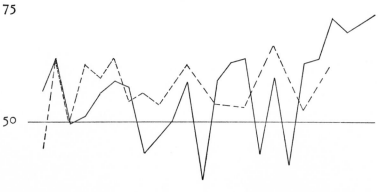

YEAR   '90 '92 '94 '96 '98 '00 '02 '04 '06 '08 '10 '12 '14 '16 '18 '20 '22 '24 '26 '28 '30 '32 '34 '36
'91 '93 '95 '97 '99 '01 '03 '05 '07 —'11 —'15 —'19 —'23 —'27 —'31 — — —

Chart III:3   (*continued*)

JEWISH-AREA DEMOCRATIC VOTING

NEGRO-AREA DEMOCRATIC VOTING

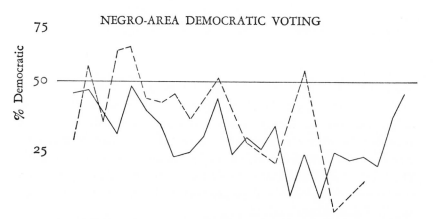

'90 '92 '94 '96 '98 '00 '02 '04 '06 '08 '10 '12 '14 '16 '18 '20 '22 '24 '26 '28 '30 '32 '34 '36
'91 '93 '95 '97 '99 '01 '03 '05 '07 —'11 —'15 —'19 —'23 —'27 —'31— — —

Chart III:3   (*continued*)

CZECHOSLOVAKIAN-AREA DEMOCRATIC VOTING[2]

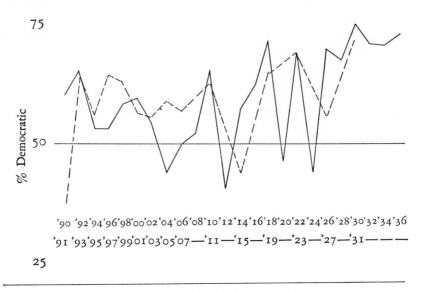

’90 ’92 ’94 ’96 ’98 ’00 ’02 ’04 ’06 ’08 ’10 ’12 ’14 ’16 ’18 ’20 ’22 ’24 ’26 ’28 ’30 ’32 ’34 ’36
’91 ’93 ’95 ’97 ’99 ’01 ’03 ’05 ’07 —’11 —’15 —’19 —’23 —’27 —’31 — — —

[2] Bohemian-area vote to 1916; Czechoslovakian vote from 1918.

cent). Thus the 1920 national vote did not carry over to the local election of 1923. It was, however, repeated in 1924, where Democratic voting decreased from 1920 levels. The Italians voted the same as in 1920, but the other groups were two to six points less Democratic. Thus even the Lithuanians failed to return a Democratic majority for president. The Czechs and Lithuanians did vote Democratic for senator and governor (between 51 percent and 59 percent), while the other three groups were Republican for all offices.

There was a significant difference from 1920, however, in the effect of the Robert M. La Follette candidacy for the Progressive party. Thus, while none of the five groups voted Democratic for president, three of them failed to vote Republican either; and among the more Democratic

Czechs and Lithuanians, the Democratic presidential candidate received more votes than the Republican. Consequently, both Republican and Democratic presidential voting declined among the newer immigrants in 1924. This does not mean that La Follette ran strongly among the newer immigrants; he simply attracted enough votes to decrease major party totals from the 1920 levels. He received an average of 18 percent among them (from 15 percent to 20 percent), which was his average in the city at large, and well below that among some other groups. Since the Democratic total decreased only very slightly from 1920 at the presidential level, the La Follette vote among newer immigrants seems primarily to have come from 1920 Republican voters. But there were no significant differences in La Follette voting between groups which were relatively more or less Democratic before 1924. And therefore Progressive voting in 1924 hinged on reasons other than previous party identification.

The 1927 mayoralty saw a continuing decrease in Democratic voting among newer immigrants: only three of the five groups voted Democratic, and in each case by less than 60 percent. The average decrease from 1923 Democratic totals was twenty-four percentage points (varying from fifteen to thirty-eight points—a rather wide range). Again the degree of decrease is not explicable in terms of previous level of Democratic or Republican voting. The five groups together voted 49.6 percent Democratic, and thus overall local voting had reached the same side of the balance as national.

In the 1928 presidential election all five groups went strongly Democratic, with a combined average of 68 percent. Increases over 1924 Democratic voting were very large, averaging thirty-three percentage points (and varying little: from twenty-nine to thirty-six points). As compared to 1920, Democratic presidential voting increased thirty points. The vote for senator and governor was essentially the same as that for president, and Democratic senatorial candidate Anton Cermak led the ticket with 71 percent. The Yugoslavs, with the lowest Democratic vote for president, comprised the only group that failed to produce a Democratic majority for any of the three offices (49 percent for governor).

This 68 percent Democratic vote was still six points under the 1918 level, but was nonetheless probably the highest Democratic presidential vote these groups had ever delivered. The increase in Democratic voting over 1920 was only four points less than the decrease from 1918 to 1920.

Interestingly, the five newer immigrant groups voted closer together in 1928 (a range of nineteen points) than in any other election of the period.

This strongly resurgent Democratic voting did not flag in succeeding elections. In the 1930 national elections each of the groups increased its Democratic vote in each of the three major contests. Their average in the senatorial election was 80 percent Democratic (the Republican candidate was female), and in the congressman-at-large race the Democratic vote was 70 percent. In the locally important race for president of the Cook County Board of Commissioners, Anton Cermak received 74 percent of the newer immigrant vote. Thus the new Democratic voting strength was becoming increasingly firm.

The 1931 mayoralty also contributed to this trend. Four of the five groups went Democratic, the exception being the Italians. The five groups averaged 65 percent Democratic, fifteen points more than in 1927. This ranged from the Italians' low of 47 percent to the Czechs' high of 84—again demonstrating the greater similarity to be found in national than in local voting behavior. All the groups, however, increased their Democratic voting materially from the levels of 1927, and for all except the Italians the 1931 mayoralty marked the third straight Democratic voting majority.

Finally, the national elections of 1932 and beyond continued the Democratic trend. The newer immigrants voted 76 percent Democratic for president in 1932 and only slightly less for senator and governor. Each of the groups was more Democratic for president than in 1928, and all but the Czechs, who dropped only one point, exceeded their 1931 Democratic vote as well. Variations between the groups were about the same as 1928 and the fact that all went Democratic in landslide proportions further minimizes the significance of the range.

By 1932, then, the newer immigrant groups had already voted Democratic through four successive elections. And the indecisive pattern of their voting at the beginning of the period had given way to an ever-growing Democratic allegiance, which continued into 1934–1936 and beyond.

The Germans and Swedes of Chicago, as older immigrants, had much in common: socioeconomic status, assimilation into the general population of the city, participation in the prevailing value structure, place of residence, and a political tradition of firm Republicanism. The Swedes were traditionally somewhat more Republican than the Germans, however, and they would be less affected by the political forces of the time.

In the wartime elections of 1918 the Germans went Democratic for senator, at 54 percent, while the Swedes went Republican (44 percent Democratic). For congressman-at-large and sheriff both groups went Republican. And in all three contests the Germans were about ten points more Democratic than the Swedes.

This difference between the two groups continued into the 1919 mayoralty, with the Germans at 51 percent Democratic and the Swedes at 35. But in the Republican sweep of 1920 the difference virtually disappeared: the Germans voted only 18 percent Democratic, and the Swedes 17 percent. The same difference obtained in the senatorial vote, and in the gubernatorial the Germans were three points less Democratic (at 31 percent) than the Swedes. Most important, both groups voted over 66 percent Republican in all three contests.

Democratic strength increased slightly in the 1923 mayoralty—the Germans at 45 percent and the Swedes at 42. But in the 1924 national elections Democratic voting dropped even below 1920 levels. The Germans voted 14 percent Democratic for president, and the Swedes 15; for senator and governor the two groups voted between 30 and 37 percent Democratic, about the same as in 1920. There was an important difference between the two groups in 1924, however, in terms of their responses to La Follette. Thus while the Germans and Swedes were only one point apart in Democratic presidential voting, they were twelve points apart in Republican (53 percent for the Germans, 65 percent for the Swedes) since the Germans gave La Follette 33 percent, his highest total among all groups, while the Swedes gave him only 19, his fifth highest.

Since Swedish and German voting for senator and governor were about the same, it appears that German voters for La Follette were essentially Republican at the presidential level. But they were less firmly attached to that party than the Swedes; this would be seen again in the future. La Follette's appeal was not constant or universal to all middle-class ethnics.

In the 1927 mayoralty the two groups voted together again, and again were firmly Republican: the Germans voted 37 percent Democratic and the Swedes 38. But in the 1928 presidential contest they were wider apart than at any other time. The Germans gave Smith 58 percent, the Swedes 34. This divergence was slightly smaller in voting for senator and governor. And in the former, the Germans gave Democrat Anton Cermak an even higher vote (64 percent) than they gave to Al Smith. Comparing the 1928 presidential vote with that of 1920 (to eliminate the La Follette factor in 1924), German Democratic voting increased by forty percentage points, more than any other group except the Jews. At the same time, Swedish Democratic voting increased by only seventeen points, less than any other group except the Negroes.

This Democratic trend increased among the Germans in 1930, and even the Swedes participated in it, although to a lesser extent. The Germans voted 85 percent Democratic in the male-female senatorial contest, the Swedes 73 percent. And the Germans voted over 70 percent Democratic for congressman-at-large and president of the County Board as well. In these two contests the Swedes were just over 50 percent Democratic—probably the first time they had ever voted so generally Democratic. Thus it appeared in 1930 that the Germans had entered the new Democratic coalition, and that the Swedes were flirting with it as well.

In the 1931 mayoralty both groups continued Democratic, now at the local level. German voters gave Anton Cermak 58 percent of their mayoral vote, and Swedes gave him 53 percent; respective increases over 1927 were twenty-one and fifteen percentage points. And in the 1932 national elections the Germans once again delivered a landslide Democratic vote: between 65 and 69 percent for president, senator, and governor. The Swedes, as in 1928, were well behind; they gave Roosevelt 51 percent, and 51 percent to the Democratic candidate for governor, but voted only 42 percent Democratic for senator.

Thus by 1932 the Germans had joined with the newer immigrants in moving strongly since 1928 into the Democratic column. And they seemed there to stay, as 1934 and 1936 voting indicates. The Swedes, at the same time, had continued to be more Republican, and their future political course was unsure. Even they, however, had voted Democratic in six of seven contests from 1930 to 1932 and if they could not be called

Democrats, neither was their traditional Republicanism any longer secure.

Chicago's Jews remained a distinct group in this period for a number of reasons: although some had been in the city for a long time, most were recent immigrants; there were relatively great divisions and animosities within the group, between the older and newer immigrant Jews; despite their recent immigration, the Jews were among the socioeconomically most advanced of the groups; and finally, they made a more complete political change in this period than any other group in the city.

Like other Chicago ethnic groups, the Jews leaned toward the incumbent Democratic party in the wartime election of 1918; this was a deviation from their traditionally strong Republicanism. They voted 60 percent Democratic for senator and 54 percent Democratic for Anton Cermak for sheriff, but only 45 percent Democratic for congressman-at-large. The next year they voted only 40 percent Democratic for mayor.

In 1920 the Jews voted 15 percent Democratic for president and were, after the Negroes, the most Republican ethnic group in the city; for governor and senator their Democratic vote was slightly higher, but still second most Republican. In 1924 Jewish Democratic voting rose slightly, to 19 percent, at the same time that all other ethnic groups were slightly decreasing their Democratic vote; there were three groups more Republican than they. And in the voting for senator and governor, the Jews—at 40 percent Democratic—were among the least Republican. Here, as always, the Jewish vote showed considerable selectivity and intragroup variation. The Jews voted 27 percent for La Follette, his second best showing in the city. Thus a bare majority of 52 percent went to the Republican presidential candidate.

This selectivity had been demonstrated the year before, in the 1923 mayoralty. Here the Jews had voted 57 percent Democratic, almost as Democratic as they had been Republican four years earlier. But in the mayoralty of 1927, when Republican Thompson was again a candidate, Jewish Democratic voting reached a new local low—39 percent. By no means, then, had the Jews made any party shift by 1927.

In the presidential election of 1928 Chicago's Jews voted 60 percent Democratic, an increase of forty-one percentage points over 1924, and forty-five over 1920. With the Germans, they showed the largest such increase of all Chicago ethnic groups (thus the highest La Follette voters made the greatest pro-Democratic shifts in 1928). Jewish Democratic voting in 1928 was even greater in the senatorial race, where Anton Cermak received 64 percent; but for governor it was smaller, at 53 percent. This trend continued in 1930: 83 percent Democratic for senator, 77 percent for president of the County Board, and 70 for congressman-at-large. Local voting came into alignment in the 1931 mayoralty; the Jews deserted Thompson and gave Cermak 61 percent (precisely the total they had given Thompson four years earlier). In the 1932 national elections the trend continued: 77 percent Democratic for president, 73 percent for senator, and 83 percent for the Jewish Democratic candidate for governor.

The voting behavior of Chicago's Jews, then, rivaled that of the Germans in the dramatic nature of its development: almost universally Republican in the first half of the 1920s, and from 1928 progressively more and more Democratic, with national and local allegiance becoming quite close by 1932.

Chicago's Negroes were an even more distinctive ethnic group in politics. They were the oldest in terms of residence in the nation, but the newest in Chicago; yet, as with the Jews, there were some among them who had been in the city for generations. Socioeconomically, they were the lowest of the ethnic groups, and politically they were the most Republican. Their political behavior changed less during this period than that of any other group, and the very fact that they were largely unaffected by the forces affecting the other groups is significant.

In all but one of the elections considered here, the Negroes were the least Democratic of all voters. They were not much affected by the general proadministration wartime sentiment in 1918, voting only 35 percent Democratic for senator and 30 percent or less for governor and congressman-at-large. Even this, however, was somewhat above their usual Democratic level, which suggests that no group is totally immune to the forces operating in American politics.

In the 1919 mayoralty Negroes voted strongly for Republican Thompson and gave his opponent only 22 percent. (Thompson had received about ten points less in 1915.) In the 1920 presidential election Negro Democratic voting decreased: 11 percent for president, 12 percent for senator, and 19 percent for governor (James Hamilton Lewis, the same man to whom they had given 35 percent for senator in 1918). The Democratic presidential vote, low as it was, fell by another percentage point in 1924, to 10 percent; the gubernatorial vote remained the same as in 1920 and the senatorial vote rose slightly, to 20 percent. All in all this was an overwhelming commitment to the Republican party. Negroes were not attracted to La Follette and gave him a lower vote (10 percent) than any other ethnic group in Chicago.

Between these two national elections came the only instance of Negro Democratic voting in the entire period, in the 1923 mayoralty. The 53 percent Negro Democratic vote was not, however, a sign of disaffection from Republicanism; rather it was a sign of loyalty to former Mayor Thompson. In 1927, when Thompson ran for and won his third term as Republican mayor, Chicago's Negroes gave him an almost unbelievable 93 percent of their vote.

Negroes were not entirely unaffected by the Al Smith candidacy. They voted 23 percent for him, and a little less for his running mates. This was obviously not large, but compared to preceding elections it did show some attraction to the Democratic candidate. The same level of Negro Democratic voting was maintained in 1930, when Democrat James Hamilton Lewis received 24 percent for the Senate, and his running mates slightly less. This 1930 senatorial vote showed a real alliance with Republicanism, since Mayor Thompson was supporting the Democrat.

In the 1931 mayoralty, Negroes again supported Thompson, this time with 84 percent of their vote. And in the 1932 national elections Negro Democratic voting decreased slightly from the levels of 1928–1930. Franklin D. Roosevelt received 21 percent, and his running mates a point or two less.

Thus with the exception of the 1923 mayoralty, where a very unusual situation prevailed, Negroes never voted more than 35 percent Democratic through 1932, and in eighteen of the twenty-one contests were below 25 percent. They remained relatively unaffected by the forces of change in Chicago politics in the 1920s, and at the end of the period were outside the Democratic consensus. However, the figures for 1934 and 1936 (Chart III:3) show the steady increase in Negro Democratic voting that led to solid Democratic majorities in the second half of the decade.

In summary, while there were variations among the groups, almost all underwent important voting changes during the period 1918–1932, and these changes overall were in the same direction. Averaged together, they tended to support the party in power in the wartime elections of 1918 and to be fairly evenly divided in the 1919 mayoralty. In the national elections of 1920 and 1924, however, they were strongly Republican, but both less Republican and less Democratic in 1924 than in 1920, due to an average La Follette vote of 19 percent. Meanwhile, they had delivered a strong Democratic majority in the 1923 mayoralty, but would turn around and vote a Republican majority almost as strong in 1927.

In the 1928 national elections the ethnics greatly increased their Democratic voting to a position about the same as that of 1918, in what was probably the highest Democratic vote they had ever delivered in a presidential contest. This uptrend continued in the first Depression-time election of 1930, the defeat of Thompson in the 1931 mayoralty, and the national elections of 1932, creating in the process a Democratic tradition, which expanded in 1934 and 1936.

The overall trend of the 1920s is clear: starting in 1928 a switch in ethnic voting behavior began; it was reinforced by the succeeding elections of 1930, 1931, and 1932 and resulted in the ethnic Democratic consensus that provided the crux of Democratic voting strength from that time forward. None of these groups, it should be noted, followed a consistently predictable pattern. Just as politics combines rational and irrational factors, so too does political behavior. That the patterns are not neat or completely comprehensible reflects the fact that voters, as people, operate under conflicting and not always decipherable motivations.

These tendencies can be made clearer, perhaps, by comparing the voting of the nine groups with that of a sample of Native-Americans (see Table III:2). By and large the ethnics were consistently more Democratic than were the Native-Americans (the exceptions being instances where Thompson or his ally Governor Len Small were running on the Republican ticket). But the extent of this difference varied from election to election. The ethnics were sixteen percentage points more Democratic in the 1918 senatorial contest, but only seven and nine points more Democratic in the presidential elections of 1920 and 1924. This rose to a seventeen point differential in 1928 and twenty-three points in 1932, as

TABLE III:2 *Ethnic and Native-American Voting Patterns, 1918-1932*
            (Percentage Democratic)[*]

Election	Nine ethnic groups	Native-Americans
1918: Senator	62	46
1919: Mayor	51	42
1920: President	27	20
1923: Mayor	62	43
1924: President	25	16
(*1924:* La Follette	19	11)
1927: Mayor	41	55
1928: President	57	40
1930: Senator	74	68
1931: Mayor	57	61
1932: President	66	43

[*]Percentage Democratic of the two-party vote, except for 1924—the three-party vote. Figures in parentheses are La Follette's percentages of the three-party vote.

the ethnics entered the Democracy and drew further and further away from the Native-Americans. Locally, the ethnics were nine points more Democratic in the 1919 mayoralty and nineteen points more Democratic in 1923. But in 1927, when Thompson sought his third term as Republican mayor, the ethnics supported him and were fourteen points less Democratic than the Native-Americans. The weakening of Thompson's ethnic attraction in the next four years is seen in the 1931 vote, where the ethnics were only four points less Democratic than the Native-Americans.

To summarize the individual groups, the traditionally more Democratic Czechs, Poles, Lithuanians, and Yugoslavs tended to vote Republican in the early 1920s, but were pulled strongly into the Democratic party in 1928, and from that time forward steadily increased their Democratic voting and stayed Democratic at all levels. The primarily Republican Italians followed a less rational course and were less firmly

Democratic in 1932; but they nonetheless demonstrated a felt effect of the same forces from 1928 on. The Germans and Jews made the clearest shifts of all: traditionally strong Republicanism through 1927, a very strong pro-Democratic shift in 1928, and Democratic voting from that time forward. The Swedes, on the other hand, were less affected by these forces and made no significant shift in 1928. They did become more Democratic in 1930–1931–1932, but their party allegiance was not clear at the end of the period. And the Negroes were least affected of all by the forces of the time; they were about as Republican in 1932 as they had been in 1918.

Voting patterns clearly point to 1928 as the most significant election of the period. Here came the largest break with recent past voting behavior among the ethnics. Before this election one could not really generalize about an "ethnic vote"; but from this election forward the concept had real meaning. This was the real significance of the 1928 election—in creating an ethnic vote. And because these new patterns continued into succeeding local and national elections, 1928 is a major political turning point.

Finally, the question of the one important third-party movement of the decade remains: what if any effect did the 1924 La Follette candidacy have on later political changes? On the whole its effect was not great. There is no meaningful overall relationship between the La Follette voting and the Al Smith voting, for example. But if the phenomenon was not generally important, it does appear to have been selectively important among the traditionally Republican groups which did vote strongly Progressive in 1924. Thus the Jews and Germans were the highest La Follette voters and also the two groups which made the strongest Republican-to-Democratic switch when comparing 1920 or 1924 with 1928. For these basically middle-class ethnic groups (but not for the equally middle-class Swedes) the La Follette movement played a role in breaking their allegiance to the Republican party and was a kind of steppingstone to Democratic voting. There is some evidence against overstressing this factor in data on party membership among Jews and Germans.

The "voting" of the ethnic press is another indicator of changing ethnic political allegiance. The ethnic press and ethnic voters were to some extent in political accord. The ethnic press, like its readers, was

TABLE III:3 *Election Recommendations of Chicago Ethnic Newspapers for Leading Contests, 1918-1932 (Party of leading candidate)*[*]

Election	Dziennik Chicagoski	Dziennik Zwiazkowy	L'Italia	La Trib. Ital. Trans-Atlantica	Abendpost	Svenska-Trib.- Nyheter	Jewish Courier	Jewish Forward	Defender
1918: Senator	D	—	N	R	D	—	D	S	R
1919: Mayor	D	—	R	—	(R)	—	D	S	R
1920: President	D	(R)	R	R	R	R	D	S	R
1923: Mayor	D	—	—	D	R	—	D	S	N
1924: President	D	N	R	R	(P)	R	D	P	R
1927: Mayor	D	N	R	D	N	—	D	S	R
1928: President	D	N	N	D	D	R	D	S	D
1930: Senator	D	N	—	R	D	—	D	S	N
1931: Mayor	D	D	R	R	D	—	D	S	N
1932: President	D	(D)	R	—	D	—	D	S	(R)

[*]D = Democratic
R = Republican
P = Progressive
S = Socialist
N = Neutral
— = no interest or missing
() = leaned but did not specifically endorse

often more interested in individual candidates than in parties. Of interest here is the party affiliation of the major candidates supported by the press —generally, the men who topped the ticket[3] (Table III:3).

For the newer immigrants, two Polish-language newspapers were studied throughout. The *Dziennik Chicagoski* was always Democratic when it was interested at all in an election. *Dziennik Zwiazkowy,* the official organ of the Polish National Alliance, was generally neutral and often uninterested in politics; by the end of the period, however, it grew more political, definitely endorsed Democrat Cermak for mayor in 1931, and clearly leaned Democratic in 1932. The leading Italian-language paper, *L'Italia,* was never Democratic, but was sometimes significantly neutral, as in the election of 1918 and the presidential contest in 1928. *La Tribuna Italiana Trans-Atlantica* pursued a less predictable course. It was Republican in all national elections (1932 missing) except 1928, where it endorsed Smith. On the local level it wavered considerably, for example opposing Thompson in 1927 and supporting him in 1931—and thus bucking the trend in both elections. In this respect the paper reflected the enigmas of Italian voting behavior; both the paper and the people were probably affected by outside, nonpolitical forces. By the end of the period, however, the Italian and Polish press were both pretty well in accord with the Democratic leanings of the groups they represented.

For the older immigrants, the only major German-language paper in Chicago was the *Abendpost* (on Sundays called the *Sonntagpost*), and it, too, seemed to follow the same process of development as its readers. Generally Republican at the outset, it leaned toward La Follette in 1924, supported Smith in 1928, and then became strongly Democratic at all levels. The Scandinavian press was not systematically studied, but one leading Swedish-language paper, the *Svenska-Tribunen-Nyheter,* was found to remain Republican in the presidential elections of 1920, 1924, and 1928, as did Swedish voters (the owner of this paper, however, personally supported Smith in 1928).

The Yiddish-language press seemed more independent of its readership. The two major Yiddish papers in Chicago were the *Jewish Courier* and the *Forward* (a Chicago edition of the New York *Forward*). The *Jewish Courier* was always Democratic and the *Forward* was always

---

[3] A more complete and systematic study of the ethnic press will be found in succeeding chapters.

Socialist; neither ever varied, except that the *Forward* followed the Socialist party in supporting La Follette in 1924. But it is worth noting that the *Forward* was the most widely circulated Yiddish paper in Chicago and the United States, and its inculcation of liberal, democratic-socialist ideas probably had an overall effect moderately helpful to the Democratic party.

The leading Negro paper, the *Defender,* was by no means Democratic at the end of the period, but it was less firmly Republican than before. Through 1927 it was always Republican, except for its neutrality in the 1923 mayoralty when Negroes supported the Democratic candidate. But it was strongly anti-Republican and pro-Smith in 1928. It ignored the 1930 election and was neutral in 1931, but leaned Republican in 1932. The *Defender* did not become really Democratic at the local level until 1935, and at the national until after the election of 1936. Thus, although its Republicanism was weakened after 1928, it was like its readers in its reluctance to leave traditional political loyalties.

The ethnic press, then, did follow the same pattern and was susceptible to the same influences as its readers. In the press, as among the voters, there was a greater change, and a more permanent one, in 1928 than in any other year. Despite exceptions, the general trend of press-reader accord is clear. Whether leading or following, or both, the ethnic press reacted to the political forces of the time in essentially the same manner as its readers.

IV. *Some Measures of Ethnic Voting Behavior*

This chapter will endeavor to clarify and systematize the data already presented through the use of additional statistical measures. The models used should be testable and replicable, and thus contribute to the search for measures for the comparative study of voting behavior. The search for the most "critical" elections, i.e., those that led to the greatest change, cannot follow Key's model, as MacRae and Meldrum, Shover, and others have done.[1] This is because the data in this study concentrate not on the most Republican and most Democratic areas, but on ethnic areas and groups; thus the problem of criticality or significance is approached from a different subject-specific angle. What should emerge from this concern with the elections which most affected ethnic voters is an ethnic variant of the Key model.

The data in Table IV:1 present the coefficients of correlation (Pearson's r)[2] for every presidential election with every other presidential election, 1920–1936, in terms of Democratic voting of the nine ethnic groups. Here is a clear ethnic model of a major part of Key's definition of criticality for 1928: it produces a change in pattern and correlates at a higher order with succeeding elections than with preceding ones. Moreover, again following Key, the changes appear to be long-lasting, insofar as 1928 correlates at as high an order with 1936 as with 1932 (and studies of the Roosevelt coalition suggest that this continued into later elections as well).

Table IV:2 expands these presidential election correlations over the period 1892–1936 for the seven groups for which there is data for this entire period. This supports the above model when the relationships between 1928 and the pre-1920 elections are compared; not until as far back as 1900 is there a coefficient as high as 1928–32/36 (although it comes close in 1916). Thus in terms of this important statistical measure of association, this ethnic model points to 1928 as a "critical election," or as part of a critical period of voting change for the ethnic groups of Chicago.

A couple of other points are salient here. First, there is considerable consistency in waxing and waning of the Democratic vote of the seven groups over this forty-four-year period. Almost every election correlates significantly (i.e., over +.75) with every other, and there are no negative correlations. The major exception to this generalization is a second point of interest: the progressive era elections of 1904–1908–1912, which comprise a block that correlates relatively less highly with the rest. This is especially true of 1912, where Roosevelt's third-party popularity certainly affected general voting patterns. But while these elections are interesting they cannot be described as critical, since they had no long-term effects, as seen by the high order of correlation between the elections before 1908 and those after 1912.

Table IV:3 concentrates again on the 1920s and adds to presidential elections the top contest in off-years, so that the measure is biennial and

---

[1] V. O. Key, Jr., "A Theory of Critical Elections," *Journal of Politics* 17 (Feb. 1955); Duncan MacRae and James A. Meldrum, "Critical Elections in Illinois, 1888–1958," *American Political Science Review* 54 (Sept. 1960); John L. Shover, "Was 1928 a Critical Election in California?" *Pacific Northwest Quarterly* 58 (Oct. 1967); Bruce M. Stave, "The 'La Follette Revolution' and the Pittsburgh Vote, 1932," *Mid-America* 49 (Oct. 1967).

[2] Pearson's *r*, or the product-moment correlation is one of the most useful and popular of the correlation coefficients and is ideal for the kind of data used here, where all variables are interval in nature. The coefficient in fact measures the amount of spread around a linear least-squares equation and indicates the strength of a relationship between two variables (in this chapter: voting Democratic in one election and voting Democratic in another, for ethnic groups). Pearson's *r*, like other correlation coefficients, is a measure of relationship and not of causation. It varies between -1 (perfect negative correlation) and $+1$ (perfect positive correlation). It is most simply expressed by the formula:

$$r = \frac{N\Sigma XY - (\Sigma X)(\Sigma Y)}{\sqrt{[N\Sigma X^2 - (\Sigma X)^2][N\Sigma Y^2 - (\Sigma Y)^2]}}$$

Calculations of Pearson's *r* throughout this book were done on an Underwood-Olivetti Programma desktop computer, using the program instructions provided by the manufacturer. See Hubert M. Blalock, *Social Statistics* (New York, 1960), pp. 285–92, and Richard Jensen, "Methods of Statistical Association for Historical Research," Mimeo. (St. Louis, Mo., 1968), pp. 8–14.

TABLE IV:1   *Coefficients of Correlation of Presidential Elections, 1920-1936, for Nine Ethnic Groups*[*]

	1920	1924	1928	1932	1936
1920	—	.99	.82	.69	.65
1924		—	.84	.72	.71
1928			—	.95	.95
1932				—	.96
1936					—

[*]Calculations of Pearson's r for percentage Democratic of vote of each of nine ethnic groups for each election with each other election. For clarity only one side of table is given, since the two sides are identical.

relates different types of elections to one another. This does confuse the picture somewhat, especially since 1928 correlates at a higher order with the off-year elections of 1926 and 1922 than that of 1930, contrary to expectations, especially since 1930 has a high order correlation with 1932. On the other hand, though, there is a near-perfect relationship between 1928 and 1934. There is no ready explanation for these figures, except to note that the constituencies and situations of off-year elections are not the same as those of presidential years and that we are probably on firmer footing when we compare elections of the same type. For example, with the exception of 1930 (where the contest pitted a male against a female for the United States Senate, a quite unusual situation), every off-year election correlates at .90 or higher with every other off-year election, while the relationship to presidential elections is generally lower, until 1928, which has an overall closer relationship to off-year Democratic voting than any other presidential election of the time.

Correlation coefficients can be used to illuminate the La Follette phenomenon of 1924, particularly to determine whether levels of La Follette voting bear any relationship to Democratic voting among the nine ethnic groups. The coefficients are: 1918: .09; 1920: —.19; 1922:

TABLE IV:2   Coefficients of Correlation of Presidential Elections, 1892-1936, for Seven Ethnic Groups*

	1892	1896	1900	1904	1908	1912	1916	1920	1924	1928	1932	1936
1892	—	.96	.98	.79	.87	.74	.93	.90	.94	.94	.87	.88
1896		—	.95	.85	.85	.75	.83	.92	.94	.83	.73	.73
1900			—	.73	.82	.76	.93	.90	.94	.95	.83	.87
1904				—	.94	.82	.72	.60	.67	.61	.61	.61
1908					—	.90	.88	.64	.73	.75	.76	.80
1912						—	.83	.52	.67	.62	.53	.66
1916							—	.73	.84	.92	.86	.95
1920								—	.99	.82	.69	.65
1924									—	.84	.72	.71
1928										—	.95	.95
1932											—	.96
1936												—

*Calculations of Pearson's r for percentage Democratic vote of each of seven ethnic groups for each election with each other election. For clarity only one side of table is given, since the two sides are identical.

TABLE IV:3   Coefficients of Correlation of National/State Elections, 1918-1936, for Nine Ethnic Groups*

	1918	1920	1922	1924	1926	1928	1930	1932	1934	1936
1918	—	.87	.94	.90	.93	.95	.71	.87	.93	.88
1920		—	.94	.99	.80	.82	.53	.69	.81	.65
1922			—	.95	.91	.94	.71	.86	.93	.83
1924				—	.84	.84	.54	.72	.85	.71
1926					—	.93	.84	.91	.94	.88
1928						—	.81	.95	.99	.95
1930							—	.94	.77	.84
1932								—	.92	.95
1934									—	.94
1936										—

*Calculations of Pearson's r for percentage Democratic of vote of each of nine ethnic groups for each election with each other election. For clarity only one side of table is given, since the two sides are identical.

TABLE IV:4 *Coefficients of Correlation of*
Mayoral Elections, 1919-1931,
*for Nine Ethnic Groups**

	1919	1923	1927	1931
1919	—	.75	.87	.72
1923		—	.64	.35
1927			—	.89
1931				—

*Calculations of Pearson's r for percentage Democratic of vote of nine ethnic groups for each election with each other.

.08; 1924: —.18; 1926: .32; 1928: .31; 1930: .62; 1932: .46. The answer is negative; there are no statistically significant relationships between Democratic voting among the nine ethnic groups and voting for La Follette in 1924. The increasing high order after 1924 is suggestive, but the figures are too small to merit any conclusions about meaningful relationships between voting for La Follette in 1924 and voting Democratic in any ensuing election. This again would tend to deny that the La Follette candidacy was important in breaking the ethnic groups as a whole out of the Democratic party; it does not deny, however, that this might have applied to individual groups.

Finally, the coefficient of correlation for the seven groups voting for Roosevelt in 1912 and La Follette in 1924 is —.25, both statistically insignificant and negative. In the ethnic model, and to Chicago's ethnics, the Progressive movements of 1912 and 1924 were totally unrelated.

Tables IV:4 and IV:5, which deal with the relationships of mayoral elections to one another and to presidential elections, show perhaps most clearly the difficulty of comparing different types of elections with one another. Table IV:4 gives the coefficients for the four mayoral elections of 1919–1931 with one another, in terms of percentage Democratic of the vote of the nine ethnic groups. The highest order correlations are

TABLE IV:5   *Coefficients of Correlation of Mayoral with Presidential Elections, 1919-1932, for Nine Ethnic Groups* *

		Presidential Elections			
		1920	1924	1928	1932
Mayoralties	1919	.90	.90	.91	.82
	1923	.86	.91	.74	.53
	1927	.84	.85	.90	.92
	1931	.59	.60	.79	.91

*Calculations of Pearson's r for percentage Democratic of vote of nine ethnic groups for each mayoralty with each presidential election.

between the various elections when William Hale Thompson ran as the Republican candidate: 1919, 1927, and 1931; although between the first and last of these the correlation is not quite significant. The table does suggest that the ethnics tended to vote similarly when Thompson was a candidate in a mayoralty. It also points to the unusual character of the 1923 campaign. Beyond this, the data do not indicate much; mayoral elections were on the whole less closely related to one another than state and national contests.

Table IV:5 seeks relationships in Democratic voting for the nine groups between mayoral and presidential elections. It suggests nothing spectacular, but does reinforce the logical assumption that mayoral results are nearer in nature to the presidential elections closest to them in time. The 1931 mayoral Democratic vote correlates at a higher order with the 1928 and 1932 presidential elections than with the earlier ones. Even the .79 correlation between 1928 and 1931 indicates that Democratic voting for Al Smith in 1928 "explains" 62 percent of the ethnic vote for Cermak in 1931. Although the high order 1928–1919 correlation fuzzes the pattern, the data to a degree do supplement my previous conclusions about the change effected by 1928; the pattern is by no means indisputable, however.

In addition to correlation coefficients, which measure association between pairs of elections, a couple of other measures can be used to indicate the extent of agreement between and within ethnic groups for each election. To say, for example, that the ethnics voted 57 percent Democratic for president in 1932 infers two things: 1) this is a mean, the arithmetic average of the Democratic vote of each group divided by the number of groups; and 2) the percentage Democratic for each individual group is also a mean, the arithmetic average of the Democratic vote of the sample areas for each group. These means are standard measures of central tendency; it is also worthwhile to look into measures of dispersion.

The range between the voting of the various groups is an example of such dispersion. Some groups were consistently more Republican and some more Democratic, and changes in this measure could be significant. This can be regularized by using the standard deviation, which is the most widely used measure of dispersion and one quite well suited to these data. The intuitive meaning of the standard deviation's numerical expression is not too important here; it can be used as an abstract number, which is a function of the range, which makes for ready comparisons of one election to another.[3] What is important is that the smaller the standard deviation (s), the less the dispersion, or greater the agreement, between voting units.

[3] The standard deviation (s) is defined as the square root of the arithmetic mean of the squared deviations of each score from the mean. It can be expressed algebraically as follows:

$$s = \sqrt{\frac{\Sigma X^2}{N} - \overline{X}^2}$$

While extreme values can give a misleadingly high s, the picture is less distorted and more useful than its alternatives. In conjunction with the means, given in Chapter 3 and the Appendix, s provides much useful information. Calculations of s were done on an Underwood-Olivetti Programma desktop computer, using the program instructions provided by the manufacturer. See Blalock, *Social Statistics*, pp. 67–70.

TABLE IV:6   *Standard Deviation for Ethnic Group Democratic Voting,*
             1890-1936

Election	s for all groups*	s for five recent immigrant groups
1890: State Treasurer	10.0	
1892: President	9.7	
1894: State Treasurer	7.2	
1896: President	8.7	
1898: State Treasurer	8.2	
1900: President	10.0	
1902: State Treasurer	9.7	
1904: President	6.8	
1906: State Treasurer	11.4	
1908: President	8.9	
1910: State Treasurer	14.3	
1912: President	5.0	
1914: Senator	15.4	
1916: President	17.7	
1918: Senator	15.8	8.5
1920: President	14.6	11.8
1922: State Treasurer	18.0	14.5
1924: President	12.4	10.6
1926: Senator	15.2	11.8
1928: President	18.0	9.2
1930: Senator	20.0	8.8
1932: President	20.0	9.4
1934: State Treasurer	17.6	11.4
1936: President	14.8	4.9

TABLE IV:6   *(continued)*:

Election	s for all groups*	s for five recent immigrant groups
MAYORALTIES:		
1891	8.7	
1893	9.6	
1895	7.6	
1897	9.4	
1899	7.2	
1901	9.1	
1903	7.9	
1905	10.6	
1907	11.2	
1911	8.4	
1915	11.7	
1919	17.5	8.5
1923	15.8	12.1
1927	15.6	10.1
1931	18.6	13.4

*Computed for seven ethnic groups, 1890–1916, and for nine ethnic groups, 1918–1936; s computed for the Democratic vote percentage of each of the groups per election.

TABLE IV:7   Standard Deviations of Democratic Vote of Individual Ethnic Groups, 1918-1936*

Election	Czechoslovaks	Poles	Italians	Yugoslavs	Lithuanians	Germans	Swedes	Jews	Negroes
1918: Senator	6.4	12.6	17.6	12.1	11.0	15.5	11.6	7.0	16.0
1920: President	9.3	18.2	15.5	4.0	4.7	6.6	9.7	2.9	8.2
1922: St. Treas.	8.0	18.0	16.7	8.5	3.6	22.3	9.8	13.8	14.7
1924: President	9.0	14.6	12.8	7.0	19.8	8.4	8.3	11.5	3.5
1926: Senator	5.6	17.9	18.2	3.8	6.2	19.1	9.4	16.5	10.3
1928: President	4.2	10.4	9.5	5.8	7.6	22.8	7.6	8.5	6.4
1930: Senator	2.9	6.8	11.4	14.6	10.8	5.4	8.4	4.7	8.8
1932: President	1.9	5.6	10.2	6.6	3.3	14.4	6.0	3.2	6.2
1934: St. Treas.	7.1	6.3	10.2	5.0	4.8	7.4	5.7	6.6	11.2
1936: President	1.5	2.9	6.7	1.2	2.9	8.5	9.9	5.3	5.5

MAYORALTIES:

1919	6.4	18.9	12.3	5.6	5.4	20.4	11.4	6.6	14.2
1923	12.5	18.4	12.3	7.5	7.4	24.1	12.5	22.0	17.3
1927	6.3	9.1	13.3	5.5	8.8	22.4	14.6	16.7	3.6
1931	5.5	8.3	7.0	1.0	8.0	11.7·	8.0	15.2	6.3

*Three areas (Czech El, Polish El, and Jewish Cl—see Appendix) were excluded from computation because they are not usable for the entire eighteen years and thus would throw calculations off if used here.

Table IV:6 gives s for the voting of the ethnic groups 1890–1936, plus s for the five recent immigrant groups (excluding Germans, Swedes, Jews, and Negroes from the computation) for 1918–1936. The figures for all groups do indicate the elections where the greatest changes seem to have taken place: disagreement increases and dispersion is greater. Thus s for state and national elections tends to be higher in the period 1918–1932 than in the prewar period; and within the former period s is at its highest in 1928–1932. This is logical, since it was at this time that most groups were greatly increasing their Democratic vote, pulling away from more Republican groups such as the Negroes and Swedes.

For this reason I have separately computed s for the five newer immigrant groups for 1918–1936. Here there is a drawing together in the later elections for national office. Interestingly, s is lower for 1928 than for any other presidential election of the period through 1932; the Smith election served to draw recent immigrants closer together in their voting behavior. So if 1928 and succeeding elections saw increased voting division between ethnic groups as a whole, they also saw increased voting agreement between the newer immigrant groups on whose allegiance the New Deal coalition would be built.

The s pattern in local elections is less clear. Again, s does increase over time, and there is a direct similarity to the national election picture of 1928–1932 in the 1931 mayoralty, where ethnic Democratic voting and s both reach new highs. This tends to support our data and assumptions in Chapter 3. But the figures for s of recent immigrant groups only do not decrease as might be expected; this reflects the strength of Republican "Big Bill" Thompson's hold on some newer immigrants, especially the Italians, all the way through the 1931 election.

Our dispersion measure can be carried to a more intensive expression by showing s for each individual ethnic group's Democratic voting. This is done in Table IV:7. These figures give the dispersion in Democratic voting between the several areas that make up the sample for each group. Generated here is a considerable increase in data. The figures are useful both to illuminate voting agreement over time of each group, and to permit a more ready remanipulation of the data by those who would care to do so.

For the five newer immigrant groups, 1928 does see more agreement within groups than was usual in the decade preceding it, thus reinforcing my conclusion from Table IV:6. This is also true for Jews. But quite the contrary prevails among the Germans, suggesting that the great increase in German Democratic voting in 1928 came from only parts of the German-American community; the difference was socioeconomic, and perhaps also religious. By and large s continued to diminish after 1928, particularly in presidential years. Indeed, several of the groups show consistently higher s in off-year elections. This does not necessarily suggest that such elections were more controversial; rather, interest was often considerably less, and interest groups less active, so that constituencies likely varied in off-year elections. This points again to the difficulty of comparing different kinds of elections.

The mayoralties show a general decrease in s over time, especially in comparing 1931 to its predecessors. Thus while the 1931 mayoralty did not diminish intergroup dispersion among recent immigrant groups (Table IV:6), it did see a real decrease in intragroup dispersion and in that respect corresponds to the national/state elections of 1928–1932. Overall, then, it shows further support for the contention that the period of increased Democratic voting starting with 1928 was also a period of increasing agreement both within and between ethnic groups, particularly the recent immigrants.

Another way of seeking the same kind of information found with standard deviations is through the use of a success score or measure of cohesion. Table IV:8 is based on the Rice Index of Cohesion, a very convenient and straightforward measure of agreement/disagreement. C (cohesion) is computed by subtracting the number of areas with a Democratic majority (plurality in cases of the three-party race of 1924) from those with a Republican majority (or vice versa, whichever yields a positive result) and dividing the result by the total number of areas. The index produces a number between zero and one, wherein a score of one would mean that all the areas voted the same way. We thus have either a Democratic or a Republican C, in an index which portrays very simply the extent of agreement of more than forty areas (precincts and groups of precincts) which comprise the sample of the nine ethnic groups.[4]

[4] The Rice Index of Cohesion, as used here, is by no means a perfect measure, since I have engaged in no weighting to compensate for the fact that there are more areas for some ethnic groups than for others. Thus Poles (seven areas) will have more weight in the index than Yugoslavs (three areas). But since I am

TABLE IV:8   *Rice Index of Cohesion for Voting of Nine Ethnic Groups, 1918-1936*[*]

Election	Number of Democratic areas	Number of Republican areas	Index and party of cohesion
1918: Senator	30	11	.46 Democratic
1920: President	7	34	.66 Republican
1922: State Treasurer	22	21	.02 Democratic
1924: President	10	33	.54 Republican
1926: Senator	27	17	.23 Democratic
1928: President	29	15	.32 Democratic
1930: Senator	39	5	.77 Democratic
1932: President	37	7	.68 Democratic
1934: State Treasurer	35	9	.59 Democratic
1936: President	39	5	.77 Democratic
MAYORALTIES:			
1919	24	17	.17 Democratic
1923	31	12	.44 Democratic
1927	19	25	.14 Republican
1931	31	13	.41 Democratic

[*]Total number of areas varies from 41 to 44 because of three areas which are added to sample during the period.

Unfortunately, methodological limitations on the data for 1890–1916 preclude their inclusion in this measure; but this index can be used to make another inquiry into the 1918–1936 period.

The data in Table IV:8 are self-explanatory. They reinforce the conclusions of my other measures and are particularly congruent with the percentage figures in Chapter 3. The data indicate the fairly high wartime Democratic support, followed by strong Republican cohesion in the early 1920s. The cohesion index does indicate the questionable nature of stressing 1928 as a sole turning point, although—as with percentage figures—1928 does end the cycle of off-year Democratic voting followed by presidential-year Republican voting. This points to a critical period of voting change, wherein 1928 plays the single largest role. And if this measure points somewhat less to the influence of 1928 than others do, it also points somewhat more to the influence of the 1931 mayoralty in bringing local ethnic voting behavior into line with state and national. My main concern, obviously, is with the extent of congruence of the several measures, and this is reasonably clear.

---

using the index for comparisons within the same data, and the universe remains the same, the measure is certainly valid. See Jensen, "Methods of Statistical Association," p. 65.

V. Ethnic Group
Party Identification

Voting returns comprise the best but not the only data source for studying changes in political behavior among ethnic groups. Party membership or identification of the ethnic masses and their leaders is another significant indicator. Did ethnic attachments to political parties, either in terms of mass party identification or that of group political leaders, change from 1920 to 1932? Were those changes consistent with changes in voting behavior?

Registration records provide information about party identification. In 1928 and thereafter Chicago had closed primaries; voters were obliged to register in advance and declare their party membership in order to vote in the primary. Here, then, was a positive act, a commitment, on the part of the voter, and a definite indication of his party identification. Unfortunately, we are obliged to use a less exact measure prior to 1928.[1]

The major difference between ethnic voting returns and data on party identification is that according to the latter the ethnic switch to the Democratic party came later and was less dramatic. Thus while only the Negroes—and, in part, the Swedes—delivered Republican voting majorities in 1932, these two groups and two others still had Republican registration majorities in that year.

There was a reasonably strong similarity between a group's voting and its party identification (see Table V:1). The newer immigrants were more Democratic in both; and those groups which voted most Democratic were also most Democratic in party identification. The Lithuanians, for example, showed strong Democratic identification from 1918 to 1924—more than 67 percent in each year. But they were the only group with Democratic identification majorities over all five elections to 1924. The Czechs and Poles, predictably, were next most Democratic, but neither showed Democratic majorities in 1920. The Italians were Democratic in 1918 and 1919, but then switched dramatically. And the Yugoslavs were strongly Republican throughout.

Generally, newer immigrant Democratic identification, like voting, decreased steadily in the early 1920s. Thus highs in Republican voting and identification occurred at the same time many newer immigrants were just starting to vote, and many were beginning their participation in American politics with Republican allegiances. By the primary of 1927 all the newer immigrant groups (indeed, all ethnic groups) showed Republican identification majorities. The Czechs, Lithuanians, and Poles were above 40 percent Democratic then, and the Yugoslavs and Italians were well below. In the spring of 1928 (the first year for which the data become more accurate) every group except the Czechs fell even further in Democratic party identification. Thus, on the eve of their major voting shift into the Democratic party, Chicago's newer immigrants reached new lows in terms of identification with that party. This makes the 1928 pro-Democratic switch even more impressive.

The 1928 election produced some change in this: total percentage strength of newer immigrant Democratic registration rose thirty-three points in the 1930 primary. Even so, only the Czechs showed Democratic majorities at that time. The election of 1930, despite the highest Demo-

[1] The City of Chicago was not completely consistent in the way it kept its records during this period. Through the election of 1927, the official election returns for primaries did not list the number in each ward and precinct registered in each party; rather, they listed the total number voting in each primary contest. This is not as accurate a figure as the total registered (which was given from the 1928 primary on), but represents what was generally the same thing, so is being used. However, data from 1928 on are clearly more reliable. Both of these figures, but particularly the former, were affected by the amount of interest in a given primary election, and since Democratic primaries during the period tended to be cut-and-dried affairs, while Republican factionalism made their primaries always hotly contested, there is a certain prejudicing of the data in favor of unrepresentatively high Republican party membership on the part of all ethnics. I decided to use these data despite these qualifications, because they do have value for our understanding of developing party membership; it is necessary only to remember that this is another of the indicators for ethnic political behavior, and that since it is one of many, we are less likely to be misled by it. Furthermore, its innate prejudice toward indicating Republican membership will serve to give my conclusions about the development of the Democratic consensus the added weight of conservatism. I use the term *identification* rather than *membership* because prior to 1928 I do not really have membership data.

TABLE V:1   *Ethnic Party Identification, 1918-1932 (Percentage Democratic of declared members of the two major parties*)*

Group	1918	1919	1920	1923	1924	1927	1928	1930	1931	1932
Czechs	81	62	39	62	58	41	50.4	60	69	72
Poles	63	53	47	56	55	46	39	41	40	64
Lithuanians	81	81	68	78	69	46	46	45	36	65
Yugoslavs	37	35	15	27	34	22	13	15	26	38
Italians	71	62	38	34	39	22	15	35	29	46
Germans	50.1	54	30	28	31	19	16	30	29	59
Swedes	27	25	14	21	23	21	12	16	16	32
Jews	43	37	22	38	39	37	29	36	50.4	67
Negroes	25	22	11	13	12	5	8	11	12	23
Native-Americans	38	26	27	26	25	21	16	21	16	36

*Party membership calculated on basis of: total number voting in relevant primary contest, 1918 to 1927, inclusive; total number of names on poll book (i.e., number of declared party members), 1928 to 1932. Source: Official election returns, City of Chicago.

cratic vote of the period, did not produce increased newer immigrant Democratic registration (three groups decreased and two increased in the 1931 primary). But the 1931 mayoralty, and the accession of the Democrats to power locally, was very effective: percentage strength of newer immigrant Democratic identification rose among all five groups, a total of eighty-five points, in the 1932 primary. The Czechs, Poles, and Lithuanians now showed strong Democratic majorities, while the Italians and Yugoslavs, despite large Democratic increases, were still Republican.

Two conclusions emerge from this data. First, growing newer immigrant Democratic party identification was created not by any one election, but rather by the cumulative effect of the several general elections starting with 1928. The 1928 national and 1931 local elections were particularly successful in producing increased Democratic registrations. Second, the large Democratic voting majorities given by the ethnics in the 1928, 1930, and 1931 elections did not immediately translate themselves into majorities in party identification. The cumulative effect just noted and the passage of time were necessary before the newer immigrants were persuaded that they were not simply Democratic voters, but were Democrats as well. The idea of a critical period of political change, rather than a single election, is thus reinforced.

Party identification among the older immigrants and the Jews was roughly similar to that among newer immigrants, although a little closer to voting behavior. The Germans were barely Democratic in 1918 and 1919, and then clearly Republican until 1932—the same pattern as their voting except that the Democratic voting shift preceded the registration shift by four years. The Swedes were strongly Republican throughout, but they, too, increased their Democratic registration in 1932, just as their Democratic voting increased in the same year. And the Jews were firmly Republican until 1931, when they showed a slight Democratic registration majority, which jumped further in 1932.

The older immigrants also reached a low point in Democratic identification in the spring of 1928 and then began to rise. The 1928 election led to a percentage strength Democratic increase of eighteen points. As with the newer immigrants, this decreased after the 1930 election (one point), but then jumped after the 1931 mayoralty by forty-six points, so that in the spring of 1932 two of the three groups had Democratic registration majorities. The Jews varied slightly: their Democratic registration did not decrease in 1931, but continued its steady increase, thus showing the best example of the cumulative effect on party identification. And in party identification, as in voting, the Jews and Germans made very clear and dramatic shifts.

This party identification measure denies any profound effect by the La Follette candidacy on party loyalties of the most pro-La Follette groups. Germans, for example, were 31 percent Democratic in the 1924 primary and this decreased to 19 percent in 1927 and to 16 percent in 1928. And Jewish Democratic identification also decreased during the same period, although to a lesser extent. Thus while the La Follette candidacy did serve to make 1928 Democratic voting easier for Germans and Jews, it did not have any immediate effect on their party identification. They seemed content to remain renegade Republicans until the cumulative effect of several Democratic voting experiences resulted at last in their identifying with the Democratic party.

The same general conclusions about party identification apply to the older immigrants and Jews as to the newer immigrants. This is true also of the Negroes, whose party identification closely reflected their voting. Never did Negro Democratic identification exceed 25 percent, and it fell as low as 5 percent in the middle of the decade. The increase to 23 percent by 1932 still left Negro party identification overwhelmingly Republican.

Like the ethnic voter, the ethnic press could well "vote" for candidates of one party while identifying with the other. The extent to which the ethnic press identified with, or felt it belonged to, one major party or the other will serve as a further indication of ethnic party allegiance.

Ethnic newspapers often considered themselves basically nonpartisan, and to second-guess them is not easy. Issues and personalities do not concern us here. We are interested in press identification with the party, as party, apart from issues or candidates. Ethnic press party identification will also contribute to understanding the pictures of the two parties which ethnics, or their influentials, had over time.

The Polish press reflected Polish voting behavior, if not Polish party registration, in consistently seeing the Democratic party as the party of the Poles. At the start of the period the *Dziennik Chicagoski* was issue-oriented rather than party-oriented, but by the mid-1920s its identification with the Democrats was strong. At the time of the 1923 mayoralty, it saw the Democratic party as the only "popular" one and in 1924 identified it generally with "a better living for the future."[2] Similarly, in the same year a Republican Polish politician ruefully acknowledged that most Poles identified with the Democratic party.[3] This continued into 1928, 1930, and 1932, with the paper supporting the entire Democratic ticket in each election and endorsing the Democratic side of every issue.[4]

The most politically interested representative of the Polish press, then, did identify strongly with the Democrats. This did not, however, denote change, since the same was true in 1920 as in 1932. The same consistently Democratic identification was probably true for the Czech press as well—it seemed generally to see the Democratic party as "ours." Other Slavic groups were similar; in fact, by the end of the period, the large Slavic Alliance of America was virtually a Democratic appendage.[5]

The case of the Italians was somewhat different, in that the basic identification of the press remained Republican. As Italian party identification stayed Republican while Italian voting became more Democratic from 1928 on, the Italian press agreed with the former rather than the latter. *La Tribuna Italiana Trans-Atlantica* demonstrated a strong emotional Republicanism at the beginning of the period, in 1918. Many issues were debated, some of them real and some imagined (Senator James H. Lewis's "partisan opposition to McKinley and the Spanish-American War"), but basically it was a case of devotion to the "glorious past" of the Republican party.[6] This identification continued into 1919 and 1920, for *L'Italia* as well as *La Tribuna.* For both papers only the Republican party had virtues and qualified as the Italians' political home; as *L'Italia* put it, a Republican vote in 1920 was a "duty to party."[7]

This allegiance continued into the mid-1920s. For example, *La Tribuna,* which really ignored the 1924 campaign, at the last moment simply reassured Italian voters that even though Calvin Coolidge looked

[2] *Dziennik Chicagoski,* Mar. 30, 1923, p. 1; Nov. 4, 1924, p. 1.

[3] Chicago *Tribune,* Sept. 24, 1924, p. 1; Nov. 1, 1924, p. 2.

[4] *Dziennik Chicagoski,* Nov. 5, 1928, p. 1ff.; Oct. 21, 30, and 31, 1930, p. 1; Nov. 2, 1932, pp. 2, 5.

[5] *Jugoslavenski Glasnik,* 31:14 (April 2, 1936), WPA. Also: *Denni Hlasatel,* April 1, 1923, WPA; *Osadne Hlasy,* Oct. 17, 1930, WPA.

[6] *La Tribuna Italiana Trans-Atlantica,* Nov. 2, 1918, p. 1.

[7] Ibid., Oct. 9, 1920, p. 7; *L'Italia,* Mar. 30, 1919, p. 1; Oct. 31, 1920, p. 1; Sept. 21, 1920, WPA.

like a "puritan," they should continue to support the Republican party, and that was all.[8] *L'Italia* told Italian voters that the Progressive party existed only "to place a stick in the wheels of the national party."[9] The fact that the editor did not feel it necessary to put "Republican" after "national" demonstrates that he thought in Republican terms. And in the 1927 mayoralty, *L'Italia* endorsed Thompson in the process of being "faithful to our Republican program."[10] Similarly, the attractiveness of Al Smith in 1928 did not really mean that Italians had changed their party identification. When *L'Italia* shattered precedent by not endorsing the Republican presidential candidate, it nonetheless supported all other Republican candidates, and its owner personally supported Hoover as well.[11] The same sentiment was expressed by *La Tribuna* two years later; in supporting an Italian Democrat for Congress it made it clear that this did not mean any shift in basic party loyalty.[12]

The German press, like its readers, was more politically sophisticated and issue-oriented, and therefore its party identification is less clear. Its consistent support of Democrats at the end of the period, contrasted to its generally Republican leaning earlier, does indicate that the German press agreed with its readership in its conception of the two major parties.[13]

The Swedish press and Scandinavian opinion leaders demonstrated a more determined emotional attachment to party, and this, of course, was Republican. The Dovre Club, the leading Norwegian-American organization, and the John Ericsson League, its near-equivalent among the Swedes, were both virtual appendages of the Republican party. This phenomenon went back to the late nineteenth century.[14] Both organiza-

---

[8] *La Tribuna Italiana Trans-Atlantica,* Oct. 11, 1924, p. 2.

[9] *L'Italia,* Nov. 2, 1924, p. 1.

[10] Ibid., April 3, 1927, p. 1.

[11] Ibid., Nov. 4, 1928, p. 1; *La Tribuna Italiana Trans-Atlantica,* Nov. 3, 1928, p. 7; Mrs. Oscar Durante, personal interview.

[12] *La Tribuna Italiana Trans-Atlantica,* Nov. 11, 1930, p. 1. Unfortunately, neither paper could be located for 1932. *L'Italia* did remain Republican in that election, however; Mrs. Oscar Durante, personal interview.

[13] See *Abendpost,* Nov. 3, 1929, WPA; Nov. 7, 1932, p. 1; Nov. 3, 1934, WPA.

[14] Gustave E. Johnson, "The Swedes of Chicago" (Ph.D. diss., University of Chicago, 1940), pp. 39–43 and 53–54. The 1910 constitution of the Dovre Club stated that its object would be "to inculcate the political principles on which the Republican Party is founded" (Birger Osland, *A Long Pull from Stavanger* [Northfield, Minn., 1945], p. 48).

tions were issue-oriented, supporting the progressive wing of the Republican party, but when this wing did not prevail they still remained Republican.[15] Similarly, the *Svenska-Tribunen-Nyheter* preferred La Follette to Coolidge in 1924, but endorsed the latter out of a desire to maintain Republican party strength; the John Ericsson League agreed.[16]

The limited Swedish leaning to Smith in 1928 was personal and not partisan in nature. When the owner of *Svenska-Tribunen-Nyheter* (but not his paper) endorsed and worked for Al Smith, it seemed to the other leading Swedish paper, *Svenska-Kuriren,* that something really dismaying had taken place.[17] This view of the Republican party as the Swede's party continued through 1932. As one student of the group put it in 1940, "The story of the Swedes in politics [in Chicago] is the story of loyalty to the Republican Party."[18]

The dramatic change in Jewish voting and party membership from 1928 to 1932 was not reflected in the Yiddish press, since the Democratic *Courier* and Socialist *Forward* maintained consistent party identifications from the start of the period to its end. As the *Courier* believed in 1924 ("The Democratic Party has always been and we hope always will be the torchbearer of true liberalism"), so too did it believe in 1932.[19] And the *Forward* was likewise consistent in its disdain for all capitalist parties.

Jewish opinion leaders, however, did follow the trend of Jewish voting and party identification. And the more conservative and issue-oriented German Jews began, after 1928, to join the newer immigrant Jews in identifying with the Democratic party.[20]

[15] Thus the Dovre Club worked mightily to defeat Thompson in the 1919 Republican primary, but endorsed him when he got the nomination (*Skandinaven,* Sept. 12, 1920, WPA; *Scandia,* Mar. 8, 1919, WPA). This tendency changed somewhat in later elections, in that the animosity of the "respectables" to the Thompson-Small organization became so great that they would sometimes endorse Democrats, as in 1924, which was the first time in thirty years that the Dovre Club supported any Democrat (Chicago *Tribune,* Oct. 8, 1924, p. 4; Oct. 21, 1924, p. 6; Oct. 28, 1924, p. 4).

[16] Reuel G. Hemdahl, "The Swedes in Illinois Politics: An Immigrant Group in an American Political Setting" (Ph. D. diss., Northwestern University, 1932), p. 435; Chicago *Tribune,* Oct. 21, 1924, p. 6.

[17] Johnson, "The Swedes of Chicago," pp. 53–54.

[18] Ibid., pp. 54, 103.

[19] Chicago *Jewish Courier,* Oct. 29, 1924, p. 8; Nov. 4, 1932, p. 8.

[20] Dr. Louis L. Mann, personal interview; see also M. R. Werner, *Julius Rosenwald: The Life of a Practical Humanitarian* (New York, 1939), passim.

Party identification in the Negro press and among Negro opinion leaders complemented the voting and identification of the mass of Negroes, in firm adherence to the Republican party. Despite occasional attraction to Democratic candidates and issues, this did not really waver. In 1920 the *Defender* said that "the Democrats have frankly told us that we are not wanted."[21] And its 1928 support of Smith was strictly personal and not partisan.[22] It was not really surprising in 1930, when Mayor Thompson supported the Democratic candidate for the Senate, that Negro political leader Oscar De Priest called him a "sick man" for expecting Negroes to do likewise.[23] And in 1932 the *Defender* felt just about the same as it had in 1920: "Every right we enjoy in this country was bestowed upon us by the Republican Party."[24]

Further indications of ethnic political allegiance exist at the party leadership level. The proportions of ethnic candidates and officeholders in the two major parties at chosen points in time indicate whether ethnic political leaders remained within the same party or made a shift similar to that of their constituents. This points not only to which party ethnic political leaders felt would prevail but also which they felt commanded the allegiance of their own strongest supporters, the members of their respective groups.

The party allegiance of ethnic political leaders is as well a cause as an indicator of political change (see Chapter 8). Here, however, we are interested only in the latter, effective aspect of the phenomenon.

Through listing the names of candidates in the ten elections studied and tagging the applicable names with one of five ethnicities (German, Scandinavian, Italian, Jewish, Slavic), we arrive at a quantitative measure of ethnic party leadership. The same procedure was followed for everyone to hold the post of ward committeeman (party leader at the ward level, an elective position) during the same period. Tables V:2 and V:3 summarize these data.[25]

---

[21] Chicago *Defender,* Oct. 30, 1920, p. 12.
[22] Ibid., Nov. 3, 1928, Pt. 2, p. 2.
[23] Chicago *Tribune,* Oct. 27, 1930, p. 8.
[24] Chicago *Defender,* Nov. 5, 1932, p. 1ff.
[25] This includes most candidates for most offices, but not all of them. Particularly to be missed are precinct captains, whose names were not available, and aldermen (members of the city council, one elected from each ward), who

TABLE V:2   Ethnic Composition of Party Slates, 1918–1932 (Number of candidates; D = Democratic; R = Republican)

Election year and no. of contests	German		Scandinavian		Italian		Jewish		Slavic		Total	
	D	R	D	R	D	R	D	R	D	R	D	R
1918: 58	5	4	0	3	1	1	2	1	6	5	14	11
1919: 41	7	5	1	1	1	0	1	2	5	7	15	15
1920: 50	6	10	0	5	1	1	4	3	2	1	13	20
1923: 3	0	1	0	0	0	0	0	0	1	0	1	1
1924: 46	6	8	2	4	0	1	2	0	4	1	14	14
1927: 3	0	0	0	1	0	0	0	0	1	0	1	1
1928: 33	3	7	0	8	2	0	1	1	4	1	10	17
1930: 57	9	13	0	3	2	2	3	1	6	2	20	21
1931: 4	1	0	0	0	0	0	0	0	2	0	3	1
1932: 61	5	5	0	2	2	4	4	4	10	3	21	18
TOTAL	42	53	3	27	9	9	17	12	41	20	112	119

TABLE V:3 *Ethnicity of Chicago Ward Committeemen, 1918–1932 (Number of ward committeemen; D = Democratic; R = Republican)*

Year and no. of committeemen	German D	German R	Scandinavian D	Scandinavian R	Italian D	Italian R	Jewish D	Jewish R	Slavic D	Slavic R	Total D	Total R
1918: 35	4	10	0	3	0	0	2	2	5	1	11	16
1919: 35	3	11	0	3	0	0	2	2	4	1	9	17
1920: 35	3	11	0	3	0	0	2	2	4	1	9	17
1923: 50/35*	5	11	0	3	0	0	3	2	5	1	13	17
1924: 50/35*	6	6	0	1	0	1	3	1	5	3	14	12
1927: 50/35*	6	6	0	1	0	1	2	1	5	3	14	12
1928: 50	5	12	0	3	0	1	2	2	6	2	13	20
1930: 50	6	12	0	0	0	2	2	2	7	4	15	20
1931: 50	6	12	0	0	0	2	2	2	7	4	15	20
1932: 50	5	13	0	1	1	4	3	1	7	2	16	21
TOTAL	49	114	0	18	1	11	23	17	55	22	129	172

*Chicago was redistricted in 1921 and changed from thirty-five wards to fifty. The Democrats immediately followed suit in terms of organization. But the Republicans were so divided by faction at this time that they could not agree on reorganization until 1928; thus there continued to be only thirty-five Republican Committeemen, as opposed to fifty Democrats, from 1921 to 1928.

The data in the two tables are not definitive. But they do not conflict with our other measures. That is, the data on ethnic party leaders generally complement the data on ethnic voting and party identification and reflect the same forces in operation at the same times.

Thus among the Scandinavians, who were quite Republican throughout on our other measures, the overwhelming majority of officeseekers and officeholders remained within the Republican party. And the moderate decrease in Scandinavian Republican voting that began in 1930 was reflected in the diminishing number of Republican Scandinavian candidates and ward committeemen at the same time. Like the Scandinavian voters, their political leaders seemed more to be leaving the Republican party than joining the Democratic—leaving what appeared to be a losing cause.

The same lingering Republicanism can be seen, without late fading, among Negro political leaders. The lack of characteristic names prevents a quantitative study of the party affiliations of Negro candidates and committeemen, but the overwhelming majority remained in the Republican party in 1932 as in 1920. Their party change came between 1934 and 1940.

In the case of the Germans, the pattern is considerably less clear, since German political leaders played important roles in both parties, without major changes over time. There were greater numbers of German political leaders in the Republican party than the Democratic, and thus they did not reflect the same forces as German voters. They probably did not feel a need to do so. As members of a well-assimilated and secure ethnic group, such considerations were less important to German politicians than, for example, to Polish ones; the German political leader could well expect in 1932 to appeal to the electorate at large and thus was less strongly reliant upon his own group than was his equivalent among the newer immigrants.

The relatively unpredictable nature of Italian voting was well reflected by the fact that there were relatively few Italian politicians in the offices studied here. At the same time, the relative Republicanism of the

---

could not be used since aldermanic elections after 1921 were officially nonpartisan, and party membership of each alderman could not be obtained. Also, names of candidates for the state legislature were not always available. Source: *Chicago Daily News Almanac,* for the relevant years.

Italians, among newer immigrants, was in accord with the party membership of most Italian political leaders. But the majority of Italian voters were voting Democratic at the end of the period, and this was not reflected in the allegiance of Italian politicians at that time.[26] The voters, then, had made their party shift ahead of their own political leadership.

The Slavic data, which include all Slavic names and thus a large proportion of newer immigrants, are more clearly similar to the voting of the group involved. Almost equally divided between the parties in 1918–1920, the proportion of Democratic Slavic candidates grew progressively larger. For ward committeemen, the proportion of Democratic Slavs was greater throughout, with little change. There was a clear similarity, then, between the party preference of Slavic voters and of Slavic political leaders, with each reinforcing the other.

Jewish political leaders, on the other hand, were more like the Germans. They were found in roughly equal numbers in both parties throughout the period. There was relatively little change over time, but what change there was, was toward the Democratic party. And larger numbers of both candiates and ward committeemen were found, overall, in the Democratic party than in the Republican party. Thus the political behavior of Jewish voters and Jewish politicians was complementary.

It is significant, in considering these five ethnic categories together, that in 1920 thirteen ethnic candidates ran on the Democratic ticket and twenty on the Republican; and in 1932, twenty-one ran as Democrats and eighteen as Republicans (this difference was not seen among ward committeemen, who were much more secure in their positions). There was, then, an overall ethnic swing to the Democratic party, similar to that among ethnic voters; further, the swing of political leaders was again like that of voters in tending to develop from 1928 on.

Another indicator of the same phenomenon emerges from considering the ethnicity of the ward committeemen of selected ethnic wards. Thus if the Democratic committeeman of a Slavic ward was a Slav, while his Republican counterpart was not, this, too, indicated ethnic party

[26] This generalization would have to be somewhat qualified had it been practicable to include *all* candidates in these tables. In lesser offices, for example the Illinois state legislature, the Italians were becoming more and more represented in the Democratic party by about 1930. Another factor of importance here is the role of organized crime as a political control, especially on the Italians. Some illumination on this point will be provided in Chapter 9.

TABLE V:4   Ethnicity of Ward Committeemen of Selected Ethnic Wards at Selected Points in Time
(Ethnicity of Committeemen; D = Democratic; R = Republican)

Group & ward		1918	1924	1928	1932
Germans Ward 24/45*	D	German	German	German	German
	R	Scandinavian	Scandinavian	German	German
Swedes Ward 23/46*	D	Anglo-Saxon	Anglo-Saxon	Anglo-Saxon	Anglo-Saxon
	R	Swedish	Swedish	German	Swedish
Jews Ward 34/24*	D	Jewish	Jewish	Jewish	Jewish
	R	Polish	Polish	Jewish	Jewish
Italians Ward 18/25*	D	Irish	Irish	Irish	Irish
	R	Anglo-Saxon	Anglo-Saxon	Anglo-Saxon	Anglo-Saxon
Poles Ward 17/31*	D	Polish	Polish	Polish	Polish
	R	Anglo-Saxon	Anglo-Saxon	Swedish	Anglo-Saxon
Czechs Ward 12/22*	D	Czech	Czech	Czech	Czech
	R	German	German	German	German
Negroes Ward 2	D	Anglo-Saxon	Anglo-Saxon	Anglo-Saxon	Anglo-Saxon[†]
	R	Irish	Negro	Negro	Negro

*The two ward numbers represent pre-1921 and post-1921 numbers of single wards whose boundaries remained essentially unchanged during the period. The Republicans continued to operate organizationally along the old lines to 1928.

[†]Possibly Negro; odds very great that he was white.

affiliation. It is also an important cause of political change (see Chapter 8). We can isolate wards where each of the selected ethnic categories dominated, and look at the ethnicity of their ward committeemen (Table V:4).

The data in the table do not provide any new information and again are not definitive. There is little change over time. But they at least do not conflict with what we have previously concluded. Ethnic political leaders did move in the same direction as ethnic voters. They recognized where their constituents were going, politically, and identified with the same party. Which movement came first—that of the politicians or that of the voters—is not too important, although it seems that at least in some cases it was the voters who led the way. It is the fact of the congruence of these several factors (ethnic voting and the "voting" of the ethnic press, ethnic party identification and that of the ethnic press, and the political allegiance of ethnic political leaders) that is most significant in delineating the political behavior of Chicago's ethnic groups from 1918 to 1932. The fact that the data in this chapter generally reinforce the voting data of the previous chapters makes the generalizations offered there more meaningful.

VI. *Political Party Self-Conceptions*

Each major political party necessarily has a conception of itself, its constituent parts, and the groups in American life which are important to it. Thus party self-conception provides an interesting, if elusive, measure of political change; it can also be a cause of political change, as groups respond to developments in party self-conception. What, for example, did the parties of the 1920s construe themselves to be? Whom did they feel they represented? How did this change over time, especially in terms of the role they allotted to the ethnics? We want especially to see if there were changes in Democratic party self-conception which mirrored the growing ethnic identification with that party from 1928 on.

There are two simple measures for investigating this problem of party self-conception or self-identification: First, once every four years the national party organizations are forced to come to terms with themselves, in the drafting of platforms and nominating of presidential tickets. Here a statement is hammered out, either through compromise among factions or by the dominance of one or more factions over others. In either case the platform and the candidates are, by definition, reasonably accurate pictures of the parties' self-conceptions at the time, since the common denominator of belief, or the belief of the most powerful group(s) in the party, is thus expressed. This is found by looking at the national platforms and presidential tickets of the 1920s for this kind of information.[1]

A second indicator of party self-conception consists in what candidates say, directly or implicitly, about their parties. In many respects candidates make the party, and their conception of it—whether in accord or in conflict with the platform—can be determining. The voter is often more conscious of party through its candidates than through its organization. Moreover, candidates at the state and local level often differ with the national organization in conception of the party and thus intrude important variations at these levels which are closer to the voter.

In both of these approaches it is necessary to deal with issues, but in a special way: How do the values represented in the issue-stands of each party contribute to an understanding of which party was more receptive to the ethnics? Should the same issue be of importance for the same reason to a party as to the ethnics, it would indicate a positive sign of identification of interest.

The platforms of both national nominating conventions were conservative in 1920. They reflected the concerns of "responsible" leadership generally. Their major differences were on the question of international organization, the Democrats supporting President Woodrow Wilson and his League of Nations, and the Republicans opposing both.[2] The Republicans insisted on seeing themselves as the party of traditional American values and the Democrats as the instigators of "un-American" adventures at home and abroad. But the Democrats were radical only in Republican eyes, not their own. They emulated the Republican vagueness on organized labor and opposition to such "radicalism" as strikes. Like the Republicans they said nothing about Prohibition, even though it was the leading issue to the ethnics in 1920.

The two parties agreed in opposing Asiatic immigration, but apparently disagreed on immigration generally. The Democrats simply said nothing, while the Republicans believed that no more immigrants should

[1] Much work remains to be done in the systematic study of party platforms and platform battles over the past hundred years. Especially needed are quantitative models for analysis of the kind that are being developed in studies of the Constitutional Convention. The Democratic convention of 1924 and the Republican of 1964 are two leading examples of the kinds of basic conflict that can exist in convention and which are not necessarily seen if one looks only at the postconvention campaign.

[2] Party platforms can be found, in Kirk H. Porter and Donald B. Johnson, *National Party Platforms, 1840–1956* (Urbana, Ill., 1956). What follows is a kind of qualitative content analysis of platforms and of party decisions on candidates. The ensuing notes for this section are simply guides to major sources of information on the given convention or campaign; no effort has been made to cite all sources or be comprehensive, since the conclusions are original and taken from the surface facts of the conventions and nominations.

be admitted than could be "assimilated with reasonable rapidity" and that immigration legislation should "favor immigrants whose standards are similar to ours." The Republican party's self-conception was not one receptive to the newer immigrants. Similarly, the Republican platform had "Naturalization" and "Free Speech" planks which were essentially anti-alien and defensive of "American institutions"; the Democrats ignored these subjects.

By what they avoided saying, then, the Democrats saw themselves in 1920 in a way more representative of the ethnics, or at least less unrepresentative of them. Thus they, and not the Republicans—partially out of deference to President Wilson, but also perhaps to ethnic voters—expressed "active sympathy" with the Armenians, Chinese, Czechoslovakians, Finns, Poles, Yugoslavs, and, particularly, the Irish. For the Negro, party roles were reversed, as the Republicans continued to see themselves as his political protector, again supporting antilynching legislation. The Democrats ignored the Negro.

The tickets nominated in 1920 complemented the rather neutral, conservative policy statements of the platforms. Warren G. Harding was a compromise, chosen when the several leading candidates stalemated one another. He symbolized the regular Republican party, and particularly its congressional leadership—complacency, stability, and passivity in government.[3] The nomination of Calvin Coolidge to run with him can be interpreted as a popular delegates' rebellion against domination by the party "bosses."[4] But if so, it was a "revolt" in favor of essentially the same values personified by Harding, and indicated harmony in belief.

James M. Cox, for the Democrats, represented generally the same forces in his party—the professional politicians, who, in this case, were trying to take leadership away from President Wilson. As a mild progressive and a mild Wet, Cox was nominated after forty-three futile ballots, to compromise diverse choices. A symbol, politically, of nonadministration and non-Dry forces, he remained otherwise little different from Harding, particularly in terms of ethnic orientation.[5] Franklin D. Roosevelt, as his running mate, was selected for availability. With Cox he

[3] Wesley M. Bagby, *The Road to Normalcy* (Baltimore, Md., 1962), pp. 36–42, 85–96.

[4] Ibid., pp. 100–101.

[5] Ibid., pp. 73–76, 110–20.

represented a continuation of mild loyalty to Democratic progressivism and not a great deal more.

In 1924 the differences between the parties were even less clear. The Democrats said they were the party of human rights and change and that the Republicans were the party of material rights and stagnation. The slogan itself had some significance in terms of party self-conception, but failure to implement it specifically indicated that if some Democrats really believed it, others did not. The Democratic platform was better suited to 1912 than 1924 in the problems it saw before the nation— problems that were less relevant in 1924 and were certainly not vital to the ethnics. Again nothing was said about immigration, or the Johnson bill, and the Democratic stand on Prohibition was in effect anti-ethnic: they accused the Republicans of failing to enforce the law, and vowed to do so if they received power.

This was one sign of the lack of accord among the Democrats on what values the party should represent. An even better indication was a plank that did not appear in the platform—that on the Ku Klux Klan. The narrowness of the vote by which specific condemnation of the Klan was voted down is well known. It is also a good example of the Democrats' inability to decide in 1924 whether they were the party of Anglo-Saxon, Protestant, rural America, or of ethnic, heterogeneous, urban America. The 1924 platform and candidates clearly demonstrated that the latter elements were by no means dominant.

The Republicans were fat and happy in 1924, the Harding scandals to the contrary notwithstanding. In abbreviated form they repeated their platform of 1920 and continued to see themselves as the perpetuators of traditional American values. The new immigration restriction law was defended as a necessary protection for Americans, and laws were proposed for the "education of the alien in our language, customs, ideals and standards of life." It was as if the Democrats could not decide whether to be rural or urban, old or new, while at the same time the Republicans were trying to escape the cities and re-create their party on a nineteenth-century base.

The 1924 presidential tickets expressed the same forces as the platforms. Calvin Coolidge was simply a shoo-in, both because he was the incumbent and because he so well personified the traditional, conservative, complacent, and native-American conception that the Republicans had of themselves. This was complemented by the nomination, without much dispute, of midwestern banker and soldier Charles G. Dawes as his running mate; it was a consistent ticket.[6]

The new-old or rural-urban Democratic conflict was perfectly reflected in the excruciating battle between Al Smith and William Gibbs McAdoo for the presidential nomination. Furthermore, the equal strength of the two sides was seen in the failure of either to beat the other. Thus John W. Davis was an escape from a basic problem as well as a compromise: an honest man and loyal Democrat, but a Wall Street lawyer and a different quantity from either McAdoo or Smith. He represented honest conservatism and little more, neither Wet nor Dry, neither Klan nor anti-Klan, neither rural nor urban. And the nomination of William Jennings Bryan's brother Charles to run with him was so patently contrived as to be insignificant, except as further proof that the rural forces of the party continued strong.[7]

Finally, in 1924, there was Robert M. La Follette and his Progressive party. Both the Conference for Progressive Political Action and La Follette personally drew up platforms, and the two were essentially the same: short statements of the major ills of the time and of their proposed cures. Like the Democratic platform of 1924, those of the Progressives were probably better suited to 1912. La Follette's platform opened with: "The great issue before the American people today is the control of government and industry by private monopoly." Even if true, which is hardly likely, this statement did not express a self-conception of party cognizant of new forces in American life, particularly that of the ethnics. The issues of interest to La Follette represented values essentially foreign to most of the ethnics of Chicago.

In 1924, as in 1912, progressivism meant to La Follette a movement for political and economic reform, with a broad appeal to all well-intentioned people. The common denominator of progressivism was not social desire, nor was it ethnicity; rather, it was a middle-class concern with honesty and efficiency. In its own way, then, the Progressive party of 1924 was strictly traditionalist—in the longstanding tradition of nonpartisan middle-class American reform.[8] It had precious little in common

---

[6] John D. Hicks, *Republican Ascendancy* (New York, 1960), pp. 90–91.
[7] Ibid., p. 97.
[8] Ibid., pp. 97–99.

with most ethnics. That Germans, for example, were attracted to La Follette because of his opposition to World War I, does not negate the essentially nonethnic nature of the man and his party in 1924.

In 1928, platform differences between the two parties diminished again. The Democrats moved toward the Republican value structure, and the Republicans stood pat. The division within the Democratic party was by no means gone, but it did sink beneath the surface. The two parties agreed on limited government, economic stringency, and traditional Americanism. The Democrats even specifically supported immigration restriction, almost as strongly as the Republicans. And both supported Prohibition, although haltingly, and vowed to enforce it. Both parties, then, were oriented toward values which excluded the ethnics from consideration. The Republicans, however, continued their tradition of verbal support of the Negro.[9]

Thus the real difference between the parties seen by the voters in 1928 did not come from their platforms. And the presidential nominees, though very different types of men, were to their parties pretty much the same thing: leading political figures to be nominated simply because they were the strongest candidates, for political rather than ideological reasons. Herbert Hoover did have some opposition, for personal reasons and because his party regularity was suspect. But he was nominated easily on the first ballot. And his running mate, Charles Curtis, differed from him only in being a party regular and a little closer to the farm belt.[10]

There was no Democratic nomination battle because William G. McAdoo—traditional leader of the rural, WASP forces in the 1920s—had removed himself from contention late in 1927. This did not mean that the party was united for Smith, but it meant that he was the only strong contender, and he, too, won easily on the first ballot. Most of all, the Democrats wanted to avoid a repetition of the 1924 experience. Continuing reluctance to accept an urban, Wet, Catholic candidate was reflected in the choice of running mate: Senator Joseph T. Robinson, a southerner, a Protestant, and a Dry.[11]

Certainly many rural Democrats feared Smith's nomination—not

[9] Roy V. Peel and Thomas C. Donnelly, *The 1928 Campaign* (New York, 1931), pp. 24–27, 32–33.

[10] Ibid., pp. 8, 14, 29.

[11] Ibid., pp. 10, 33–34.

necessarily for what he was, but for what they imagined him to be. In Houston, scene of the Democratic convention, the Protestant churches were full, and "a fervent petition has been raised to the Most High against the elevation of Gov. Smith to the Presidency."[12] But inside the Democratic organization the emphasis was less on religious than on political harmony and regularity. Thus in nomination, as in platform, the basic problems that continued from 1924 were simply ignored. Perhaps the likelihood of Republican victory made self-questioning less meaningful to the Democrats in 1928.

At any rate, the changes in voting that began in 1928 were not reflected in the Democratic party's conception of itself as expressed in questioning over platform and candidates. But an urban, ethnically oriented, and ethnically attractive presidential candidate had nonetheless been nominated.

The 1932 platforms saw some changes from those of 1928, particularly in reflecting the Depression situation. The Democrats, smelling success, refused to argue with one another and issued their shortest platform of the period. The Republicans, on the defensive, issued their longest. What little the Democrats did have to say showed small change from 1928: the party still insisted on looking upon itself as a conservative force, preserving traditional values. The platform's strongest stand was on Prohibition, which it now opposed forcefully; and it returned to the 1920–1924 pattern of ignoring immigration, which was at least negatively closer to what an ethnic party should do. Finally, there were hints in the platform of new directions, as in the advocating of active governmental help to the unemployed. But that was about all there was to it. It was not a strong document.

The Republicans in 1932 firmly maintained their successful values of the previous twelve years, but they were on the defensive. They felt the need to attack, but were able only to defend. The platform again supported immigration restriction and congratulated the party on having "formulated into law the quota system." The Negro continued to be assured of a place of refuge. Previous strong support for Prohibition was replaced by a plank arguing that it was not a "partisan" issue at all, and so not worthy of discussion. They were willing that the issue be remanded to

[12] *Christian Century* (July 5, 1928), p. 847.

the states. There was no indication that this plank had anything to do with a changing party self-conception; rather, it was a hot political issue to be straddled. On the whole, the Republicans in 1932 wanted to be seen as the party of the 1920s, which would overcome the indisposition of the Depression and maintain the civilization of 1921–1929.

As in 1928 the presidential tickets of the two parties offered only small light on their self-conceptions. Hoover, as president, continued to be disliked by the professional party leadership and by the small progressive wing. But he was the incumbent, wanted renomination, and there was little to be done. Moreover, he continued to represent the mainstream of party thought and was certainly an honest representative of its platform.[13]

The Democratic contest was really between Smith and Franklin D. Roosevelt. The several other candidates had little chance unless these two stalemated one another.[14] That the Democrats ultimately chose Roosevelt over Smith was a sign basically of their desire to win: either candidate had a good chance in 1932, but surely Roosevelt had less strikes against him, and so was the more available. It would be incorrect to see much conflict in party self-conception in the selection of Roosevelt over Smith. If Smith was more ethnically oriented, for example, in his desire to stress Prohibition over all other issues, he was less so in his emotional denunciation of "setting class against class and rich against poor," and so on.[15] In fact, Smith's ethnic orientation was essentially emotional and superficial and did not really amount to commitment, while that of Roosevelt was more intellectual, and in the long run more sincere. Images often conflict with realities, however, and it is likely that to the party Roosevelt was less firmly on the ethnic-urban-Wet side of the scale than Smith in 1932, and that the selection of Roosevelt in part reflects a reluctance to move too far in new directions.

It is hard to find any dramatic differences between the self-conceptions of the two major parties, 1920–1932, as demonstrated in national platforms and presidential tickets. But this is to be expected in the American political system, where parties have traditionally stressed heterogeneity and catholicity and have not looked upon themselves as repre-

[13] Roy V. Peel and Thomas C. Donnelly, *The 1932 Campaign* (New York, 1935), pp. 19–25.
[14] Ibid., pp. 25–43.
[15] Ibid., pp. 63–64.

sentative of one particular group or interest. Differences in such a system tend to be subtle. Both parties in the 1920s saw themselves in the mainstream of American belief and values, and thus they hoped to be in the mainstream of American voting. Neither seemed to realize that this mainstream was changing course, with the coming enfranchisement of the newer immigrants.

The Democratic party did construe itself on somewhat more ethnic lines, but this prevailed no more at the end of the period than at its beginning. It seems that the ethnic voters came into the Democratic party before the party came to consider itself consciously as the party of the ethnics.[16] Truly, the voters (and the candidates) led; the party consensus followed well behind. In this phenomenon, which probably pervades American politics from its earliest history, can be found basic strengths and weaknesses of the American party system.

But if the Democratic party changed little in terms of self-conception during the period, the Republican party changed not at all—and was from the start considerably less ethnic-oriented (the Negro always excepted). Consequently the Democrats became the ethnics' party as much by default as anything else. Indeed, the major division within the Republican party in this period was between the old guard and the progressives—a division based essentially on political and economic questions, rather than social ones, and a division wherein neither side reflected ethnic interests. But the major division within the Democratic party was basically social: urban-ethnic-Wet vs. rural-WASP-Dry, and this was a division innately reflecting ethnic interest. Thus, regardless of which side was winning in this intra-Democratic battle at any given point in time, the fact remained that the ethnics at least made up one of the sides, whereas they were on the outside with the Republicans. And by 1928–1932 the urban-ethnic-Wet side of the Democratic division had more or less won out, even if this was not clear to the party at the time. Therefore party history and party self-conception during this period are congruent with changing patterns of ethnic political behavior.

[16] The 1936 platforms showed this interparty difference much more clearly. The Republicans remained the defenders of traditional American values, warning that "America is in peril," and promising to retrench. The Democrats, faced with what their administration had done over three and a half years, did seem to see themselves as a party of new values, which were at least in effect pro-ethnic. Belief was catching up with practice.

Quadrennial platforms and presidential nominations are one expression of party self-conception. Another resides in what candidates have to say about their parties. Here consensus gives way to diversity and permits local variations to appear. The party conceptions of leading national and local Chicago candidates might or might not agree with the parties' official conceptions of themselves. In either case they contribute to an understanding of party self-conception and its congruence, or lack thereof, with ethnic political behavior.

The presidential candidates of the period tended to conceive of their parties—especially in matters ethnic—much the same as the conventions which had nominated them. In 1920, for example, James M. Cox followed the platform in supporting President Wilson's League of Nations, although reluctantly, and in being otherwise not at all controversial. Like the platform, he had some general ethnic-consciousness, as in Chicago where he stressed the Irish question.[17] But he basically saw his party in traditionalistic terms. His opponent, Senator Harding, gave off an aura of even stronger traditionalism. When Illinois Senator Medill McCormick brought 1,500 representatives of thirty different nationalities to Marion, Harding told them "to love and support the old flag and all it stands for."[18]

In 1924 there were some clear-cut problems of ethnic interest, but none of the candidates saw his party as involved on the ethnics' side. The question of the Klan, for example, was important to the ethnics, but Calvin Coolidge and Robert La Follette ignored it, and John W. Davis mentioned it only to deny that it was an issue.[19] Immigration restriction was similarly ignored. In Chicago, Davis articulated the traditional Democratic argument for Irish freedom and hinted that the Democrats continued to oppose Prohibition,[20] but otherwise rivaled Coolidge in failing to make any direct appeal for ethnic sympathy. The Democrats in 1924 used former Senator James Hamilton Lewis to campaign among Chicago's immigrants, which did show a continuing concern; Lewis denounced the Illinois Republican organization for its threatened "criminal Negro domi-

[17] Chicago *Tribune,* Oct. 31, 1920, p. 1ff.

[18] Ibid., Sept. 19, 1920, p. 6; Oct. 19, 1920, p. 3.

[19] Ibid., Aug. 24, 1924, pp. 12–13. Finally, in October, the Democrats did speak out against the Klan in Chicago, after being heckled for not doing so before (ibid., Oct. 17, 1924, p. 1ff.).

[20] Ibid., Sept. 19, 1924, p. 1ff.

nation" of the state and the city.[21] This was playing on interethnic rivalries and prejudices, a game which could sometimes succeed but was innately dangerous.

The Progressives hardly saw themselves as representing ethnic America. The only exception involved German-Americans, who were looked upon as generally pro-La Follette, and whom he courted vigorously.[22] The Republicans accepted this as true; a leading Chicago German-American congressman felt obliged to tell his constituents that they need not vote for La Follette simply because he "stood by us" during the War.[23]

The 1928 presidential candidates presented a somewhat different profile, in that one of them did see his party quite differently than had its members in convention assembled. Secretary Herbert C. Hoover happily ran as the candidate of the Republican party and its platform. As he put it in his acceptance speech, "Never has a political party been able to look upon a similar period with more satisfaction."[24] He believed this and thus saw his party as it saw itself, for example, as the party of Prohibition, "a great social and economic experiment, noble in motive and far-reaching in purpose." Similarly, Hoover not only approved of immigration restriction but also felt that the use of 1890 as a base for determining quotas was just.[25] Between the candidate and the party there was harmony.

The case of Al Smith, however, was something else again. More than any other presidential candidate of the decade he seemed to see his party in a new and different way, and this helps explain the effect he had on Chicago's ethnics. The specific matters on which Smith differed from his party were questions of primary concern to the ethnics; and the sum of his alterations amounted to a conception of the Democratic party far more hospitable to ethnic voters. Smith was opposed to Prohibition and would work for its modification, if not outright repeal.[26] He acknowledged that immigration restriction was necessary, but argued that the use of the 1890 census for determining quotas was "designed to discriminate

[21] Ibid., Nov. 1, 1924, p. 6.
[22] Ibid., Sept. 24, 1924, p. 19.
[23] Ibid., Oct. 11, 1924, p. 2.
[24] Herbert C. Hoover, *The New Day: Campaign Speeches of Herbert Hoover, 1928* (Stanford, Calif., 1928), p. 12.
[25] Ibid., pp. 24, 71. (The different quota laws, and their effects, are considered in Chapter 7.)
[26] Alfred E. Smith, *Campaign Addresses of Gov. Alfred E. Smith* (Washington, D.C., 1929), pp. 14–15, 200.

against certain nationalities."[27] Thus he seemed to see his party as the protector of the interests of those who identified so heartily with him. More generally, he tended more to view his party as one of change than had the platform, and he offered a view of government which included action and a searching for new answers to the problems of the "rank and file of the people."[28]

Here is one clear instance of a presidential candidate construing his party as something quite different from the party's conception of itself; moreover, the differences revolved around matters central to the problem of the place of the ethnics in that party. To Smith the Democratic party was a party for the ethnics, while to the leadership of his party this was not the case at all; and the Republicans, by their own self-conception, offered no contest to this in 1928.[29]

One can well overstate the case here. Indeed, as his later career would indicate, Smith was never a social radical, much less a revolutionary.[30] But he certainly was a successful ethnic politician up to 1928 and saw his party (in those egocentric terms common to most successful politicians) as being likewise. And he was the Democratic presidential candidate. According to the voting returns, his party conception was shared by ethnic voters.

The situation was less clear in 1932. Herbert Hoover remained essentially the same man he had been in 1928 and continued to view his party in the same light as before. Current problems would be solved not by seeking new paths but by resolutely clinging to time-tested Republican answers. Certainly the election of 1928 had not convinced him that his party ought somehow to open its doors to the ethnics. Indeed, it seemed to him that the Democrats were advocating some conspiratorial new concept of society which, if implemented, could be disastrous to traditional American civilization.[31]

[27] Ibid., pp. 25–26.

[28] Ibid., pp. 202, 260, 293.

[29] This points to one of the most interesting and significant aspects of the 1928 campaign. It was clearly a contest between Hoover, as a representative of the Republican party, and Smith, as an individual only secondarily representing a party. The ethnics, too, saw it as a contest between a party and a man. This was the source of much of Smith's strength among them.

[30] As early as the campaign of 1932 Smith lost whatever "radical" *élan* he might have had in 1928. (See Arthur M. Schlesinger, Jr., *The Crisis of the Old Order* [Boston, 1957], p. 416.)

[31] Ibid., pp. 431, 437.

Franklin Roosevelt's conception of the Democratic party at this time is by no means clear; above all, perhaps, it was a vehicle to power. In Chicago, as elsewhere, he spoke mainly on the problems of Prohibition and the Depression and in both seemed implicitly to see his party as one of action—action which, in these cases, corresponded to ethnic belief.[32] He liked the phrase "New Deal," with its implication of operating for the mass of the people and assuaging their despair in difficult times. In this he seemed to define his party in basically human terms, quite distinct from Hoover's definition of the Republican party.[33] He had a construction of the Democracy roughly similar to that of Al Smith, but he saw it more broadly and with a more general vision. For Smith's emotional and largely unconscious ethnic sympathy, Roosevelt substituted a more conscious, calculating, and intellectual sympathy that would last far longer. If his view of the Democratic party is not clear, it was nonetheless something quite different from that of Cox or Davis, and something which did have a place for the ethnics.

Thus, in a general way, the conceptions of party of presidential candidates do correlate with ethnic voting behavior. The Republican candidates demonstrated no real qualitative change in matters of ethnic consciousness. And that of the Democrats can easily be overstated. But Smith and Roosevelt, closing out the period, seemed to conceive of the Democratic party as a house for all peoples among Americans; thus party, like voter, was changing at this time, in complementary fashion. And the rise of the ethnic Democratic consensus is further explained.

The party conceptions of presidential candidates are only part of this measure; it is important also to consider leading local candidates and officeholders, to see if their party conceptions corresponded with or varied from those of national figures. This is particularly important for understanding the party conceptions which came across to the ethnics, since their political horizons were not necessarily broad, and local party impressions were important.

William Hale ("Big Bill") Thompson, Republican, and Anton Cermak, Democrat, were the two most important politicians on the Chicago scene in the 1920s, both generally and to the ethnics. Thompson was mayor three times (1915–1923, 1927–1931), and a candidate in three

---

[32] Chicago *Tribune,* Oct. 1, 1932, p. 1ff.; Oct. 2, 1932, p. 1ff.; Oct. 3, 1932, p. 3; Schlesinger, *Crisis of the Old Order,* pp. 429–30.

[33] Schlesinger, *Crisis of the Old Order,* pp. 429–30, 433.

of the elections under study (1919, 1927, 1931). Cermak emerged into ever greater power as the decade unfolded, becoming Democratic boss by 1930 and defeating Thompson for mayor in 1931. The differences, if any, between Thompson's conception of the Republican party and Cermak's of the Democratic, in terms of the place of the ethnics in the parties, will add materially to an understanding of local party self-conception and its role in changing political behavior.

The traditional picture of Thompson as a clever ethnic politician is only partially true and is hardly true for the later stages of his career. His ethnic consciousness seemed to be working well in his much-publicized reluctance to invite the Joffre mission to Chicago during the Great War. It must be remembered, he said, that Chicago was "the sixth largest German city in the world, the second largest Bohemian, the second largest Norwegian, and the second largest Polish," and some of these groups might resent such an invitation.[34] This was perhaps attractive to the groups involved and did strengthen Thompson's appeal among the German-Americans (his 1915 and 1919 opponent was a German-American). He gained national fame as an ethnically sophisticated politician, as did one of his chief advisers, Fred Lundin, for saying that "the party that eliminated the hyphen would eliminate itself from politics."[35] Thompson's long battle with the king of England can also be construed as ethnically oriented. He first began king-baiting in 1920, and it surely pleased the Irish, and perhaps other groups as well, since monarchy was not popular with any of them.[36] It was in his reentry into politics in 1927 that Thompson really began to swing at King George, but this was simply a part of his more general "America First" campaign.

In the long run, the America First crusade signified a retreat from ethnocentric politics. The crusade made little sense to the ethnics and probably repulsed many of them. Thompson was moving away from a pro-ethnic concept of party and politics.[37]

[34] Lloyd Wendt and Herman Kogan, *Big Bill of Chicago* (Indianapolis, Ind., 1953), pp. 152–53.

[35] Chicago *Tribune,* Mar. 21, 1919, p. 1ff.

[36] William H. Stuart, *The Twenty Incredible Years* (Chicago, 1935), p. 114.

[37] "America First" was apparently Thompson's own idea. When asked what the issues of 1927 would be, he decided to center it on America First. When asked what this had to do with the campaign, he answered: "That's just it, it hasn't anything to do with it, and that is why it will make a good issue. If anyone opposes us, we will say he is not for America First; he is for America second or

This became clearer as time passed and as Thompson's career became less and less secure. It was as if he possessed a dormant nativism, which he had managed to stifle until age and pressure caught up with him. By 1931 his conception of his party, as an extension of his person, was clearly anti-ethnic. Throughout his campaign for a fourth term he insisted that no man should be Chicago's mayor who was not born in America, and he repeatedly sang of his opponent: "Tony, Tony, where's your pushcart at? Can you imagine a world's fair mayor with a name like that?"[38] He continued to be effective with the Negroes and perhaps won over the Irish with his comment on the Democracy: "From Szymczak to Zintak to Cermak and the Irish are all out."[39] But his nativism became more and more pronounced, ultimately merged with antisemitism,[40] and before the campaign was over he had excluded most ethnic groups from his Republican party.

Thus by 1931 Thompson's Republican party had no room for southern or eastern European newer immigrants (the Italians excepted), and since his was the only local Republican faction ever to have been really ethnically oriented, it seemed that they were quite excluded, that the Republicans really had "eliminated the hyphen."

This change is important, because the Democrats under Tony Cermak went in the opposite direction. Cermak was an archetypal ethnic politician—probably, with Fiorello LaGuardia, the best there ever was. His rise to power had been through championing his own Czech group and through interethnic cooperation (he was, for example, the leading figure in the United Societies, an interethnic anti-Prohibition organization

---

third or he is perhaps not a good American at all. Everybody is for America First, and if anyone is against us we will say that he is disloyal." (Charles E. Merriam, *Chicago: A More Intimate View of Urban Politics* [New York, 1929], p. 291; Stuart, *The Twenty Incredible Years,* p. 297.)

[38] Chicago *Tribune,* April 8, 1931, p. 1; Wendt and Kogan, *Big Bill of Chicago,* pp. 329–31; Harold F. Gosnell, *Machine Politics: Chicago Model* (Chicago, 1937), p. 13.

[39] *Collier's* 91 (Jan. 7, 1933): 21.

[40] His wrath was directed especially against Judge Henry Horner, who would be Democratic candidate for governor in 1932, and Julius Rosenwald, Chicago businessman and philanthropist. (See Charles E. Merriam, "Recollections" [manuscript autobiography], ch. 6, p. 14, Merriam Papers, University of Chicago; M. R. Werner, *Julius Rosenwald: The Life of a Practical Humanitarian* [New York, 1939], p. 318.) It is instructive to note, in this context, that in 1936 Thompson would run for governor on the Lemke ticket.

founded in 1906). He had risen steadily through the regular Democratic organization, becoming president and member of the Cook County Board in 1922 and soon becoming known as "The Mayor of Cook County." But at the same time he was never really close to the ruling clique of Roger Sullivan and then George Brennan, largely due to traditional Czech-Irish animosity.[41] While remaining within the organization, Cermak was also creating his own kind of Democratic party, characteristically via interethnic ties.[42]

Cermak took the initiative in getting four opinion ballots on Prohibition added to the elections of the period and brought in Al Smith to speak in favor of the one in 1922.[43] He was the leader of Chicago Wets. As head of Cook County government he created a separate and kosher Jewish section in the county poorhouse, thus endearing himself to the newer immigrant Jews and their political leaders.[44] And with a Czech-Jewish alliance he was ready to take over the party in 1928, when Brennan died. He added his own Irish ties, with Pat Nash of the twenty-eighth ward, who had been on the outs with Brennan for years.[45] Between 1928 and 1930 Cermak solidified his hold over the local Democracy. He was not Brennan's chosen successor (that honor went to a fellow Irishman, Michael Igoe), but Cermak had planned too well, and his ethnic Democratic organization was considerably more powerful than his rival's less ethnic one.[46] His ultimate victory over the Irish came in 1930 and was signified in the party's endorsement of a truly ethnic ticket of Cermak, Kaindl, Brady, Allegretti, and Smietanka.[47] In this way he came to power, reflecting the ethnics' goals. Prohibition was his issue, ethnic representation his goal (and thus he gave up the Democratic tradition of Negro-baiting, as practiced by his Irish predecessors).

In the 1931 mayoralty, Cermak reacted to Thompson's nativist taunts in a manner with which the ethnics could empathize: "He don't [*sic*] like

---

[41] Alex Gottfried, *Boss Cermak of Chicago: A Study of Political Leadership* (Seattle, Wash., 1962), p. 138.

[42] Ibid., pp. 134–37; Stuart, *The Twenty Incredible Years*, pp. 219–20.

[43] Gottfried, *Boss Cermak*, pp. 118–19.

[44] Philip P. Bregstone, *Chicago and Its Jews* (Chicago, 1933), p. 323.

[45] Gottfried, *Boss Cermak*, pp. 178–79.

[46] Harold L. Ickes, *The Autobiography of a Curmudgeon* (New York, 1943), pp. 254–55.

[47] Gottfried, *Boss Cermak*, pp. 199–203.

my name. . . . It's true I didn't come over on the Mayflower, but I came over as soon as I could."[48] In Cermak's hands and eyes the Chicago Democracy was very different from what it had been under Brennan and equally different from Thompson's Republicans. It was to him an ethnic political party; that was why he had joined it and what he had made it.

The party conceptions of any number of local political figures could be considered; none of them, however, played so central a role as the two considered above. There are other significant indications of increasingly greater Democratic identification with the ethnics, without a reciprocal concern on the part of the Republicans. Both parties had ethnic organizational systems operating during campaigns, but the Democratic system was much more active, especially toward the end of the period. The Democrats were also more attentive to building up a network of social, athletic, and other kinds of clubs among the ethnics, all of which were designed to win them over to the party and hold them there, while at the same time serving ethnic nonpolitical interests.[49]

The pro-ethnic effort permeated most levels of the local Democracy. For example, Carter Harrison II, five times mayor and leader of a small "reform" group within the party in the 1920s, argued to William Gibbs McAdoo in 1928 that the ethnics made up an important part of the Democratic party's strength and that it would be wrong to deny them their proper influence within the party.[50] The changing proportions of ethnics represented on party tickets expressed the same belief.

Democratic leaders in Chicago more and more saw their party as the ethnics' real representative in local and national politics. The Chicago delegation to Washington to testify against the Johnson bill in 1924 was led by Jacob M. Arvey, Jewish Democratic leader and Cermak ally.[51] And no one was more expressive of this feeling than A. J. Sabath, congressman from Cermak's Czechoslovakian section. Sabath was both Czech and Jew and represented both groups, as well as the ethnics generally. As

[48] Report of a student (H. Bobino), of Democratic campaign meeting, Trianon Ballroom. Gosnell materials, Merriam Papers, University of Chicago.

[49] See series of interviews in Wards 11, 12, 14, and 15 in 1934. Mary McDowell Papers, Chicago Historical Society.

[50] This was in a letter requesting that McAdoo support Smith in 1928 because Smith was the ethnics' choice. Harrison to McAdoo, Oct. 16, 1928. Harrison Papers, Newberry Library.

[51] Chicago *Jewish Courier,* Mar. 5, 1924, WPA.

ranking Democrat on the House Immigration Committee, Sabath led the battle against the Johnson bill, fighting Democrats and Republicans alike, in Congress and out.[52] Between 1918 and 1932 he introduced innumerable bills to Congress, about 80 percent of them concerning immigration, immigrants, and Prohibition. His stance on Prohibition was ferocious and unremitting, as were his efforts to obtain a national Pulaski Day, recognition of Soviet Russia, and various kinds of aid for countless individual immigrants.[53] He was striving to create a Democratic party that was a home for the ethnics—particularly the Jews, but generally as well.[54]

Sabath is a leading example of those ethnic politicians within the Democracy who served to bring the ethnics into the party, by conceiving of the party as the ethnics' true place of refuge. He was rather alone at the start of the period, but toward its end had quite a few colleagues, because the Democratic party was reluctantly coming around.

[52] See, for example, Sabath to Gompers, May 10, 1924, and speeches to House, April 4 to May 15, 1924. Sabath Papers, American Jewish Archives.

[53] See copies of bills introduced and speeches delivered in Sabath Papers, American Jewish Archives.

[54] See letter to Sabath from Harry [?], Aug. 24, 1945, Sabath Papers, American Jewish Archives.

Part Two

The Forces of Coalition

VII. *Political Issues*

Among the several forces of political change, issues are probably foremost. These are the substantive and qualitative matters important to the individual voter and to groups of voters: what should or should not be done; what would or would not serve one's interest.[1] The voter opts for that party or candidate which best represents his desires on the issues, or, negatively, which least conflicts with those desires. The voter can associate the alternatives of an issue with political parties as wholes, or simply with one of two contesting candidates, or anywhere in between.

Thus when issue considerations prompted an ethnic voter to opt for a Democratic candidate, or group of them, that voter was not necessarily persuaded that the whole Democratic party participated in that issue in the same way. Most significant, then, were those issues which were of greatest importance to the ethnics, particularly when the alternatives seemed to divide the major parties. But issue arguments in favor of leading individual candidates must also be considered, since it was of this in good part that party allegiances were eventually created.

The number of issues in which the ethnics were really involved during this period was relatively small. They were interested in matters which directly related to them, particularly in their roles as ethnic group members: immigration restriction legislation, the xenophobia of the Ku Klux Klan and other kinds of bigotry, and curtailments of their traditional practices and liberties. Prohibition was the issue in which they were involved above all others. These issues which were most important to the ethnics gave rise to strikingly similar attitudes among them. Additionally, there were some more general issues in which the ethnics also demonstrated interest: the Great War, President Wilson and the Versailles Treaty, the League of Nations, and the Depression. The effect of these latter issues was more selective, involving some of the groups and eliciting less than unanimous decisions among those involved. Thus the former can be considered "ethnic issues," while the latter were, more simply, issues in which there was ethnic interest. Both kinds of issues affected ethnic political behavior.

The ethnics were very much concerned with the outcome of the First World War, since the homelands of so many of them were involved. The war itself, and then the peace which followed, became important political issues, particularly in the elections of 1918 and 1920. And President Woodrow Wilson, as the leading American figure in the War and the peace, became himself a complex issue as a symbol of many things.

No Chicago ethnic group was as involved in these issues as were the German-Americans. Their position, especially after the United States joined the Allies, was very difficult, and their interest was very great. As early as 1916 most German-Americans considered Wilson pro-British, and preferred the election of Charles Evans Hughes to the presidency.[2] Up until the time that the United States entered the war, the *Abendpost*, like the rest of the German-language press, continued to justify the German cause; indeed, the *Abendpost* charged the United States with responsibility for the rupture of diplomatic relations in early 1917.[3]

---

[1] Distinctions have been made between actual substantive issues (Wilson's peace plans, the Depression), on the one hand, and more attitudinal, contentless issues (Al Smith as an urban politician) on the other. One group of scholars has concluded that the latter become important mainly in elections where the former are absent. (See Bernard Berelson and others, *Voting: A Study of Opinion Formation in a Presidential Campaign* [Chicago, 1954].) The distinction may not be really meaningful, however, because there were issues which straddled both categories. Prohibition is the best example; there was an actual substantive dispute involved, but there were also many qualitative ramifications.

A better distinction, I think, can be made between those issues which include cultural-social disputes and those which do not. The former tend to involve more people more deeply than the latter. In this study, Prohibition is the leading example, and religious and ethnic bigotry (the Klan, much of the criticism of Al Smith) would also be included. And these were the issues most important to the ethnics. A study of Iowa voting in an earlier period has concluded similarly (Samuel P. Hays, "History as Human Behavior," *Iowa Journal of History* 58 [July 1960]: 193–206, 196).

[2] Carl Wittke, *The German-Language Press in America* (Lexington, Ky., 1957), pp. 255–56; Andrew J. Townsend, "The Germans of Chicago" (Ph.D. diss., University of Chicago, 1927), pp. 144–48; Harold L. Ickes, *The Autobiography of a Curmudgeon* (New York, 1943), p. 186.

[3] Wittke, *The German-Language Press*, pp. 238–43, 259–61.

Overall, the problems of the war seemed to make Chicago's Germans more ethnocentric and united.[4]

Once America entered the war, however, the *Abendpost* became very patriotic and pro-Wilson, for reasons of self-preservation as well as sincere patriotism.[5] This was facilitated by the issuance of the Fourteen Points in early 1918, which the *Abendpost* accepted with great enthusiasm and which was the keystone of its support of the Democrats in the fall elections. President Wilson was a "man of peace," the paper said, who had gone to war "only against the German government, not against the German people," and who wanted a League of Nations "of all people," including the Germans. For this reason, all of "Wilson's personal candidates" should be elected.[6]

James Hamilton Lewis, campaigning for reelection to the Senate, played upon this kind of sentiment and upon German-American fears: "To Illinois—this Illinois, the largest German state of America—to this Chicago, the largest German city of America, Berlin's eyes are turned. The Kaiser and Hindenburg are watching the election."[7] These tactics were fairly successful. The *Abendpost* supported Lewis, "So he can pursue the president's policy of peace in the Senate"; a vote for his opponent (Medill McCormick, who won) was a vote for the "Roosevelts and Lodges" and other supporters of an unjust peace.[8] German voters agreed, although not overwhelmingly: these traditionally Republican voters gave Lewis 54 percent of their senatorial vote.

Other Chicago ethnic groups were also very much involved in the Great War, but they did not always relate their interest to American politics. The Swedes, like the Germans, were sympathetic to the Central Powers, out of distrust of Great Britain and Russia.[9] But they were not

[4] Townsend, "The Germans of Chicago," p. 68.

[5] The Illinois *Staats-Zeitung,* which remained more critical of the United States, was forced to suspend publication during the war and never really recovered. The implications of this were not lost on the *Abendpost.* (See Wittke, *The German-Language Press,* p. 265; Townsend, "The Germans of Chicago," pp. 178–79.)

[6] *Abendpost,* Nov. 4, 1918, p. 4.

[7] Chicago *Daily News,* Nov. 1, 1918, p. 2.

[8] *Sonntagpost,* Nov. 3, 1918, pp. 4, 8; *Abendpost,* Nov. 4, 1918, p. 1.

[9] Reuel Hemdahl, "The Swedes in Illinois Politics: An Immigrant Group in an American Political Setting" (Ph.D. diss., Northwestern University, 1932), p. 431; Ickes, *Autobiography,* p. 185.

intimately involved. The Irish, too, favored the Central Powers over their foremost enemy, Great Britain. The rest of Chicago's ethnic groups seemed pro-Ally from the start and stayed that way.[10] Some even outdid the Native-Americans in jingoism. The Czech press, for example, was virulently anti-German and participated in all the agitation in favor of restricting civil liberties to remove any pro-German sentiment in the United States.[11] By and large, however, and especially among the central and eastern European ethnics, it was a case of overwhelming interest in the course of the war itself which tended to minimize rather than accentuate questions of American politics.

Wilson's plea for a Democratic Congress in 1918 received considerable attention in the metropolitan press, as did the answers of prominent Republicans.[12] But the foreign language press refused to become involved in the campaign in any great way and devoted itself instead to straight war news, plus news of the Liberty Loan campaign and the current flu epidemic. This political apathy existed despite an alleged administration effort to pressure the foreign language press, through the machinery of the foreign language division of the Liberty Loan organization, into prominently featuring the president's appeal for a Democratic Congress.[13]

The war and looming peace did have some effect on ethnic political behavior in 1918, although less than in 1920 when the trammels on free expression were no longer felt. As with the Germans, most of this activity favored President Wilson and the Democrats, expressing the real or forced patriotism of wartime. One leading Polish newspaper, *Dziennik Chicagoski,* cautioned its readers to remember President Wilson and what he was doing for Poland on election day.[14] Even a Republican Italian paper, *La Tribuna Italiana Trans-Atlantica,* while supporting a straight Republican ticket, felt obliged to justify itself, arguing that the Republi-

[10] Ickes, *Autobiography,* p. 185.

[11] *Denni Hlasatel,* April 2, 1918, WPA. According to Cermak's biographer, he was a leading Hun-baiter during the war, although advised that this was politically dangerous. (Alex Gottfried, *Boss Cermak of Chicago: A Study of Political Leadership* ([Seattle, Wash., 1962], pp. 92–95.) This is exaggerated, however, since Cermak was close to the Germans, particularly through the United Societies, and was always treated well by the German press and German voters.

[12] E.g., Chicago *Daily News,* Oct. 25, 1918, p. 1; Chicago *Tribune,* Oct. 26, 1918, p. 1; Chicago *Daily News,* Oct. 31, 1918, p. 1.

[13] Chicago *Tribune,* Nov. 1, 1918, p. 6.

[14] *Dziennik Chicagoski,* Nov. 2, 1918, p. 1.

cans had supported Wilson more faithfully than the Democrats.[15] A Greek paper argued identically.[16] And the Chicago *Jewish Courier,* like *Dziennik Chicagoski,* reasoned that Wilson's plea for a Democratic Congress deserved to be satisfied by Jewish voters.[17] The relatively high Democratic vote among all the ethnic groups in 1918 well reflected this loyalty to the party in power during wartime.

More significantly, because it was free of wartime restraints, was the effect of this general issue on the election of 1920, and to a lesser extent on that of 1919. The whole problem telescoped into the question of a League of Nations. The Democrats were identified as the party of the League and of Woodrow Wilson, while the Republicans were identified as opposed to both. It was clear that the people as a whole were opposed to the League in 1920, and James M. Cox realized this; he complained that the Republican National Committee sent scouts out on his campaign trail to urge Republican newspapers to deluge him with questions on the League (obliging him continually to commit himself).[18]

The German-American reaction to this issue was intense; the peace treaty was far different from what they had expected, and the proposed League excluded Germany. Throughout the nation the German press rebuked "Wilsonism" in language antithetical to that of 1918; it hoped for the nomination of isolationist Hiram Johnson by the Republicans and ultimately strongly supported Warren G. Harding as the anti-Wilson candidate.[19] Chicago's Germans were very strongly anti-League in 1920.[20] To the *Abendpost,* the whole election centered on the League, and it insisted that German voters choose "Harding and staying out of the League."[21] With the Sedition Act no longer hanging over its head like a guillotine, the *Abendpost* rapidly lost its Wilsonian fervor.

[15] *La Tribuna Italiana Trans-Atlantica,* Nov. 2, 1918.

[16] *Saloniki,* Aug. 10, 1918, WPA.

[17] *Jewish Courier,* Oct. 29, 1918, p. 4.

[18] Chicago *Tribune,* Sept. 12, 1920, p. 3. On the predominance of the League issue and the general animosity to the League, see Chicago *Herald & Examiner,* Oct. 15–Nov. 2, 1920, passim, and W. R. Hearst editorial, Oct. 27, 1920, p. 1; Chicago *Tribune,* same period, passim, especially p. 1 McCutcheon cartoons; Chicago *Daily News,* same period, passim.

[19] Wittke, *The German-Language Press,* pp. 277–78.

[20] Townsend, "The Germans of Chicago," p. 180. The same seems true for New York (Chicago *Tribune,* Sept. 7, 1920, p. 9).

[21] *Abendpost,* Nov. 1, 1920, p. 4.

The Scandinavians agreed. The Norwegian Dovre Club issued an announcement saying that the only issue in the election was the defeat of Woodrow Wilson; it therefore endorsed the entire Republican ticket.[22] The Swedish-language *Svenska-Tribunen-Nyheter* endorsed Harding because of his "America First" program.[23]

The leading Italian-language newspaper, *L'Italia,* reacted profoundly against Wilson and related this to both local and national elections. Its Republican endorsements in the 1919 local election were made on international issues: vote straight Republican to rectify the "great blunders . . . made by the party now in power" and to prepare for the campaign of 1920.[24] This reasoning continued into 1920 in a bitter attack on Wilson, reflecting the feelings of Italians everywhere that the American president had betrayed them at Versailles. "Wilson has always violated international ethics." The "abuses of Wilsonism" were endless, whereas Harding had fought the "caprice of Pres. Wilson" in the Senate and had opposed the president's policy on the "Italian question," doing so "as an act of justice to Italy and all humanity." The peace conference, under Wilson's direction, had done a "grave injustice to Italy," but Harding, as an "Italophile," would rectify this, and the Republicans ought therefore to be supported and Wilsonism defeated.[25]

Chicago's other major Italian-language paper agreed. It bitterly criticized Wilson for the activities of George Creel (chairman of the Committee on Public Information), who, the paper insisted, was encouraging "bolshevism" in Italy. It supported the whole Republican ticket, telling Italian voters to "mock and snub the Democratic administration and elect . . . Sen. Harding who is the champion of Americanism against hysteria and of liberty against oppression."[26]

Italian voters, like the German and Scandinavian, articulated this reaction to the issue of Woodrow Wilson and his international policy on election day.[27] Their general attitude was well summarized in the com-

---

[22] *Skandinaven,* Oct. 29, 1920, WPA.

[23] *Svenska-Tribunen-Nyheter,* Oct. 13 and 17, 1920, WPA.

[24] *L'Italia,* Mar. 30, 1919, p. 1.

[25] Ibid., Oct. 10, 1920, p. 1; Oct. 24, 1920, p. 1; Oct. 31, 1920, p. 1.

[26] *La Tribuna Italiana Trans-Atlantica,* Oct. 9, 1920, p. 7; Oct. 30, 1920, p. 2.

[27] One national study of the 1920 election points out the "correlation between Republican gains and the percentage of German-Americans, Austrian-Americans, Irish-Americans and Italian-Americans in that state." (Wesley M.

ment of Titto Ruffo, star baritone of the Chicago Grand Opera: "*A Bas the League of Nations. It is no good. Harding and Coolidge—they will win this fall, sans doute.*"

The Negro attitude on this issue was stated in a Chicago *Defender* editorial which argued that the League was not considered a paramount issue "by us." "The More Important Issue" was seen in an accompanying cartoon, showing Harding and Cox arguing over the League while a lynched Negro hung from a telephone pole in the background.[28]

There were groups, however, to whom Wilson's policies were not offensive. This was particularly true of the submerged nationalities of eastern Europe which achieved national independence as a result of the Congress of Versailles. In Chicago, the group most affected was the Poles. The very large and prestigious Polish Roman Catholic Union, for example, had telegraphed its thanks to President Wilson in 1919 for recognizing the Polish government; Polish freedom and independence, it said, were "mainly due to you."[29] *Dziennik Chicagoski,* which had been so strongly pro-Wilson in 1918, remained so. In endorsing the Democratic candidate for mayor in 1919, it had argued that a vote for his opponent (Thompson) would be "a vote against Pres. Wilson and a free Poland."[30] In 1920, this paper recognized that Harding would probably win, but endorsed the Democratic candidates. Cox, too, was a "good friend of Poland the Polish people."[31] *Dziennik Zwiazkowy,* official newspaper of the Polish National Alliance, had been so interested in the war in 1918 that it had totally ignored American politics and was rather unclear on this issue in 1920, probably because its tradition was nonpartisan. It endorsed the League of Nations and noted that Poles were very grateful to Wilson for the League and other help; but it did not endorse Cox. In fact it grew critical of Wilson's wartime administration and, while remaining uncommitted, said that many voters would opt for the Republicans.[32] Thus devotion and gratitude to Wilson did not automatically

Bagby, *The Road to Normalcy: The Presidential Campaign and Election of 1920* [Baltimore, Md., 1962], pp. 159–60, 185 n.)

[28] Chicago *Defender,* Oct. 23, 1920, p. 12.

[29] *Narod Polski,* Nov. 5, 1919, WPA.

[30] *Dziennik Chicagoski,* Mar. 30, 1919, p. 16.

[31] Ibid., Oct. 27, 1920, p. 1; Oct. 28, 1920, p. 1; Oct. 30, 1920, pp. 1, 4.

[32] *Dziennik Zwiazkowy,* Oct. 28, 1920, p. 1; Oct. 30, 1920, pp. 5, 6; Oct. 31, 1920, pp. 1, 4; Nov. 2, 1920, p. 4.

result in support of the Democrats in 1920; and Polish voters reflected this, giving 61 percent of their presidential vote to Harding.

Roughly the same thing obtained in the Jewish press, where there was much adulation of Woodrow Wilson as a "messianic figure" of peace, particularly because of strong Jewish acceptance of the idea of a League of Nations.[33] But Jewish voters, like Polish voters, reasoned otherwise and delivered strong Republican majorities.

The issue of Wilson and his peace plans and activities was a real issue, and one with considerable effect. But it was more powerful in reinforcing the Republican-predisposed than the Democratic-predisposed voter. That is, Wilson's detractors were more strongly moved to vote Republican by the issue than were his friends to vote Democratic. The difference probably reflected the fact that other concerns of the time reinforced Republican voting and impeded Democratic. The Polish press, for example, while very grateful to Wilson, seemed by 1920 to suffer a war-weariness that led to passive acceptance of the likelihood of a Republican victory.

The effect of the issue was considerable, and to the disadvantage of the Democrats. The group that remembered it longest, the German-Americans, would continue to identify the Democrats with Wilson and the hated League for several elections to come.

Prohibition was the greatest ethnic issue, both for its precise aims and for the more general ethnic–Native-American conflict which it epitomized. This was an old conflict in Chicago, long predating the passage of the Nineteenth Amendment. In 1873, for example, Mayor Joseph Medill let himself be pressured into closing the saloons on Sunday, something which Illinois law required but which Chicago had generally ignored. This resulted in the formation of a People's party, with strong ethnic (and particularly German) support, which elected Harvey D. Colvin to the mayoralty in 1874 and reopened the saloons on Sunday.[34]

In 1906, with the Prohibition movement becoming more and more powerful, the editor of the *Abendpost* suggested a meeting which led to the formation of the United Societies for Local Self-Government. The

[33] *Jewish Courier,* Oct. 27, 1918, pp. 4–5; Nov. 2 and 5, 1920; Dr. Louis L. Mann, personal interview.

[34] Lloyd Lewis and Henry J. Smith, *Chicago: The History of Its Reputation* (New York, 1929), pp. 147–48.

United Societies was an interethnic pressure group which concerned itself with a number of immigrant problems, but especially Prohibition. It became Chicago's leading opponent of the Prohibition movement, as that movement came closer and closer to victory. By 1919, at its fourteenth convention, the United Societies allegedly comprised 1,087 separate ethnic organizations, representing a membership of 258,224 people.[35] Here there was power. The organization was officially nonpartisan, but admittedly political. As time went by it became rather pro-Democratic, partially because most Chicago anti-Prohibitionists were Democrats, and primarily because Anton Cermak was its secretary and leading figure and used the organization for his own and his party's success. The United Societies was the outstanding interethnic, or omni-ethnic, organization in the city; it continued to exist and derived its power from the fact that the overwhelming majority of Chicago's ethnics found the idea and then the actuality of Prohibition absolutely repugnant.

The effects of Prohibition in Chicago, as elsewhere, are well known: patent breaking of the law and the rise of disregard for the law; a rapid rise in the crime rate; increased drinking and alcoholism; growing resentment and dissent. A 1926 study of the problem in the Back-of-the-Yards area of Chicago (Polish, Lithuanian, and other newer immigrant stockyards workers) by the University of Chicago Settlement described the situation and the ethnics' attitudes toward it. The Settlement, which favored Prohibition, concluded that it was a "huge joke" in Chicago: countless saloons could be found in the area, often operating under police protection; much home-brewing was also discovered; there seemed to be more drinking in 1926 than ever before; women in the area felt that "neighborhood conditions were worse" under Prohibition; there was animosity between the Roman Catholic clergy, which opposed Prohibition, and the Protestant clergy, which favored it; most businessmen opposed it; and to the residents it was an insult forced upon them by the Native-Americans, which was "encroaching upon their personal liberty."[36] The frequency with which terms such as *liberty* and *freedom* were used in the anti-Prohibition struggle suggests the complexity of the issue and its social and political ramifications.

It is important that the ethnics not only opposed Prohibition but also

[35] *Abendpost,* June 9, 1919, WPA.

[36] "Prohibition Survey of the Stock Yards Community, 1926." MS in Mary McDowell Papers, Chicago Historical Society.

tended to feel that it was something willfully and maliciously foisted upon them by the Native-Americans. The battle for repeal was also a battle for the general recognition of ethnic rights.

There were opinion referenda on Prohibition at four points in time between 1919 and 1930. In each of these referenda, Chicagoans voting on the issue voted between 72 and 83 percent anti-Prohibition; thus it was not only the ethnics who were Wet.[37] The first of these ballots was included in the 1919 mayoralty and was typical. The question was: "Shall this city become Anti-Saloon territory?" Chicago as a whole voted 73 percent "No," the newer immigrants 88 percent, the older immigrants 78 percent, the Natives 58 percent. The Czechs, Germans, Lithuanians, and Italians all voted 90 percent or more against; the Yugoslavs and Poles over 80 percent, the Jews 77 percent. The Negroes were only slightly more anti-Prohibition than the city at large, 75 percent; and the Swedes were close to the Native-Americans, at 64 percent. (See Table VII:2.)

Thus the two most Protestant ethnic groups—Swedes and Negroes —were the two least opposed to Prohibition. The Germans and Czechs, on the other hand, although each group had numbers of Protestants, had long traditions of anti-Prohibition activity and were the highest "No" voters of all. Most important, of course, was the fact that great majorities among all groups were opposed to Prohibition, in this and subsequent referenda, and that all of them were considerably more opposed to Prohibition than the Native-Americans.[38]

The strength of this anti-Prohibition sentiment was important to political behavior, since the Wet cause came to be associated with the

---

[37] See Harold F. Gosnell, *Machine Politics: Chicago Model* (Chicago, 1937), p. 145. On the whole, "the Catholics, the foreign born, the unemployed, the persons who pay the lowest rents, and the non-home owners tend to be wet. Inversely, the Protestants, the native whites of native parentage, the employed, the persons paying the highest rents, the home owner, the persons with superior educational attainments tend to be the dries" (ibid., p. 149). All these generalizations are true, but within the ethnic groups I have discovered little difference in anti-Prohibition voting on the basis of socioeconomic status; the *ethnic* animosity to Prohibition was most determining.

[38] *Jewish Forward,* Mar. 26, 1919, p. 1; *Dziennik Chicagoski,* Mar. 30, 1919, p. 16, Mar. 31, 1919, pp. 1, 7; *Amerikanski Slovenec,* Feb. 17, 1926, WPA; *Denni Hlasatel,* May 21, 1917, April 23, 1917, Mar. 27, 1917, Mar. 17, 1917, WPA; *Abendpost,* Mar. 20, 1919, letters to the editor.

Democratic party, both locally and nationally. This association can be seen throughout the period, but tended to become clearer and greater as time went by, steadily contributing to ethnic Democratic allegiance.

In the election of 1920, Cox and Harding both tried to avoid the issue, but it was not easily done. Cox, whose campaign was more active, had a particularly grueling time. He was endlessly questioned in Chicago about his stand on the issue, but simply insisted that it was dead and not to be discussed.[39] The Democratic gubernatorial candidate, James Hamilton Lewis, was less fearful and campaigned strongly against Prohibition; he was rewarded with the endorsement of the United Societies.[40] This was significant and a lesson to future candidates, since Lewis led the Democratic ticket in Chicago. At the same time, he received a majority from only one ethnic group, making it clear that other issues were involved, here as in all subsequent elections. Nonetheless, Lewis's opposition to Prohibition clearly helped him, and other Democrats would profit from the example.

Again on the national level, the 1924 election did not offer any real alternatives on this crucial issue. Ethnic press involvement was primarily with the questions of immigration restriction and the Ku Klux Klan, especially since none of the candidates was speaking forcefully on Prohibition. Democrat John W. Davis, however, did argue for "personal liberty" in Chicago, and, as one reporter put it, "they all thought personal liberty meant free liquor."[41]

In 1928 the issue was joined much more vigorously, and the two sides were clearly delineated. As the generally Republican *La Tribuna Italiana Trans-Atlantica* put it in a headline: "PROHIBITION OR NO PROHIBITION!! THAT'S THE QUESTION." Not only was it the question, but it was also the main reason Italians were advised to vote for Al Smith for president and for all other anti-Prohibition candidates as well. ("Great are the merits, most numerous, of Antonio [*sic*] Cermak, the champion of personal liberty.")[42]

The larger *L'Italia* reasoned similarly. In the long run, it said, the

[39] Chicago *Tribune,* Sept. 12, 1920, p. 10; Sept. 13, 1920, p. 7.
[40] Chicago *Herald & Examiner,* Oct. 27, 1920, p. 4.
[41] Chicago *Tribune,* Sept. 19, 1924, p. 1ff.
[42] *La Tribuna Italiana Trans-Atlantica,* Sept. 22, 1928, p. 1; Oct. 6, 1928, p. 1; Oct. 20, 1928, pp. 1, 3.

issues of the campaign were simply the "dinner pail" for Herbert Hoover and anti-Prohibition for Smith. Many voters would be willing to forsake the security of Republican rule in their ardor to be rid of Prohibition. This paper endorsed the entire Republican ticket, as usual, with the exception of the presidency, where it was neutral.[43] Prohibition was clearly the main reason for its refusal to endorse Hoover.

These feelings were quite general. The Democratic *Dziennik Chicagoski* advised its Polish readers that "A big moment in your lives" approached, especially since Smith was so strongly against Prohibition.[44] The *Abendpost* placed Prohibition above all other issues; one headline proclaimed: " 'I CAN AND WILL CHANGE THE PROHIBITION LAW—AL SMITH.' " Hoover, on the other hand, was a "tool of the Anti-Saloon League." Cermak, like Smith, was a "fighter against Prohibition" and was thus endorsed, as were larger numbers of Democrats than ever before.[45]

The widespread effect of this issue in 1928 was seen in the editorial of a nonpartisan Danish paper, which reasoned exactly as had *L'Italia:* voters would be deciding between Republican prosperity and Democratic Wetness.[46]

The Democratic *Jewish Courier* also devoted a great deal of space to the Prohibition issue, to the advantage of Smith and the Democrats.[47] The Negro Chicago *Defender,* on the other hand, while making its first Democratic presidential endorsement, concentrated on other issues. It thus reflected the milder repeal feelings of Negro voters.[48] And a leading Swedish paper, reflecting the voting of Chicago's Swedes, was not very Wet at all and stayed Republican in 1928.[49]

After a general and vacillating identification of the Democrats with

[43] *L'Italia,* July 15, 1928, p. 2; Oct. 14, 1928, p. 1; Oct. 21, 1928, p. 1.

[44] *Dziennik Chicagoski,* Nov. 2, 1928, p. 7; Nov. 4, 1928, p. 24; Nov. 5, 1928, p. 1ff.

[45] *Abendpost/Sonntagpost,* Nov. 4, 1928, p. 1ff.; Nov. 5, 1928, p. 1ff.; Nov. 3, 1928, p. 9. Given the rather overwhelming qualitative and quantitative evidence for the role of the Prohibition issue in 1928 which is in this chapter, one is rather unimpressed by suggestions that it was an "insignificant" correlate of Smith voting, even when buttressed by partial analysis (e.g., Ruth C. Silva, *Rum, Romanism and Votes* [University Park, Pa., 1962], p. 43). Cf. Table VII:1.

[46] *Danske Tidende,* Oct. 19, 1928, and Oct. 26, 1928, passim.

[47] *Jewish Courier,* Oct. 17, 1928, p. 8; Nov. 4, 1928, p. 8.

[48] E.g., editorial of Nov. 3, 1928, Pt. 2, p. 2.

[49] *Svenska-Tribunen-Nyheter,* Oct. 26, 1921, Feb. 15, 1922, WPA; Oct. 31, 1928, p. 1.

the anti-Prohibition cause, this became very well articulated in 1928. Alfred E. Smith's stand on this issue played an important role in the voting changes of that year. The only two groups which failed to give Smith majorities in 1928—the Swedes and the Negroes—were also the two ethnic groups which voted least anti-Prohibition in the referenda on that question. Similarly significant was the fact that Cermak, the local Wet leader, did even better than Smith among ethnic voters in 1928.

This emphasis on Prohibition continued into the 1930 elections, attracting much more attention than did the Depression; and the ethnics continued to associate the Democrats with repeal. To some groups it was the only real issue. For example, *La Tribuna Italiana Trans-Atlantica,* which returned to the Republican party in 1930, cautioned its readers that: "We renew our prayer to the Italian voters that, whatever their party, they . . . respond with a YES to all the [anti-Prohibition] questions on the REFERENDUM ballot."[50] In supporting Ruth Hanna McCormick for the Senate, rather than "J. Ham." Lewis, *La Tribuna* assured Italian voters that she would vote against Prohibition and that Lewis really could do nothing to get it abolished.[51] Thus, albeit negatively, here was an admission that most Italians did look upon the Democrats as the real Wets.

The Germans continued to be the leading battlers against Prohibition. Mrs. McCormick, in seeking their votes, allegedly said that "No German should sell his soul for a glass of beer."[52] But the *Abendpost* was unruffled by this admonition and concluded that Prohibition was the great issue of the election, noting that most of the real anti-Prohibitionists were Democrats.[53] The paper worked mightily to secure Lewis's election, basically on this one issue, as did a newly organized German-American Liberty League, which campaigned for Lewis because of his "fight for individual freedom."[54]

When the election was over, a leading Slovak paper decided that the returns demonstrated that "the public has proved what it thinks of the

[50] *La Tribuna Italiana Trans-Atlantica,* Nov. 1, 1930, p. 1. There were three Prohibition questions on a special ballot; a "Yes" vote was a vote against Prohibition. See also *Dziennik Zwiazkowy,* Nov. 3, 1930, p. 7.
[51] *La Tribuna Italiana Trans-Atlantica,* Nov. 1, 1930, p. 1.
[52] *Abendpost,* Nov. 6, 1930. WPA.
[53] Ibid., Nov. 2, 1930, pp. 1–3, 4.
[54] Ibid., Nov. 2, 1930, p. 20; Nov. 6, 1930, WPA.

present administration and prohibition."[55] Even the Republican *Svenska-Tribunen-Nyheter,* which was relatively friendly to Prohibition, admitted that the issue was a major factor in diminishing Republican power.[56]

Finally, 1932 was but a continuation of 1928 and 1930: continuing great attention focused on Prohibition and continuing identification of opposition to it with the Democratic party. By this time all congressional candidates from Chicago—of both parties—were acknowledged Wets, a strong indication of voters' wishes; in the state, all Democratic congressional candidates were Wet, while twelve of the twenty-eight Republicans refused to commit themselves.[57]

The German press had moved, by 1932, into a position of real Democratic party support because of the issue: "ONLY THE DEMOCRATIC PLATFORM GIVES THE GUARANTY OF ABOLISHING THE COERCION LAWS, The Main Issue of the Whole Campaign is the Prohibition Question." Thus German voters should "Vote the Whole Democratic Ticket"—the first time this paper had ever made such a recommendation.[58] The effect of this one issue on German political behavior could hardly be overestimated. A leading Polish paper reasoned similarly in 1932: Prohibition had given "a bad name to our country," and a straight Democratic vote was the only answer.[59]

The major Italian papers are missing for this election, but certainly they continued to be concerned with Prohibition. Which party this led them to in 1932, however, is not known. The Yiddish-language press did continue to cite Prohibition as a major reason for its Democratic endorsements.[60]

In local politics Prohibition also served the Democrats, but it took some time before this became clear. When Mayor Thompson campaigned for reelection in 1919, he was criticized for having inaugurated Sunday-closing in 1915, after promising to oppose it. But he managed nonetheless to appear Wet. The very anti-Prohibition *Abendpost,* for example, decided that he and his Democratic opponent, Robert M. Sweitzer, were equally "respectable" on the issue, and simply urged its readers "many

[55] *Osadne Hlasy,* Nov. 7, 1930, WPA.
[56] *Svenska-Tribunen-Nyheter,* Nov. 12, 1930, WPA.
[57] Chicago *Tribune,* Sept. 10, 1932, p. 7.
[58] *Abendpost,* Nov. 7, 1932, pp. 1, 4.
[59] *Dziennik Chicagoski,* Nov. 2, 1932, p. 2.
[60] *Jewish Courier,* Oct. 19, 20, 25, 26, 1932, p. 1; Nov. 1, 1932, p. 4.

hundred thousand times" to vote against Prohibition on the opinion ballot.[61] Other ethnic newspapers also saw the candidates as equally Wet and the issue was therefore minimized in 1919. (Overwhelming ethnic interest in European events tended to overshadow the mayoralty, anyway.) It is worth noting, however, that all the candidates endorsed by the Anti-Saloon League for the Illinois General Assembly in 1920 were Republicans.[62]

In 1923, when Thompson was not a candidate, roughly the same situation prevailed. Neither candidate made Prohibition an issue. But in 1927, when Thompson returned to confront Mayor William Dever, Prohibition was very important. Dever was not a Dry, but he had tried to maintain an honest administration and to enforce the law. The results of his effort had been "disastrous"—the reformed police department had closed thousands of liquor places, and, to some, Chicago had become "the driest large city in the country."[63]

For this reason Thompson combined a "wide-open town" appeal with that of America First in the 1927 campaign. He promised his Negro audiences, for example, that he would end the "police terror" in Chicago: "Wherever Bill Dever closes up one [liquor] joint, I will open up two. Wherever he closes up one wet place, I will open two. . . . I will break any cop I catch on the trail of a lonesome pint into a man's house or car. I will put them on the street and they must catch hold-up men."[64]

Dever assured the ethnics that he was as Wet as Thompson, or wetter. He told a Czech audience that Thompson only talked while he, as mayor, had gone to Washington to testify against Prohibition; to German and Polish audiences he pointed out the number of Drys in the Illinois Republican party, hoping to taint his opponent with their dryness.[65]

[61] *Abendpost,* Mar. 31, 1919, p. 4.

[62] Chicago *Tribune,* Sept. 13, 1920, p. 7. This says as much about the Anti-Saloon League as it does about the Illinois Republican party.

[63] *Literary Digest* 79 (Dec. 15, 1923): 16. The statement was more wishful thinking than anything else, but Dever did try to live up to his "reform" image. See also Kate Sargent, "Chicago, Hands Down—'Big Bill' and Politics," *Forum* 78 (Nov. 1927): 708–24, 711; Dever Papers, folders 32–34, Chicago Historical Society.

[64] Chicago *Defender,* Mar. 19, 1927, p. 1ff.; Merriam, "Recollections" (MS Autobiography), ch. 7, p. 7, Merriam Papers, University of Chicago; William H. Stuart, *The Twenty Incredible Years* (Chicago, 1935), p. 297; *Literary Digest* 93 (April 16, 1927): 6.

[65] Chicago *Tribune,* April 1, 1927, p. 12.

Clearly both candidates sensed the importance of the issue. The United Societies, which was by then pretty well controlled by Cermak, advertised in the German press that a Thompson who had gone back on his anti-Prohibition pledge in 1915 could not be trusted in 1927, whereas Dever was a real fighter against Prohibition.[66] Perhaps this had some effect: the *Abendpost* refused to endorse either candidate, arguing that there were no important differences between them.[67]

The issue received much attention in 1927, but the Democratic press tended to stay with Dever and the Republican with Thompson. To each side, its champion was the real Wet of the two. Most indicative was the neutrality of the *Abendpost,* which could always be counted upon to support the wetter candidate. Thompson's victory, and his support from lower-class ethnics, who had the hardest time in circumventing Prohibition, was certainly facilitated by Dever's effort to enforce the law and Thompson's promise to flout it.

By 1930 Thompson lost this issue, because one of the nation's leading Wets now controlled the local Democracy. Cermak had played a leading role in placing the anti-Prohibition referenda on ballots earlier in the decade and continued to epitomize organized political Wetness.[68] In March of 1931, one month before Cermak defeated Thompson for the mayoralty, the Illinois Senate passed the O'Grady-McDermott bill, and Illinois became the sixth state to repeal its enforcement laws. All thirteen Cook County Democrats voted for the bill, as did five of the six Cook County Republicans.[69]

In 1931, the issue of Prohibition was rather overshadowed by that of ethnic intolerance, but Cermak did profit from his long years of leadership. As the German-American Liberty League put it, Cermak was "our trustworthy old leader,"[70] and his years of fighting the ethnics' greatest battle paid off.

Because ethnic voters were able to express their feelings about Prohibition in the voting booth, it is the one issue of the period for which we can construct quantitative models. In Table VII:1 are listed Pearson's *r*

[66] *Sonntagpost,* April 3, 1927, p. 12.
[67] *Abendpost,* April 4, 1927, pp. 1, 4; *Sonntagpost,* April 3, 1927, p. 1.
[68] See Gottfried, *Boss Cermak,* pp. 118–19.
[69] Chicago *Tribune,* Mar. 26, 1931, p. 1.
[70] *Abendpost,* April 4, 1931, p. 7.

TABLE VII:1   *Correlations between Voting against*
              Prohibition, 1919, and Voting for
              Leading Candidates, 1919-1932*

Candidate, Office, Year	r with voting against Prohibition, 1919
Cox, President, 1920	.62
Davis, President, 1924	.20
La Follette, President, 1924	.25
Smith, President, 1928	.75
Roosevelt, President, 1932	.58
Thompson, Mayor, 1919	-.80
Dever, Mayor, 1923	.60
Thompson, Mayor, 1927	-.52
Cermak, Mayor, 1931	.45
Thompson, Mayor, 1931	-.45

*Calculation of Pearson's r between percentage voting "No" on proposition, "Shall This City Become Anti-Saloon Territory" in 1919, and percentage voting for named candidate, for nine ethnic groups.

correlations for ethnic voting against Prohibition in the 1919 elections with ethnic voting for leading candidates of the period. And in Table VII:2 there are percentage figures for voting on this proposition, as well as standard deviations for each group and between groups.

The correlations for national voting clearly agree with our qualitative data of the role of the Prohibition issue in the Smith campaign. Of the contests shown, only the Smith candidacy has a really statistically significant relationship with voting against Prohibition in 1919; the anti-Prohibition vote "explains" 56 percent of the Smith vote of 1928. Even Roosevelt in 1932 appears to have benefited far less from anti-Prohibition sentiment, as did all the other presidential candidates of the time.

In mayoral voting there is a striking lack of positive relationship between anti-Prohibition voting and pro-Thompson voting, which is quite opposite from what one would expect in looking at the rhetoric of the decade. The 1919 contest saw a significant negative relationship; the 1927 "wide-open town" campaign resulted in relatively little change; and Cermak voting clearly related more highly—albeit not very strongly—to anti-Prohibition voting than did Thompson voting in 1931. Here there is a strong hint of the weak foundations of Thompson's relationship with most of Chicago's ethnic groups: while individual groups (e.g., the Germans) may have seen him as a Wet leader, the ethnics as a whole did not make him their champion in the one issue which meant the most to them.

The importance of this issue to them is indicated in Table VII:2. We have already noted the size of the anti-Prohibition voting majorities. The relatively small standard deviations reinforce this. The s of 10.1 for all nine groups was the lowest s among them for any election between 1914 and 1936. And the s of 5.5 for the five recent immigrant groups was lower than that for any election except the 1936 presidency. Within groups also, s was unusually low. The ethnics were both strong and strongly united in their opposition to Prohibition. And the Democrats were profiting from this by the end of the 1920s.

There were a number of complementary ethnic issues that can be called "ethnic interest and defense." These include such problems as immigration restriction and various forms of real and imagined ethnic and religious prejudice. These issues tended to wax and wane in impor-

TABLE VII:2   *Percentages and Standard Deviations of Ethnic Group*
               *Vote against Prohibition, 1919**

Group (s)	Percentage Anti-Prohibition	Standard deviation
Nine ethnic groups	83	10.1
Five recent immigrant groups	88	5.5
Czechoslovaks	95	2.3
Italians	90	4.0
Poles	83	13.2
Lithuanians	91	4.5
Yugoslavs	82	10.7
Germans	93	3.8
Swedes	64	8.7
Jews	77	5.8
Negroes	75	8.6

*Based on percentage voting "No" on proposition, "Shall This City Become Anti-Saloon Territory," in 1919. Standard deviation computed between ethnic groups and between areas comprising sample of each ethnic group, as indicated.

TABLE VII:3   *Immigration into the United States Based on Varying Scales,*
1922-1929

Country of origin	Actual immigrants fiscal 1923	Annual quota 1921-1924	Annual quota 1924-1929
Great Britain	48,277	77,206	34,007
Sweden	17,918	19,956	9,561
Norway	11,745	12,116	6,453
Denmark	4,523	5,644	2,789
Germany	48,277	68,039	51,227
Czechoslovakia	13,840	14,269	3,073
Poland	26,538	20,019	5,982
Yugoslavia	6,181	6,405	671
Lithuania	1,828	——	344
Russia	17,507	34,247	2,248
Italy	46,674	42,021	3,845
Jews	49,719	——	11,483[*]

Source: *World Almanac* and *Chicago Daily News Almanac* for relevant
years.

[*]There was no quota for Jews; this number represents the actual number
of Jewish immigrants, fiscal 1928, within the quotas of the various nations
from which they came.

tance, but all had political effects at one time or another (a prime
example is seen in Cermak's defeat of Thompson in 1931). None of
these issues, however, was as omnipresent, nor as omnipotent, as Prohibition.

Immigration restriction was a very real problem, especially after the
passage of the Johnson Act in 1924. The 3 percent quota established in
1921 was based on the census of 1910 and greatly diminished the
number of immigrants allowed into the United States. The Johnson Act
created an even more restrictive 2 percent quota based on the census of
1890 (see Table VII:3).

The table makes clear the difference between the two quota laws. All immigrant groups except the Germans were to be allowed fewer immigrants under the Johnson Act than had actually entered in fiscal 1923 (and the number in fiscal 1923 was by no means high for any group). Moreover, the newer immigrants would suffer most of all, as the law had intended.

It was not surprising, then, that the Chicago Italian Chamber of Commerce formally protested the proposed immigration law in 1920 and emotionally denounced the 1924 Johnson bill as meaning that "the American nation will brand millions of its citizens as belonging to an inferior race."[71] This reaction was typical. More to the point was the fact that the Chicago delegation to testify against the Johnson bill was dominated by Democrats and led by Alderman Jacob M. Arvey, and that the battle in the House was often led by Chicago Democratic Congressman Adolf J. Sabath, who was probably the most vociferous opponent of restriction in the entire Congress.[72] The major restriction legislation was passed by a Republican Congress, under Republican presidents, and this was equally important.

The strong ethnic opposition to immigration restriction included older as well as newer immigrants: both the John Ericsson Republican League of Illinois and the Danish-American Citizens League of Chicago denounced the restriction laws, as did countless newer immigrant organizations.[73] It does seem that ethnic opposition to restriction was led by the Democrats, who in turn profited therefrom. When a joint committee of Poles, Czechs, and Slovaks was formed in 1927 to create a united Slavic-American opposition to restriction, the temporary president was none other than Tony Cermak.[74] As with Prohibition, Cermak put himself on top of a major ethnic issue to the advantage of his own career and that of his party.

[71] Chicago Italian Chamber of Commerce *Bulletin,* March 1920 and March 1921, WPA; Chicago Italian Chamber of Commerce to Senate Immigration Committee, April 1924, WPA.
[72] See, e.g., speech before the House, May 18, 1928, Sabath Papers, American Jewish Archives. Sabath also strived to associate opposition to immigration and to immigrants with the Republican party (see *Jewish Courier,* Oct. 25, 1932, p. 4).
[73] Hemdahl, "The Swedes in Illinois Politics," p. 230; *Danske Tidende,* Sept. 17, 1926, WPA.
[74] *Dziennik Zjednoczenia,* Oct. 18, 1927, WPA.

The problem was complicated by the reluctance of either of the national parties to take a stand against restriction. But the Republicans more clearly supported it during the early 1920s, and the Democrats profited from simply saying nothing. For this reason a Polish paper supported John W. Davis in 1924.[75] And an Italian paper that supported Calvin Coolidge argued in his defense that the Johnson Act had been passed over his veto;[76] this, too, showed the importance of the issue. When both parties supported restriction in their 1928 platforms, the studiedly nonpartisan *Interpreter,* official journal of the Foreign Language Information Service, printed one of the very few political editorials of its history, saying that neither party could any longer be looked to for help in alleviating the quota laws.[77]

Al Smith did commit himself against discriminatory restriction legislation, and this had some effect in 1928. A Polish paper argued that the Republicans were against immigration from Poland, while Smith was "fair" on the issue.[78] An Italian paper also endorsed Smith for this reason, but noted with some fear late in the campaign that he seemed to be weakening.[79] Unlike the John Ericsson League, the *Svenska-Tribunen-Nyheter* did not see anything wrong with restriction; indeed, it looked upon it as a safeguard of the "mixture of races which makes up the American people" and cited it as one of the reasons for staying Republican.[80] This agreed, however, with the ethnic conception of the Democrats as the antirestriction party.

In 1932 the Democrats returned to their earlier policy of saying nothing about restriction, while the Republicans continued to support it. Thus the Democrats continued to appear as the immigrants' only hope. The ethnic press did not devote much attention to the issue after 1928. It

---

[75] *Dziennik Chicagoski,* Nov. 4, 1924, p. 1.

[76] *La Tribuna Italiana Trans-Atlantica,* Oct. 11, 1924, p. 2. This was not true; Coolidge had signed the bill. The other Italian paper argued similarly, saying that more Democrats than Republicans had voted for the bill (*L'Italia,* Nov. 2, 1924, p. 1).

[77] *The Interpreter* 8 (June 1928): 3–6.

[78] *Dziennik Chicagoski,* Nov. 4, 1928, p. 24.

[79] *La Tribuna Italiana Trans-Atlantica,* Oct. 20, 1928, p. 3. For this reason, probably, the Smith forces ran an ad in *L'Italia* on election eve (a day that *La Tribuna* was not published) strongly reasserting his stand against the Johnson Act.

[80] *Svenska-Tribunen-Nyheter,* Oct. 31, 1928, p. 4.

was always there, implicitly, but was seldom specifically mentioned. When the leading Chicago Yiddish paper devoted two major editorials to an assurance that "Gov. Roosevelt Speaks for Humanitarian Immigration Law—Is Against Registration [*sic*] Law," it was concentrating on an issue that most other ethnic papers had apparently given up as lost.[81]

But immigration restriction had been an issue of some importance and as such worked to the Democrats' advantage. It was they who articulated what little opposition there was to restriction, and ethnic voters recognized this.

The Ku Klux Klan also aroused ethnic interest, particularly in 1924 and, to a lesser extent, 1928. The issue helped neither party in 1924, since neither was willing to take a strong stand against it. Candidate John W. Davis, for example, asked Coolidge to agree that the Klan was not an issue; the president wisely declined to answer, leaving Democrats to stew in essentially Democratic juices.[82] The *Abendpost* complained about the weakness of both parties here; Robert M. La Follette seemed to it the only candidate really against the Klan.[83] A Democratic Yiddish paper, on the other hand, argued that it was Davis who was really anti-Klan, while Coolidge refused to do anything about it and La Follette had Klan-like views himself.[84] A Republican Italian paper said that Coolidge was the Klan's real enemy.[85] Thus there was no consensus, simply because neither party was truly committed on the issue.

The Klan was, however, basically a Democratic problem in 1924, and the party was hurt by it. As the Negro Chicago *Defender* put it, "The Klan was born in the stronghold of the Democratic Party, and flourishes there today."[86] The issue might well have hurt the party more, in the long run, were it not for the fact that the Klan became effectively Republican in 1928, due to its animosity to Smith's Catholicism. Thus the *Defender* would argue in support of Smith because he had "denounced in no uncertain terms the Ku Klux Klan."[87] The Smith candidacy had the effect

[81] *Jewish Courier*, Oct. 26, 1932, p. 1; Nov. 7, 1932, p. 4.
[82] Chicago *Tribune*, Aug. 24, 1924, pp. 12–13.
[83] *Abendpost*, Aug. 25, 1924, WPA.
[84] *Jewish Courier*, Oct. 16, 1924, p. 8; Oct. 17, 1924, p. 4; Oct. 26, 1924, p. 1.
[85] *La Tribuna Italiana Trans-Atlantica*, Oct. 11, 1924, p. 2.
[86] Chicago *Defender*, Oct. 4, 1924, p. 16.
[87] Ibid., Nov. 3, 1928, Pt. 2, p. 2.

of removing the Klan from around his party's neck, and this did work to the party's advantage with ethnic voters.

On the whole it was not a major issue, because it was short-lived. But it does help explain ethnic Republican voting in 1924 and Democratic voting in 1928. After that time, the issue was dead in Chicago.

Religious bigotry was a related issue. It, too, came and went in Chicago politics for both local and national elections. Most of this bigotry was anti-Catholicism, and in the long run it, too, aided the Democrats with the largely Catholic newer immigrants. The first of William Hale Thompson's successful contests for the mayoralty (1915) was marked by religious acrimony. Local Republicans allegedly mailed thousands of letters to voters, pointing out Democratic candidate Robert Sweitzer's Catholic loyalties. Reciprocally, Democrats publicized Thompson's Masonic support.[88] Similar developments took place when the two met again in 1919; both were accused of injecting the "religious issue" into the campaign.[89] But the ethnic press was not very involved in this and drew no conclusions from it; and Thompson won both times.

In 1923, when Catholic Democrat William E. Dever ran against Lutheran Republican Arthur Lueder, religious bigotry again entered a mayoral campaign. There was considerable anti-Catholic publicity against Dever, as in a broadside distributed around the city by the "Committee of Public School Teachers":

> NON-CATHOLICS: If you want Rome to run our Public Schools and City Government vote for WILLIAM E. DEVER, Democratic candidate for Mayor. He is a Roman Catholic and a member of the Knights of Columbus.[90]

The campaign itself was rather dull, and the effects of this publicity were probably not too great. It was noticed, however. One Italian paper felt that the "religious question . . . did much to influence the foreign element, especially the Jews, to vote for Mr. Dever."[91] And it is true that

---

[88] Lloyd Wendt and Herman Kogan, *Big Bill of Chicago* (Indianapolis, Ind., 1953), pp. 107–108; Lewis and Smith, *Chicago,* p. 375; Stuart, *The Twenty Incredible Years,* p. 15.

[89] Chicago *Tribune,* Mar. 22, 1919, p. 7; *Jewish Courier,* Mar. 28, 1919, p. 1.

[90] A copy can be found in the Agnes Nestor Papers, Chicago Historical Society.

[91] *La Parola del Popolo,* April 7, 1923, WPA.

Dever became, in 1923, the first Democratic mayor in eight years. Anti-Catholic politics was a two-edged sword in highly Catholic Chicago.[92]

In the 1928 presidential campaign religious prejudice reached its political zenith. The criticism of Al Smith because he was a Catholic contributed to the size of his vote and on the whole served the Democratic party in Chicago. The religious issue received a great deal of publicity. Some of this sentiment came from nonpolitical sources, but much of it did come from Republican partisans.[93]

The largely Catholic immigrant groups were understandably pleased that a coreligionist might become president and were sensitive to the anti-Catholicism of the campaign. The generally Republican *La Tribuna Italiana Trans-Atlantica* decried opposition to Smith on social and religious grounds and felt that "independent Americans" would have to vote for him to demonstrate that religious bigotry was a thing of the past.[94] The Polish-language *Dziennik Chicagoski* said that Republicans were warring against "all Catholics, foreigners and Negroes," and it was essential that Smith be elected.[95] Even the very Republican *L'Italia*, which was neutral in the presidential contest, was affected by the religious issue and vigorously applauded Smith's denunciation of religious bigotry in one of his major addresses.[96] Smith's religion, like his stand on Prohibition, pushed this paper out of the Republican column for the presidency for the first time.

Non-Catholic ethnic groups were also affected by the religious issue in 1928. A Yiddish newspaper was very concerned with "the issue of all issues—religion" and denounced Hoover for his reticence in condemning

---

[92] There were some allegations of anti-Catholicism being used against Dever in 1927, when he lost to Thompson. These were not great, however, and Thompson's America First campaign cannot really be called anti-Catholic in any but the most general and implicit sense. (See *Jewish Courier*, Mar. 18, 1927, p. 14.)

[93] See John M. Allswang, "Portrait of a Campaign: Alfred E. Smith and the People of Chicago" (M.A. thesis, State University of Iowa, 1960), pp. 26–35. There was little anti-Catholicism in the press of Protestant ethnic groups, but see Nov. 10, 1928, editorial of *Svenska Kuriren*, reprinted in Gustave E. Johnson, "The Swedes of Chicago" (Ph.D. diss., University of Chicago, 1940), p. 54.

[94] *La Tribuna Italiana Trans-Atlantica*, Nov. 3, 1928, p. 1.

[95] *Dziennik Chicagoski*, Nov. 2, 1928, p. 7; Nov. 4, 1928, p. 24.

[96] *L'Italia*, Oct. 14, 1928, p. 1; Oct. 21, 1928, p. 1.

the religious attack on Smith.[97] Rabbi Stephen S. Wise campaigned in Chicago for Smith and used the same arguments.[98] This was a matter of practical as well as ideological importance to Chicago's Jews: "Today a Roman Catholic will be disqualified from holding public office. Tomorrow a Greek Catholic will be disqualified, and the day after, a Jew will suffer the same fate."[99] The *Abendpost* also considered the issue and argued that Smith, whom it favored, was religiously "liberal" and that there was no need to fear him on this account.[100] The Scandinavian press, on the other hand, did not devote much attention to the issue. The Negro press did stress it, however: in making its first presidential endorsement of a Democrat, the *Defender* was impressed by Smith's opposition to "racial and religious bigotry"; hopefully, his suffering of the latter would make him active against the former.[101]

The religious question did not reappear in significant form subsequent to 1928. It was not as long-lived an issue as Prohibition, nor as influential, but it did play a role in both local and national elections. Most important, it was another of the ethnic issues that worked to the advantage of the Democratic party.

The Depression was not an "ethnic issue," but it was an issue of considerable interest to the ethnics. It was frequently mentioned in the campaigns of 1930 and 1932, but in both instances Prohibition was of much greater concern, despite the severity of the Depression among the ethnics of Chicago.

Inevitably the Depression was associated with the party in power, and the Republicans had the misfortune to be in power nationally, locally, and at the state level. Thus in the 1930 campaign, *Dziennik Chicagoski* charged that the full dinner pail had become the empty dinner pail and that the Republicans were responsible.[102] In 1932 it said the Depression was worsening and that the answer was political change: "With Demo-

---

[97] *Jewish Courier,* Oct. 3, 1928; Nov. 4, 1928, p. 1.
[98] Chicago *Tribune,* Oct. 26, 1928, p. 8; *Jewish Courier,* Oct. 28, 1928.
[99] *Jewish Courier,* Nov. 1, 1928, p. 8.
[100] *Abendpost,* Oct. 31, 1928, p. 3.
[101] Chicago *Defender,* Nov. 3, 1928, Pt. 2, p. 2.
[102] *Dziennik Chicagoski,* Oct. 21, 1930, p. 1; Oct. 30, 1930, p. 1; Oct. 31, 1930, p. 1.

crats—Better Times."[103] A Slovak paper, also generally Democratic, similarly blamed the Republicans for the Depression in both campaigns.[104] And a Greek paper said the same thing in 1932, arguing that the "Republican administration has done nothing to alleviate depression ills," but rather had "accentuated them."[105]

The Italian press, on the other hand, was so fully involved in the problem of Prohibition in 1930 that it simply ignored the Depression. The same was true of the *Abendpost,* which was becoming more and more Democratic in 1930 and 1932. Only when the Prohibition question was fully settled did it consider the Depression, and then it argued the issue in favor of the Democrats.[106] A Swedish paper did see the 1930 results as an economic protest against the Depression.[107] The Yiddish press and Jewish opinion leaders felt the same in 1932.[108]

Local elections, too, were affected by the Depression, again to the Democrats' advantage. The ethnic press was primarily concerned with purely ethnic problems in 1931, but the ethnics participated in the general worker alienation from the Republican party. Many labor organizations supported the Cermak candidacy in reaction to the "Republican Depression," and there was more worker involvement in this campaign than in any other local election of the period. An "A. J. Cermak for Mayor Union Labor Club" was organized, financed by a group of a hundred unions and representing over 300,000 workers.[109] Many of Chicago's ethnics were involved in this and other labor organizations active in the election, virtually all of which supported Cermak.

These are the issues that most affected Chicago's ethnic voters between 1918 and 1932 and the political response that emanated from them. Certainly there is nothing here which conflicts with our quantitative data on ethnic political behavior. Indeed, most of these issues, and the

[103] Ibid., Nov. 2, 1932, pp. 2, 5.
[104] *Osadne Hlasy,* Nov. 7, 1930, Oct. 17, 1930, Feb. 24, 1933, WPA.
[105] *Hellenic Center News,* Oct. 1, 1932, WPA.
[106] *Abendpost,* Nov. 3, 1934, WPA. Cf. Nov. 3, 1930, p. 1ff., and Nov. 7, 1932, pp. 1, 4.
[107] *Svenski-Tribunen-Nyheter,* Nov. 26, 1930, p. 1.
[108] *Jewish Courier,* Oct. 19, 20, 25, 1932, p. 1; Oct. 26, Nov. 1, 1932, p. 4. Dr. Louis L. Mann, personal interview.
[109] Chicago *Tribune,* Mar. 14, 1931, p. 8.

most important and latest of them, clearly help to explain the rise of the Democratic party among the ethnics of Chicago. The only major issue which ran contrary to this trend was the series of questions revolving around Woodrow Wilson and his international policies. But this issue died over time, and by the end of the period was virtually gone. Other issues that persisted, and new ones that arrived, tended to reinforce ethnic Democratic voting and to increase it from year to year, particularly from 1928 on.

VIII. *Political*
Organization

Ethnic membership in and identification with political parties are not only indexes of political change but are also forces promoting such change. Thus the ethnic press's conception of the two major parties demonstrated its party loyalty over time, and it also served as an influence on ethnic voting behavior. The same forces, then, were indicators and agencies of change—both cause and effect.

This is evident in the phenomenon of the ethnic composition of party tickets, which is an important indicator of ethnic political allegiance (see Tables V:2 and V:3) and also a major determinant of ethnic political motivation. As a force for change, ethnic representation on party tickets and in political office has a twofold importance: ethnics tend to vote for members of their group, regardless of party affiliation; and ethnics tend to support whichever party affords the greatest representation to their group.

The situation of the Negro was typical. In 1920 a Republican Italian judge upbraided a Negro audience for not forcing one of their own onto the Municipal Court; every Italian, he said, had ensured his election by voting for him. Negroes should do the same. Reporting this, the *Broad Ax* complained: "The Irish-Americans, the German-Americans, the Swedish-Americans, the Italian-Americans, the Jewish-Americans, the Polish-Americans, And All the Other Nationalities Amounting to Anything in This City, Aside from the Japanese, Chinese and the Colored Race, Have Representatives on the Municipal Court Bench."[1] Twelve years later, Negroes would make the same plea, as the *Defender* said during the 1932 campaign: "We are entitled to a Judge."[2] A similar source of Negro resentment was the prevalence of whites as precinct captains in Negro areas.[3] Both parties were guilty here, but continuing

Negro Republicanism was logical enough: in 1930 the Republicans slated a Negro for the Municipal Court (who lost), along with eight other Negro candidates, including the only Negro congressman in the country and the only Negro state senator in Illinois. The Democrats in 1930 did not have one Negro candidate.[4]

The same forces operated among the rest of Chicago's ethnic groups. The Czechs, for example, entered the Democratic party when they arrived in the 1880s, in good part because Czechs were nominated for office by the Democrats.[5] This continued through the years, and the Czechs remained Democratic. One Czech newspaper, strongly recommending Cermak for the presidency of the County Board in 1922, also noted: "All Czechoslovak voters, both men and women, should forever bear in mind that there are four of our countrymen on the Democratic ticket and not one on the Republican—and act accordingly next Tuesday."[6] Czechs, like other ethnics, expected their representation to increase steadily. The Slovaks, who fared less well in this regard, were threatening to "join the other side" as late as 1930, "if the Democrats fail to recognize us."[7] A few years earlier, the leaders of the Chicago Hungarian Republican Club had

[1] *Broad-Ax,* Oct. 23, 1920, p. 3. This is a good example of the operation, among ethnic groups, of the concept of "relative deprivation." The concept has been characterized as an "interpretative variable," "a provisional after-the-fact interpretative concept which is intended to explain the variation in attitudes." In this case, with all ethnic minorities considered as one reference group, Negroes are affected by the fact that all other members of the group are faring better than they, and they feel deprived relative to the others. The feeling would tend to reinforce Negro Republican voting, since their better representation in that party would result in the feeling operating less in the Republican than in the Democratic context. (See Robert K. Merton, in collaboration with A. Rossi, "Contributions to the Theory of Reference Group Behavior," in *Social Theory and Social Structure,* rev. ed. [Glencoe, Ill., 1957], esp. pp. 227–30; James A. Davis, "A Formal Interpretation of the Theory of Relative Deprivation," *Sociometry* 22 [Dec. 1959]: 280–96.) The concept has potentialities for the study of ethnic group history that deserve intensive exploration and refinement.

[2] Chicago *Defender,* Sept. 17, 1932, Pt. 2, p. 2.

[3] Harold F. Gosnell, *Negro Politicians* (Chicago, 1935), p. 137.

[4] Chicago *Tribune,* Oct. 16, 1930, p. 6; Frances W. McLemore, "The Role of the Negroes in Chicago in the Senatorial Election, 1930" (M.A. thesis, University of Chicago, 1931), p. 12.

[5] Alex Gottfried, *Boss Cermak of Chicago: A Study of Political Leadership* (Seattle, Wash., 1962), p. 42.

[6] *Denni Hlasatel,* Nov. 5, 1922, WPA.

[7] *Osadne Hlasy,* Oct. 17, 1930, WPA.

threatened to join the Democrats if they did not get three political jobs; and they probably so joined.[8]

The Republican Italian press generally endorsed the entire Republican ticket, but always with the exception of any Italian Democrats. Italian candidates always came first. And when an election was generally uninteresting, they tended simply to publicize the Italian candidates of both parties, and to ignore the rest.[9] The relative Republicanism of the Italians in 1932 is partially explained by the fact that they were still better represented by the Republicans than by the Democrats. But they were becoming better represented in the Democratic party under Cermak, and for this reason many Italians were switching.[10] The more Democratic Poles responded in a similar fashion. When a Polish-American Democratic congressman supported a Jewish Democrat for the state senate, rather than his Polish Republican opponent, the newspaper of the Polish Roman Catholic Union protested vigorously.[11] And as a progressively higher proportion of Polish candidates appeared on the Democratic ticket, the Polish press became progressively more attached to the party. The generally nonpartisan paper of the Polish National Alliance became partisan indeed when Democrat M. S. Szymczak ran for city treasurer in 1927; the importance of this ethnic attraction was clear in the fact that Thompson advertisements in this paper endorsed Szymczak rather than Thompson's own running mate.[12] The most partisan Polish newspaper always lost its partisanship when a Polish candidate ran for the other party.[13]

This ethnocentricity in politics was not confined to less assimilated ethnic groups. The *Abendpost,* for example, took an unprecedentedly strong stand in local politics when Arthur Lueder ran for mayor in 1923, and as late as 1934—when it was a Democratic paper—it recommended the election of all German-American candidates, regardless of party.[14] In 1928 the *Abendpost* warned Thompson that, in return for their support in 1927, German-Americans wanted more political representation than

[8] *Magyar Tribune,* Mar. 12, 1926, WPA.
[9] *L'Italia,* Mar. 30, 1919, p. 1; Oct. 26, 1930, p. 11.
[10] George L. Spatuzza, personal interview.
[11] *Dziennik Zjednoczenia,* April 7, 1922, WPA.
[12] *Dziennik Zwiazkowy,* April 4, 1927, pp. 7, 9.
[13] E.g., *Dziennik Chicagoski,* Nov. 3, 1930, pp. 6–7.
[14] *Sonntagpost,* April 1, 1923, p. 1; *Abendpost,* Nov. 3, 1934, WPA.

they were receiving.[15] And the *Abendpost* supported Cermak in 1931. This problem was not as great among the Germans as among some other groups because they were pretty well represented in both parties by 1932; but it was always an issue.

For the Jewish press, increasing Jewish representation in the Democratic party was important. The *Jewish Courier* felt this to be true always, and it reached its highest point in 1932, when a Jew received the Democratic nomination for governor ("forget everything in order to give your vote to the Democratic candidate for governor, Henry Horner").[16] Even at this point, the Democratic *Courier* supported all Jewish candidates, regardless of party, but the fact that most of them were Democrats was important.[17]

In this context, the data in Tables V:2 and V:3 assume a new importance, as reasons for ethnic voting changes. The differences between the two parties were not overwhelming. But there was a steady rise in ethnic representation in the Democratic party, particularly for the newer immigrants. Given the intense importance attached to this factor by the ethnic press and other ethnic spokesmen, this development is a significant force for change in ethnic political behavior. Other aspects of political organization will further clarify the forces of change.

The development of local party organizations is an indicator of changing ethnic-consciousness in party self-conceptions. Ethnic reactions to these developments were instruments of political change. That is, in Big Bill Thompson's career we can see not only his organization's reaction to the ethnics but also the ethnics' reaction to his organization. The same, obviously, also applies to Cermak's Democratic organization. And a climax was reached when the two men confronted one another in the mayoralty of 1931.

Thompson's antiwar stand in his first term in office (1915–1919) probably lost him more ethnic support than it gained. His enforcement of Sunday closing laws in 1915 was also resented by the ethnics. When he

---

[15] *Abendpost,* April 6, 1928, WPA.

[16] *Jewish Courier,* Nov. 3, 1918, p. 1; April 6, 1923, WPA; Oct. 28, 1932, p. 1.

[17] In 1932, for example, Republican Samuel Heller was strongly supported for the Municipal Court in the same preelection editorial which endorsed Roosevelt and Horner. (*Jewish Courier,* Nov. 7, 1932, p. 4.)

tried to get the Republican nomination for the United States Senate in 1918, he suffered the first loss of his political career: in the primary he carried the city with 57 percent, but lost the state with only 40 percent. His alleged pro-Germanism was resented by newer immigrant leaders.[18] The same held true in his successful campaign for reelection in 1919. Fred Lundin, one of his leading advisers, felt his strength for the campaign would be among selected ethnics: the Negroes and the anti-British Irish and Germans.[19] Lundin was only partly right. There was considerable German support for Thompson, then and later. The *Deutsch-Amerikanischer Bürgerbund,* for example, reminded German voters that it was Thompson who had kept the city safe for them during the war. And the *Abendpost* agreed.[20] But only half of the German voters felt the same. Thompson's 1919 victory was essentially a party victory, in that he did best among the traditionally most Republican groups—Jews, Swedes, and Negroes. There was no strong ethnic break in his favor.

Thompson's 1919 victory was actually built on a weak alliance— weak because it pretty well excluded the newer immigrants and also because its reliance on the Negro vote alienated other ethnic voters.[21] Moreover, further weakness came from the disruptive effect that Thompson was beginning to have on the Illinois Republican party. By 1920 this animosity was open and sufficiently bitter that the Republicans were unable even to agree on where and when to hold their preelection convention.[22] Things got worse as time passed. Throughout the 1920s there were generally three strong factions in the party and sometimes more; occasionally two or more would work together for one campaign, but the fragmentation always returned. This made the party less effective than it might have been, and in some campaigns ethnic spokesmen specifically cited Republican factionalism as a reason for supporting the Democrats.[23]

[18] Chicago *Daily News,* Oct. 6, 1918, p. 1; Lloyd Wendt and Herman Kogan, *Big Bill of Chicago* (Indianapolis, Ind., 1953), pp. 161–62.

[19] Wendt and Kogan, *Big Bill of Chicago,* pp. 167–68.

[20] *Abendpost,* Mar. 2, 1919, WPA; April 2, 1919, WPA.

[21] The *Abendpost,* for example, noted that efforts had been made to dissuade Germans from voting for Thompson because he was pro-Negro. (Mar. 31, 1919, WPA.)

[22] Chicago *Tribune,* Sept. 20, 1920, p. 1.

[23] E.g., *Jewish Courier,* Mar. 25, 1923, p. 8, Nov. 4, 1932, p. 8; *Dziennik Chicagoski,* Mar. 30, 1923, p. 1; Chicago *Defender,* Mar. 31, 1923, p. 10. A

Internecine Republican conflict partially dictated Thompson's decision not to try for a third term in 1923; it was reinforced by the aura of corruption around his chief allies and himself. Fred Lundin had just been indicted for fraud of three million dollars in School Board expenditures, and Thompson was fearful. More scandal had appeared in the gubernatorial administration of his ally, Len Small. And, for the time, the Robert E. Crowe and Edward Brundage factions of the party were fighting him. So Thompson removed himself from active politics for four years, another factor which probably weakened his position in the long run.

Nonetheless he was triumphant when he reentered politics in 1927 to run for a third term as mayor. One contemporary analyst of his "America First" campaign felt that it exerted a strong ethnic appeal because it was not really anti-English, but rather anti-American English—the white Anglo-Saxon Protestant culture dominating American life.[24] But this kind of analysis was at most only partly right. Thompson did not carry the votes of the Czechs, Poles, or Lithuanians in 1927, and his vote among all the newer immigrants was only 50.4 percent; this certainly demonstrated no strong hold on ethnic sympathies. He profited greatly from the Negro vote, and from continuing German loyalty, which was greater in 1927 than in 1919—and here, perhaps, Prohibition was the crucial issue.[25]

While winning a third term, Thompson was also creating the forces that would undercut him. In 1926 he had broken with Fred Lundin, who supported his own candidate in 1927: Dr. John Dill Robertson, formerly Thompson's health commissioner. Thompson bitterly attacked Lundin during the campaign, in one of his famous exhibitions (debating two rats in cages, one called "Fred" and the other "Doc"). Chicago's Swedish-Americans were offended at this treatment of one of their more famous countrymen.[26] Thompson had also broken relations with Governor Small

---

convenient summary of the factions in the Republican party can be found in Carroll H. Wooddy, *The Chicago Primary of 1926* (Chicago, 1926).

[24] Editorial in the New York *Evening Post,* quoted in *The Interpreter* 6 (Nov. 1927): 3–5. One ethnic newspaper came to the same conclusion: *Magyar Tribune,* Feb. 25, 1927, WPA.

[25] Chicago *Tribune,* Mar. 21, 1927, p. 5; *Abendpost,* Dec. 7, 1926, WPA, April 6, 1928, WPA.

[26] The Swedish Club of Chicago voted to "censure William Hale Thompson for calling a Swede a rat." Chicago *Tribune,* Dec. 18, 1926, quoted in Reuel G.

in 1925–1926, creating another faction; they came back together for the 1927 campaign, with Thompson promising to support Small's reelection in 1928. But it would be an uneasy reconciliation, and, moreover, it was a reconciliation that required Thompson to break an earlier promise of 1928 gubernatorial support to Illinois Attorney General Oscar Carlstrom. He was in a bind, with no easy way out.[27]

Newer immigrant resentment of Thompson's Negro alliance also emerged in 1927. Italian and Polish newspapers used this as a reason for endorsing Dever. To *La Tribuna Italiana Trans-Atlantica*, Thompson was making Chicago "the Mecca and Paradise Land of the Negro." Negroes were infiltrating Italian neighborhoods, depreciating property values, and competing with Italian workers for jobs. And "promiscuity of races" threatened—all due to Big Bill's friendship for the Negroes.[28] *Dziennik Chicagoski* agreed: a front-page cartoon showed Big Bill kissing a "Colored Thompsonite" while a "White Thompsonite" said "America First."[29] Ethnic animosities were real and put Thompson in a difficult position, but he needed his Negro votes too badly to do anything about it.

The relationship between Thompson and Chicago's Negroes was clearly of the first importance, especially in its dual role of creating Thompson's strength and of maintaining Negro Republicanism. It was also important because of the effect this alliance had on the other ethnics of Chicago. From the start of his career, Thompson had been oriented in this direction: in his first term as alderman (1900–1902) he introduced a bill for the building of the city's first public playground—in the heart of the Black Belt.[30] When he first ran for mayor, he enlisted the aid of Bishop Archibald Carey, a leading Negro clergyman, and this alliance was maintained throughout his career. He made alliances with rising Negro politicians, such as Oscar De Priest, and gave City Hall jobs to many Negroes to help Negro politicians build a going organization.

Hemdahl, "The Swedes in Illinois Politics: An Immigrant Group in an American Political Setting" (Ph.D. diss., Northwestern University, 1932), p. 417. See also Gustave E. Johnson, "The Swedes of Chicago" (Ph.D. diss., University of Chicago, 1940), pp. 45–46, 48–49.

[27] See William H. Stuart, *The Twenty Incredible Years* (Chicago, 1935), pp. 226–27, 327–28, 335–36.

[28] *La Tribuna Italiana Trans-Atlantica*, April 2, 1927, p. 2.

[29] *Dziennik Chicagoski*, Mar. 19, 1927, p. 1.

[30] Wendt and Kogan, *Big Bill of Chicago*, p. 42.

The mayor made frequent trips to the Black Belt to maintain his rapport with the mass of the Negro electorate.[31]

Thompson's opponent of 1915 and 1919, Robert M. Sweitzer, doubted his sincerity: "He talks church, home and civil service in Hyde Park; in the First and Second Wards it is, 'I am for prize fights, dice games and jobs for you colored boys.' "[32] But Thompson was effective, as when he told a Second Ward audience in 1919: "Enemies have tried to divide us—they are trying to divide us now, but we have always stood together and we always will. I've given you a square deal, and you've given a square deal to me."[33] To this, a man in the audience cried out, "You're our brother," expressing the feeling that many Negroes had for Thompson throughout his career. He received 78 percent of the Negro vote in 1919, and the city's leading Negro newspaper exulted that, "It was a victory, not only for Mayor Thompson, but for the Chicago *Defender* as well."[34]

Thompson's hold over Negro voters was convincingly demonstrated in 1923, when he did not run for reelection. His role in the campaign is not clearly known, but he did oppose Republican nominee Arthur Lueder, who represented the rival Brundage faction of the party. By implication at least (and perhaps quite openly in private councils) Thompson supported Democrat Dever.[35] This primarily affected Negroes: Oscar De Priest openly bolted and endorsed Dever as did Alderman Louis B. Anderson, who shared control of Second Ward politics with him.[36] And the Chicago *Defender* refused to endorse anyone, bemoaning the factionalism that was hurting the local Republican party.[37]

[31] McLemore, "The Role of the Negroes," p. 3; Lloyd Lewis and Henry J. Smith, *Chicago: The History of Its Reputation* (New York, 1929), pp. 392–94.

[32] Lewis and Smith, *Chicago*, p. 374.

[33] Chicago *Tribune*, Mar. 25, 1919, p. 7.

[34] Chicago *Defender*, April 5, 1919, p. 1. The elaborateness of Thompson's Negro organization was already great by 1919, as the following perhaps apocryphal report of that year demonstrates. "Oscar De Priest . . . was reading election returns. One precinct showed 272 votes cast, of which 271 were for Thompson. Oscar turned to a henchman. 'I know who double-crossed there,' he said. 'Go out and find Mose Jackson and give him a raking over the coals.' " (*Literary Digest* 76 [Mar. 3, 1923]: 54.)

[35] Stuart, *The Twenty Incredible Years*, pp. 186–87. Stuart was a Hearst reporter and Thompson apologist; he was apparently as close to Thompson as any Chicago reporter.

[36] *Broad-Ax*, Mar. 22, 1923; Gosnell, *Negro Politicians*, p. 44.

[37] Chicago *Defender*, Mar. 31, 1923, p. 10.

Dever received 53 percent of the Negro vote (and 69 percent in the Second Ward). Clearly, the Thompson-Negro alliance was strong enough to persuade a majority of Negro voters to switch their party loyalty in a local election.[38] It was the combination of Thompson and Negro politicians, working together, that accomplished this, but Thompson made the mistake of thinking that he had done it alone.

Negro support was crucial in Thompson's bid to return to the mayoralty in 1927, and both parties knew it. The Democrats, still under the leadership of George Brennan, unwisely chose the path of prejudice. Calliopes went through the streets playing "Bye, Bye Blackbird," and distributing cartoons showing a trainload of Negroes coming up from Georgia, piloted by Thompson: "This train will start for Chicago, April 6, if Thompson is elected."[39] When, early in the campaign, Thompson apparently embraced a Negro child, Brennan distributed cartoons picturing this, and reading, "Do you want Negroes or White Men to Run Chicago? Bye, Bye, Blackbirds."[40] In a speech Brennan cautioned his listeners not to turn the city over to "the black belt." Numbers of Negroes were jailed during the campaign, in an apparent effort to exert political pressure.[41]

The Democratic campaign backfired, since it solidified Thompson's Negro support and did not arouse other ethnics to the degree necessary to defeat him. It was a stupid policy in the politics of a pluralistic society, where the louder prejudice becomes the less effective it tends to be. Brennan's successor would know better.

Thompson built on the situation presented by the Democrats in his campaign. All over the city he called his critics "lily white gentlemen" and "traducers and liars." He anticipated ethnic sympathy for his stand.[42] When Brennan talked about "Black Belt Rule," Thompson replied that "The black finger that is good enough to pull a trigger in defense of the American flag is good enough to mark a ballot."[43] And at a Negro mass

[38] See St. Clair Drake and Horace R. Cayton, *Black Metropolis* (New York, 1945), p. 347.

[39] Gosnell, *Negro Politicians*, p. 54.

[40] Wendt and Kogan, *Big Bill of Chicago*, p. 256.

[41] George C. Hoffman, "Big Bill Thompson, His Mayoral Campaigns and Voting Strength" (M.A. thesis, University of Chicago, 1956), pp. 36–38; Chicago *Tribune*, Mar. 1, 1927, p. 1ff.

[42] E.g., Chicago *Tribune*, Mar. 19, 1927, p. 6.

[43] Chicago *Defender*, Mar. 5, 1927, p. 1.

meeting, attended by both Thompson and Oscar De Priest, one speaker said: "You must either vote for Thompson or else die."[44]

With this and his promise of a wide-open town, Thompson's Negro support reached its apogee in 1927. The *Defender* called it "one of the dirtiest political campaigns ever held in the city of Chicago" and in its own desire to ensure Thompson's election enjoined its readers to vote a straight Republican ticket.[45] Thompson received 90 percent of the Negro vote (94 percent in the Second Ward, and as high as 98 percent in two precincts of the Nineteenth Ward), and this was his margin of victory.[46]

In the disastrous 1928 primary Thompson and his allies still had very strong Negro support, and he continued sure of his invincibility with the Negroes. But in 1930 it became clear how little he really knew of ethnic politics.

Between Thompson and Ruth Hanna McCormick (widow of former United States Senator Medill McCormick, and daughter of Mark Hanna), there had never been friendship. This turned into real hostility in 1930, when Mrs. McCormick was Republican nominee for the Senate and Thompson sought to defeat her by delivering the Negro vote to Democrat "J. Ham." Lewis. De Priest and other Negro leaders would not join him, but he was implacable in his overconfidence. He arranged to have a handbill, which attacked Mrs. McCormick as anti-Negro and endorsed Lewis, distributed by an "Uncle Tom" float and uniformed policemen at the doors of Negro churches on a preelection Sunday.[47] And the plan backfired tremendously.

Oscar De Priest made a clear break with his old ally, saying repeatedly: "I was surprised to find the mayor a sick man. He certainly is not the same man we elected mayor three times. No sane man, unless

[44] Chicago *Tribune,* Mar. 26, 1927, p. 5.

[45] Chicago *Defender,* April 2, 1927, p. 1ff., and Pt. 2, p. 2.

[46] Another impressive indication of this strength: Edward H. Wright, a leading older Negro politician, broke with Thompson in 1927 and supported Robertson. He was able to get Robertson only 526 votes in the entire Second Ward and only seven votes in his own precinct, despite the fact that his family numbered eight! Wright was replaced as Second Ward committeeman by Daniel Jackson, who toured the Black Belt promising that Thompson would reopen policy stations closed by Dever. (See McLemore, "The Role of the Negroes," pp. 19–22; Wendt and Kogan, *Big Bill of Chicago,* p. 249; Gosnell, *Negro Politicians,* ch. 8.)

[47] McLemore, "The Role of the Negroes," pp. 17–18, 24; Stuart, *The Twenty Incredible Years,* pp. 412, 437–39.

ill-advised or sick, would ask the colored people to vote for a Demo-crat."[48] De Priest stumped the state for Mrs. McCormick, telling Negroes that to vote for Lewis would be to lose the franchise in the North.[49] He put out a special campaign newspaper, *The Plain Truth,* and set up mass meetings in the Black Belt to reiterate these charges and to revive the charges of racism which had been raised against Lewis, with justification, in 1920.[50]

The Chicago *Bee,* a relatively new Negro paper, also denounced Thompson for misleading Negroes and praised De Priest for his inde-pendent Negro leadership.[51] Even the very nonpolitical Chicago branch of the NAACP bitterly attacked the mayor for opposing Mrs. McCormick, and questioned his general comportment as well.[52] The *Defender,* Thompson's greatest journalistic support, said absolutely nothing.

The results showed how weak Thompson was without the support of Negro politicians. Mrs. McCormick received 76 percent of the Negro vote, while Lewis was carrying the city and every other ethnic group by better than two-to-one. Thompson was the big loser. His Negro support would never again be as great as it had been, and a number of his close Negro allies left him. Even before election day he had acknowledged defeat: he requested a meeting with De Priest and guaranteed he would make no reprisals.[53] At last it should have been clear to Big Bill that his control over Negro voters was based on reciprocity, as are all political

[48] Chicago *Tribune,* Oct. 27, 1930, p. 8; Wendt and Kogan, *Big Bill of Chicago,* pp. 318–19. De Priest, of course, had openly supported Democrat Dever in 1923, and perhaps covertly Smith, in 1928.

[49] Chicago *Tribune,* Oct. 22, 1930, p. 9.

[50] McLemore, "The Role of the Negroes," pp. 42–47, 62–71 (she attended these meetings, as a student of Harold F. Gosnell). A copy of *The Plain Truth* can be found in the Gosnell materials, Merriam Papers, University of Chicago. In the 1920 campaign, Lewis had said: "This is a white man's government and as long as I have voice or power to protest, I will never permit the criminal, lawless Negro to overrun the righteous, law-abiding Negro or drive the white man from the polls." (Chicago *Defender,* Oct. 30, 1920, p. 12. A slightly different but essentially similar version is in Chicago *Tribune,* Oct. 26, 1930, p. 7. And see also McLemore, p. 8n.)

[51] Chicago *Bee,* quoted in McLemore, "The Role of the Negroes," p. 55n.

[52] Chicago *Tribune,* Nov. 2, 1930, p. 11.

[53] McLemore, "The Role of the Negroes," pp. 48–49; Stuart, *The Twenty Incredible Years,* pp. 437–39. One important white ally lost here was George F. Harding, longtime boss of the Negro Fourth Ward, and one of Thompson's earliest backers.

relationships; but he was not a man to learn lessons this late in his career.

The 1930 campaign signified Thompson's reentry into political life, despite the fact that he had been mayor since 1927. He had suffered the greatest defeat of his career in the 1928 primary and remained very inactive from that time until the fall of 1930. Chicago hardly had a mayor during much of this time. The 1928 primary sheds considerable light on the relationship between Thompson and the ethnics of Chicago.

Confident after his 1927 triumph, Big Bill immersed himself in national issues, looking once again to a place for himself in national politics. He became a flood-control enthusiast and a leading supporter of a Great Lakes to the Gulf waterway. He also participated in a "Draft Coolidge" movement, hoping to defeat Hoover's bid for the 1928 presidential nomination.[54] More controversially, in the fall of 1927 he tried to implement his America First program in the Chicago public schools. He harassed the Superintendent of Schools and finally had him put on trial, primarily because school textbooks and the superintendent were allegedly insufficiently patriotic and too anglophile. The school purge was followed by a public library purge for similar reasons; book burning was threatened. The whole affair was nationally publicized and kept the mayor on the nation's front pages. It also disrupted Chicago's schools.[55] Thompson apparently expected ethnic support from this campaign—he was careful to insist that America's foreign heroes were also inadequately honored.[56] But the ethnic press, at least, was unimpressed.

At the same time, Republican factionalism grew worse. Thompson had reneged on his earlier promise of 1928 gubernatorial support to Oscar Carlstrom, switching to Len Small in order to have the latter's support in the 1927 mayoralty. This renewed the anti-Thompson feelings of a large segment of the party. State's Attorney Robert Crowe—previously a Thompson opponent—had joined Thompson and Small in a rather unholy alliance, which prepared to do battle with the rest of the party in the 1928 primary. All the other factions (the Charles Deneen group, the Edward Brundage group, and various lesser ones) were united

---

[54] Stuart, *The Twenty Incredible Years*, pp. 351–55.

[55] The best coverage of this whole affair is in George S. Counts, *School and Society in Chicago* (New York, 1928). See also Wendt and Kogan, *Big Bill of Chicago*, pp. 284–302; John Bright, *Hizzoner Big Bill Thompson* (New York, 1930), chs. 15, 18, 19; Stuart, *The Twenty Incredible Years*, pp. 339–46.

[56] Counts, *School and Society in Chicago*, pp. 280–83.

under Deneen against them. The Thompson-Small-Crowe combine did not help themselves by choosing Frank L. Smith as their senatorial candidate. Smith had been elected to the Senate in 1926 in what was generally called an "Insullized" primary. The Senate twice ruled his election invalid because of Samuel Insull's huge investment in his candidacy, and Smith was ultimately and decisively ejected from that body in January 1928.[57]

Chicago's gangsters were also active in the 1928 primary, although their exact role remains unclear. But Al Capone was involved, and the primary campaign was characterized by bombings, murders, and general violence. It was called the "Pineapple Primary" because of the bombings of the homes of Senator Deneen and his state's attorney candidate, John A. Swanson, the leaders of the anti-Thompson group. When Crowe and Thompson charged that the Deneen forces had engineered the bombings to win voter sympathy, they chose a bad strategy, which backfired.[58] The leading candidates in the primary were Thompson-Small-Crowe: Small for governor, Crowe for state's attorney, Smith for senator; Deneen group: Louis L. Emmerson for governor, John A. Swanson for state's attorney, and Otis F. Glenn for senator. The vote was a disaster for the Thompson combine, both in the city and the state. In Chicago, Small received 38 percent to Emmerson's 62, and Crowe received 39 percent to Swanson's 61. Small and Crowe received strong majorities only among the Negroes (68 percent) and the Italians (74 percent)—the former was a pro-Thompson vote and the latter was probably influenced by the gangsters. Otherwise, Thompson's candidates received bare majorities among some relatively Democratic ethnic groups and did very poorly among the most Republican. Table VIII:1 compares the vote received by Thompson in the 1927 mayoral primary with that received by Small and Crowe in the 1928 primary for a graphic demonstration of how the mayor and his allies slipped in the course of this one year.

Thompson lost ground with every ethnic group in the city, only one year after his triumphal return to the mayor's office. The decline among the most Republican groups (Jews, Germans, Swedes, Native-Americans,

[57] Stuart, *The Twenty Incredible Years*, pp. 327, 335–36, 358; Wooddy, *The Chicago Primary of 1926*, and *The Case of Frank L. Smith* (Chicago, 1931).

[58] Wendt and Kogan, *Big Bill of Chicago*, pp. 304–305; Stuart, *The Twenty Incredible Years*, pp. 362–63; Lewis and Smith, *Chicago*, p. 467.

and even the Negroes) showed that the local Republican party was far from healthy. And Thompson's troubles were not over yet. Another blow came shortly after the primary. For years the "experts' fees" case had been dragging through the courts. This was a suit filed by the Chicago *Tribune* against Thompson, George F. Harding, and others, accusing them of cheating the city out of almost three million dollars through phony "salaries" paid to hired real estate experts. In June 1928 a decision emerged in the court of Judge Hugo Friend, a Deneen Republican. The defendants were found guilty and held liable for $2,245,604. Thompson was crushed, stayed away from City Hall, started drinking more, and spent the greater part of the next two years in semiseclusion. Not until the Illinois Supreme Court reversed the decision for lack of proof in the fall of 1930 did Thompson really come back to life.[59] Even then, his return was less than striking, since it was to the unsuccessful attempt to deliver the Negro senatorial vote to Democrat Lewis.

Tony Cermak's career was considerably different. It was, throughout, more ethnically oriented. Cermak's political frame of reference was an ethnic one, and he concerned himself with ethnic issues. His Democratic party was clearly more ethnic at base than Thompson's Republican party. It was also a more rational political movement.

The pre-Cermak Irish leadership of the local Democracy (by Roger Sullivan and then George Brennan, until he died in 1928) was not antiethnic. Both leaders had demonstrated considerable ethnic consciousness in making up party tickets and in seeking votes generally. But they were more interested in maintaining their own control over the party than they were in victory and were considerably less ethnically oriented than Cermak and the leaders who would rise with and after him. James Hamilton Lewis was probably the most popular older Democrat with the ethnics of Chicago, and he tended to stay away from the Brennan machine.[60]

The Irish leadership had effectively discouraged some ethnics from

---

[59] Wendt and Kogan, *Big Bill of Chicago,* pp. 311–13; Stuart, *The Twenty Incredible Years,* pp. 383–85; Charles E. Merriam, *Chicago: A More Intimate View of Urban Politics* (New York, 1929), p. 85.

[60] On Lewis's popularity with the ethnics generally, see Chicago *Tribune,* Nov. 1, 1920, p. 6.

TABLE VIII:1   *Ethnic Vote for Thompson Organization in Republican*
Primaries of 1927 and 1928 (Percentage of the vote
for the two major candidates received by candidate
named)

Group	Thompson, 1927	Small, 1928	Crowe, 1928
Czechoslovaks	86	58	56
Poles	74	53	49
Lithuanians	64	48	52
Yugoslavs	70	45	39
Italians	74	72	76
Germans	63	36	34
Swedes	60	30	25
Jews	69	37	37
Negroes	90	68	68
Native-Americans	51	21	22
CHICAGO TOTAL	68	38	39

considering the Democratic party as a group vehicle. Clearly the Brennan
organization was anti-Negro, and this reinforced the Negroes' predilec-
tion for the Republican party. It also discounted a growing and ethnocentric group, which was stupid politics and demonstrated Brennan's short-
sightedness. Other groups were similarly affected. The Swedes, for
example, moved into the Republican party in the late nineteenth century
partially out of their dislike for the Irish Catholic leadership of the
Democrats.[61] And essentially the same leadership prevailed down to
1928. Even the Czechs entered the Democratic party "in spite of" the
Irish leadership, and Slavic-Irish conflict and rivalry predated both Cermak and Brennan.[62]

[61] Johnson, "The Swedes of Chicago," pp. 39–43, 54, 103.
[62] Gottfried, *Boss Cermak,* p. 31.

The Sullivan-Brennan forces prevailed until Brennan's death in 1928 despite their failure to achieve consistent Democratic victories after the war. In good part this was due to the real political talent of the Irish leadership; inertia also helped. While the Republicans were torn by faction during this period, the Democrats were not. There was a small "reform" faction or group, led by former Mayor Carter H. Harrison and former Governor Edward F. Dunne, which opposed Sullivan and Brennan.[63] But it was a small group of older men who were neither vocal nor influential. What could have been a more severe rupture, involving Cermak or other powerful members of the local Democracy, simply did not rise above the surface. This may have kept Cermak down until Brennan died, but it also established a tradition of party solidarity from which he would profit when the time came.

Cermak's rise as an ethnic politician, his support, and the issues he employed help explain his increasing importance in the local Democracy. In 1912 he ran in his first citywide race, for bailiff of the Municipal Court, and was victorious. He held this office through 1918, when he ran for sheriff and suffered his first defeat (here, his practice of never relinquishing one office until he had a higher one paid off). He did carry the city in 1918, with 51 percent of the vote, but lost in the more Republican suburban returns. The office traditionally went to the Germans, and he had a German opponent, Charles W. Peters. But despite the wartime anti-German campaign, which his biographer says he engaged in, Cermak was supported by the *Abendpost* and by 47 percent of the German voters.[64] He had, as usual, strong support from his fellow Czechs, and from other ethnics as well. The seldom partisan organ of the Polish National Alliance, for example, called him "one of our sympathizers" and urged his election.[65] He received majorities from all of the nine groups except the Germans, Swedes, and Negroes. He led the ticket among the Czechs with 86 percent; and among the other groups that went Democratic, he stayed within five points of popular "J. Ham." Lewis. For a young man running for his first major office, this was good.

[63] See Harrison's penned comments on a Sullivan dossier of 1915 and on an undated [1920s] letter to Dever, Harrison Papers, Newberry Library.
[64] Gottfried, *Boss Cermak*, pp. 91–94; *Abendpost*, Nov. 2, 1918, WPA.
[65] *Dziennik Zwiazkowy*, Sept. 12, 1918, WPA.

In 1922 Cermak achieved real power. He was elected member and president of the Cook County Board of Commissioners, a position of great responsibility and a major steppingstone traditionally in Chicago politics. He was reelected in 1926 and 1930 and came to be known as "the Mayor of Cook County." Each time he ran for this office he set up another referendum on Prohibition—the issue and the man continued to be identified with one another, to his advantage. From his power base on the County Board, Cermak began to create an organization, and his alliances were indicative. Starting with the Jews, he approached Moe Rosenberg and Jacob Arvey of the Twenty-Fourth Ward ghetto.[66] For his Irish ties he sought out Pat Nash, who was alienated from the Brennan organization and Brennan's chosen successor (and Cermak's major rival), Michael Igoe. Significantly, Nash was also one of the few Democratic Irish politicians with a reputation of friendship with Chicago's Negroes.[67] Cermak thought ahead: in 1927, while Brennan sought to defeat Thompson with an anti-Negro campaign, Cermak put the publisher of the *Broad-Ax* on his Civic Commission. Negroes were duly informed.[68]

Thus he built an ethnic career, particularly oriented toward those ethnics who were least well represented in the political life of the city. The more advantaged ethnic groups were not ignored, however, and he tried to establish a foothold with the Native-Americans as well. In 1928, when he reluctantly agreed to run for the Senate, Cermak led the ticket in Chicago. Al Smith had more publicity and elicited more ethnic interest in the campaign, but Cermak was also noticed. And he did better than Smith among all groups except the Italians and the Negroes. He carried the city, with 53 percent (though losing the state), while Smith received just under 50 percent. The two candidates complemented one another, and each profited from the other's candidacy; neither would have fared as well if the other had not run. Both contributed to the political change that began with that election.

The same was true in 1930, when Cermak was again reelected to the presidency of the County Board. He ran slightly behind Lewis among all groups, but this was because Lewis had a female opponent. Cermak

[66] Gottfried, *Boss Cermak,* pp. 177–78.
[67] *Broad-Ax,* Oct. 26, 1918, p. 2.
[68] Ibid., April 9, 1927, p. 1.

received considerable ethnic support in this campaign and contributed to the extent of the Democratic victory.[69] Moreover, by this time he was clearly the boss of the Democratic party of Chicago and Cook County. Michael Igoe was not willing to recognize the fact, but it was true nonetheless; within two years even Igoe would be a believer.[70]

The 1931 campaign was not the first clash between Thompson and Cermak. In 1915, when Thompson enforced Sunday closing, Cermak led the United Societies' protest effort. A large number of protest meetings and demonstrations were held, culminating in a great Wet Parade, with about 40,000 marchers and over half-a-million viewers. From this point forward, the two men remained antagonists.[71]

The 1931 mayoralty was a clash of belief as well as personality. Whatever understanding of ethnic politics Thompson previously had, it degenerated in his campaign of vilification of "Tony Baloney" and his pushcart. It was a mistake from the start and backfired seriously, while Cermak's years of working with the ethnics were paying off.

The 1931 primaries were typical in the careers of the two contestants and the two local party organizations. Division among the Republicans continued, and two "reform" candidates opposed Thompson for the nomination. He managed to eke out a victory, largely due to the Negro vote, but the party did not heal its wounds after the primary. One Republican alderman, for example, said that party loyalty meant nothing after Thompson had bolted in 1930, and so he endorsed Cermak.[72] Other Republican politicians did the same.[73] And there is evidence that the

---

[69] *Dziennik Zwiazkowy,* Nov. 3, 1930, p. 4; *L'Italia,* Oct. 26, 1930, p. 1. *L'Italia* was still strongly for Thompson and noted that Cermak was "attractive to the Thompson organization." This was not true, but Cermak would take support on any terms.

[70] Harold F. Gosnell, *Machine Politics: Chicago Model* (Chicago, 1937), p. 14.

[71] Gottfried, *Boss Cermak,* pp. 82–85; Wendt and Kogan, *Big Bill of Chicago,* p. 130.

[72] Chicago *Tribune,* Mar. 17, 1931, p. 6.

[73] E.g., George Harding, who had broken with Thompson in 1930 tried to deliver the Fourth Ward for Thompson's primary opponent, Judge Lyle, but failed. Harding returned to the Thompson team for the general election, but other Republican politicians did not. (Wendt and Kogan, *Big Bill of Chicago,* pp. 328–31.)

Deneen group made a deal with Cermak and covertly supported him.

Among the Democrats all was calm. Cermak had no real competition, and no dissenting voices emerged publicly from members of the Chicago Democracy. Lesser threats were removed. Herman Bundesen, a popular former health commissioner, did threaten to run as an Independent, but Cermak offered him the health commissionership and Bundesen withdrew. A number of minor candidates filed for the election, but County Board President Cermak controlled the Board of Election Commissioners, and their petitions were adjudged illegal.[74] Thus the Democrats were in good shape even before Mayor Thompson played into their hands.

The clearly anti-immigrant stand taken by Thompson in 1931 has already been noted. But the ethnics' reaction to that stand is important in explaining the continuing alliance between the ethnics and the Democratic party.

Ethnic press reaction to Thompson's campaign was strong. *Dziennik Zwiazkowy* told its Polish National Alliance readers that "This campaign is not only against Anton Cermak, but also all of those who are not North Americans." A vote for Cermak was a vote to "Help your own kind."[75] Nothing could be more meaningful to the ethnic voter.[76] The Democratic *Dziennik Chicagoski* agreed, saying of Thompson that "the whole city bitterly hates him." A vote for Cermak and the other Democrats was "In Defense of the Honor of Poland."[77] Both papers carried on lengthy and emotional campaigns against the mayor, and both, after the election, ran front-page "pushcart" cartoons, satirizing Thompson's most disastrous anti-immigrant remarks.[78] Political recognition was also important here: an independent Polish-American Voters League endorsed Cer-

[74] Gottfried, *Boss Cermak,* p. 204.

[75] *Dziennik Zwiazkowy,* April 4, 1931, p. 4.

[76] In effect, Cermak was looked upon as a member of the general reference group of ethnic minorities, which was a real group in Chicago politics. This feeling certainly prevailed among influentials—editors of ethnic newspapers and various ethnic spokesmen and leaders; and it probably filtered down to the mass as well. It explains empathy with Cermak and his strong attraction to ethnic voters.

[77] *Dziennik Chicagoski,* April 4, 1931, pp. 4, 16.

[78] *Dziennik Zwiazkowy,* April 4, 1931, pp. 10, 14, April 8, 1931, p. 1; *Dziennik Chicagoski,* April 1, 1931, p. 1, April 4, 1931, p. 10, April 8, 1931, p. 1.

mak because Thompson remembered the Poles "only at election time," while filling offices with the Irish instead.[79]

Similarly, a White Russian newspaper called Cermak "an old friend of the White Russians" and a fellow Slav, who was supported by all "the most outstanding representatives of the White Russian colony."[80] All four Greek-language newspapers and the largest Hungarian newspaper also supported Cermak.[81] The *Jewish Courier* stressed the number of jobs Cermak had given to Jews and argued that he would "raise Chicago in the eyes of the civilized world," from the depths to which Thompson had taken it. Cermak appealed directly to the Jews and emphasized the number of jobs he had given them; this received front-page, headlined, and gratis space.[82] A large Jewish meeting at the Hotel Sherman accused Thompson of injecting bigotry into the campaign and of being anti-Semitic in his attacks on Julius Rosenwald.[83] Even the Chicago Irish-American Good Fellowship Club entered the fray, endorsed Cermak, and accused Thompson of trying to "exploit various racial groups, including the Irish, for the purposes of political gain, by fomenting prejudice and bigotry."[84]

The Germans were also active in Cermak's behalf, and the *Abendpost* was unusually interested in local politics. Thompson's administration, it said, was a disaster: "Scandals, an orgy of corruption, squandering and incapability." Cermak, however, was a friend of the Germans and a good candidate in all respects.[85]

The Italians were an exception, reflecting the closer ties which

[79] See full-page ad in *Dziennik Zwiazkowy*, April 4, 1931, p. 10.

[80] *Belorusskaya Tribune*, Mar. 30, 1931, WPA. See also *Rassviet*, April 29, 1931, WPA.

[81] *Greek Star*, Mar. 13, 1931, WPA; *Greek Press*, Mar. 12, 1931, WPA; *Democrat*, April 1931, WPA; *Greek Daily*, April 6, 1931, WPA; Gottfried, *Boss Cermak*, p. 217; *Magyar Tribune*, April 3, 1931, WPA.

[82] *Jewish Courier*, April 6, 1931, p. 4; April 1, 1931, p. 1.

[83] Chicago *Tribune*, Mar. 27, 1931, p. 2. Thompson had referred to "Tony, the Jew hater, supported by Rosenwald, the fake philanthropist." (Gottfried, *Boss Cermak*, pp. 205–206; M. R. Werner, *Julius Rosenwald: The Life of a Practical Humanitarian* (New York, 1939), p. 318.

[84] Chicago *Tribune*, Mar. 27, 1931, p. 2. Cermak was also endorsed by the Chicago Irish-American Club, the oldest Irish club in the city. (Ibid., April 5, 1931, p. 2.)

[85] *Abendpost/Sonntagpost*, Mar. 24–April 6, 1931, passim; April 4, 1931, p. 7; April 5, 1931, pp. 2, 4, 6–7; April 6, 1931, p. 4. Chicago *Tribune*, Mar. 30, 1931, p. 6.

Thompson had maintained with the group. Cermak had begun to make Italian ties and to appoint Italians to office, to bring them into the Democracy.[86] And this had some effect in 1931, in pro-Cermak activity within the Italian community.[87] But the Italian press, like the Italian voters, remained with Mayor Thompson. *L'Italia* publisher Oscar Durante had always been close to Thompson and had recently been appointed to the school board. *L'Italia* endorsed the mayor for reelection.[88] *La Tribuna Italiana Trans-Atlantica* did not formally endorse anyone, but it was nonetheless in Thompson's camp and totally forgot its opposition to his candidacy four years earlier. In a characteristic editorial/advertisement it listed some of the "1,000 Reasons for Il Simpaticone Tommasone." None of them were very much related to the election at hand. But after opposing Thompson in 1927 because he was too pro-Negro, the paper applauded him in 1931 for giving out jobs "irrespective of religion, nationality, race and color."[89]

Negroes, too, remained loyal to the mayor, notwithstanding the clash of 1930. But the relationship was not as close as before. Thompson used his traditional tactics, highlighting Democratic racism. He distributed a reprint of a page of the 1929 Report of the Forest Preserve District of Cook County (under Cermak's control) which stated that "Owing to the complaints and trouble with colored caddies, they were replaced with white boys."[90] Publicity was also given to a racist broadside allegedly distributed by the Democrats:

Wake up Democrats
to the Menace of
Thompson and his Negroes
vote for
Cermak and His Whole Democratic Ticket[91]

[86] George L. Spatuzza, personal interview. Cermak had also led in the battle for making Columbus Day a legal holiday, and this was endearing to Italian voters. (*La Tribuna Italiana Trans-Atlantica,* Sept. 22, 1928, p. 1.)

[87] Ibid.; Chicago *Tribune,* April 5, 1931, p. 2.

[88] Mrs. Oscar Durante, personal interview; Gottfried, *Boss Cermak,* p. 217. Exactly what this paper said in its endorsement is not known, since I was unable to locate issues of 1931.

[89] *La Tribuna Italiana Trans-Atlantica,* April 4, 1931, p. 2.

[90] A copy may be seen in the Gosnell Materials, Merriam Papers, University of Chicago.

[91] A copy may be seen in ibid.

The *Defender* printed news of the latter on page one, but did not comment editorially. And it gave almost equal space to Cermak's argument that the broadside was phony, put out by the Thompson forces.[92] Moreover, the paper virtually ignored the election and made no endorsements.[93] This was a clear sign that Thompson's grip on his Negro support was not what it had been. Nor were Negro politicians visibly very active.

The vote followed the campaign, with no real surprises. Cermak carried every ethnic group except the Italians and Negroes. The Czechs, Germans, Yugoslavs, Swedes, and Jews voted more Democratic than in any other mayoralty of the period. From all newer immigrant groups, except the Italians, Cermak received over 60 percent. Four groups which had gone for Thompson in 1927 rejected him in 1931: Germans, Yugoslavs, Jews, and Swedes (see Table VIII:2).

All in all it was an impressive victory. Cermak certainly profited from the Democratic resurgence of 1928 and 1930. But he also furthered that resurgence, particularly in bringing it firmly down to the local level. This was the most "ethnic" election of the period, and in it the most "ethnic" politician of the period was clearly triumphant. The cementing of the ethnic vote into the Democracy was well on its way to completion.

One additional factor in Cermak's 1931 success was his apparent deal with the Deneen Republican organization. His running mates for city clerk and a vacancy on the municipal court also won easily. But his other running mate, Edward J. Kaindl, for city treasurer, lost to Republican James A. Kearns. This was most unusual for Chicago politics, where city clerk and city treasurer are part of a ticket with the mayor, and all three almost always are elected together. But Kearns was the one Deneen Republican on the ballot, and this has led some students to suggest that the Deneen group and Cermak made a deal to trade votes at the expense of Thompson and of Kaindl.[94] The hypothesis is reasonable and may well be true. If Cermak did make the deal, it was a good one for him;

---

[92] Chicago *Defender,* April 4, 1931, p. 2.

[93] See, e.g., issues of Mar. 14, 21, 28, April 4, 1931, passim.

[94] *The New Republic,* 66 (April 22, 1931): 260–61; Stuart, *The Twenty Incredible Years,* pp. 470, 488. If there was a deal, Kaindl was probably in on it; he was very close to Cermak. Moreover, he was and remained a Democratic ward committeeman and was soon appointed city collector by Mayor Cermak.

TABLE VIII:2   *Ethnic Vote for Mayor in Three Thompson Campaigns:*
1919, 1927, 1931 (Percentage of the vote for the
two major candidates received by the candidate
named)

Group	1919 Thompson	1927 Thompson	1931 Thompson	1931 Cermak
Czechoslovaks	27	41	16	84
Poles	45	46	30	70
Lithuanians	24	43	38	62
Yugoslavs	48	64	36	64
Italians	49	58	53	47
Germans	49	63	42	58
Swedes	65	62	47	53
Jews	60	61	39	61
Negroes	78	93	84	16
Native-Americans	58	45	39	61
CHICAGO TOTAL	52	54	42	58

there is no evidence that it did Deneen much good—it may have defeated
Thompson, but Chicago has not had a Republican mayor since.

As the complete ethnic politician, Cermak immediately acted to bring
the remaining two ethnic groups into the Democratic consensus. He left
little to chance. An Italian ward committeeman soon appeared in the
Italian Twentieth Ward, and there was an increase in the number of
Italians on the Democratic ticket in 1932. The continuing battle against
the gangsters also served to free Italian voters from Republican obliga-
tions. This would prove effective by 1932.

Negroes also felt Cermak's persuasiveness. On taking office he fired
2,260 temporary employees, and, as the *Defender* put it, "The Race was

hard hit." He also cracked down on Republican Negro crime: "The entire city is closed up like a drum. The lid went on five minutes after it was certain Mayor Thompson had lost."[95] He told the bosses of policy gambling in the Black Belt that they had better change their politics if they wanted to stay in business. And he began the more important job of building a Democratic Negro political organization, with Negro leadership. His successor, Ed Kelly, continued this after Cermaks's 1933 death, and the success of the two men was marked by the number of leading Negro politicians (William Dawson and Arthur Mitchell, for example) who had switched parties by 1936.

Political organizations and leadership played their most important role on the local level. To consider ethnic reaction to every major national candidate would not add much new information here, but it is reasonable to look again at the election of 1928, and Smith's candidacy, since the ethnic reaction to Smith was tremendous and was carried over to his Democratic successors in 1930 and 1932. Ethnic support for Smith personally did not entirely transfer into ethnic support for the Democratic party, but it was a major force in breaking the ethnics loose from the Republican party. Smith and Cermak, together, are the two most important individuals in the Democratic party's success.

The 1928 campaign was unusual in many respects. Intensity of interest, particularly among the ethnics, reached new heights. Voter registration and voter turnout also set records (e.g., presidential vote in Chicago: 1920—731,795; 1924—949,302; 1928—1,270,300; 1932—1,347,709). Third parties fared less well in 1928 than in any other election of the period, again because interest was so intense in the battle between the major candidates.

Smith's stand on the issues, particularly Prohibition, produced much of his support, but ethnic identification with him was even more important. The Foreign Language Information Service participated in this empathy:

> Following the Democratic nomination at Houston, hundreds of foreign language newspapers and periodicals, irrespective of party affiliation, expressed, it is true, sentimental interest in the

[95] Chicago *Defender*, April 11, 1931, p. 1.

New York Governor on the part of the erstwhile immigrant. . . .
It is natural, perhaps, that the new American citizen should like to
think of the Governor as [one] . . . who has made good in real
Horatio Alger fashion. That he is not the son of an immigrant
seems to make little difference. The wishful thoughts of many
an editor places [*sic*] him in that light and sees him emerging
from the lower east side of Manhattan, an environment which
many of them know so well.[96]

This was true, and the ethnics of Chicago had all heard of Al Smith, even
if they were not sure just what he did. The United States Naturalization
Bureau examiner for Chicago reported that the question asking the name
of Illinois' governor was frequently answered "Al Smith."[97] The belief
that Smith was the son of immigrants was also found in Chicago and was
indicative.[98]

Dziennik Chicagoski enthusiastically informed Chicago's Poles that
the Smith candidacy was "a big moment in your lives." The Republicans
were against "all Catholics, foreigners and Negroes," but Smith was "a
friend of the Poles," a fighter against Prohibition, and, at one and the
same time, "the successor to Woodrow Wilson" and a strong opponent of
the League of Nations.[99] One could not ask for more.

Dziennik Zwiazkowy and *Dziennik Zjednoczenia,* the papers, respec-
tively, of the Polish National Alliance and the Polish Roman Catholic
Union, did not forsake their traditional refusal to endorse non-Polish
candidates. But both were unusually interested in the election and gave
Smith considerable coverage, and the latter was quite critical of the
Republican party.[100]

[96] *The Interpreter* 8 (Sept. 1928): 3–7.

[97] Chicago *Tribune,* Sept. 8, 1928, p. 4. This kind of thing was not uncom-
mon. The politically unsophisticated immigrant would know the names of one or
several politicians and associate those names with politics. The owners of those
names were the effective ethnic politicians. (See record of "Conversation with
Chief Examiner of Chicago District of the Naturalization Bureau," 1925, Gosnell
Materials, Merriam Papers, University of Chicago.)

[98] E.g., *Jewish Courier,* Oct. 29, 1928; *La Tribuna Italiana Trans-Atlantica,*
Nov. 3, 1928, p. 1.

[99] *Dziennik Chicagoski,* Nov. 2, 1928, p. 7; Nov. 4, 1928, p. 24; Nov. 5,
1928, p. 1ff.; Nov. 6, 1928, p. 14; Oct. 15–Nov. 5, 1928, passim.

[100] *Dziennik Zwiazkowy,* Nov. 6, 1928, p. 14; Oct. 15–Nov. 5, 1928, passim.
Dziennik Zjednoczenia, Mar. 15, 1928; April 10, 1928; May 12, 1928; Oct. 1,
1928, WPA.

There was equivalent Polish organizational support. In anticipation, a "Polish-American Al Smith for President and Anton Cermak for Governor Club" had been organized in 1927 (before it was decided that Cermak would run for the Senate).[101] Similar organizations sprang up in 1928. When Smith visited Chicago during the campaign, 3,500 Polish businessmen gave him a dinner. Other Slavic groups were also active in his support. Among the Slovaks, White Russians, and Yugoslavs there was strong journalistic and popular enthusiasm for his candidacy.[102]

L'Italia publisher Oscar Durante remained Republican in 1928, as did his paper for all offices except the presidency, where it was silent. *L'Italia* was very critical of the Coolidge administration as the campaign wore on, and did specifically endorse Smith's stand on Prohibition. Moreover, the campaign was characterized as one where a "farmer of Iowa" faced a "paper boy of the New York slums"; where the "spirit of the Quaker pioneers" was confronted by the "elastic and aggressive spirit of the immigrant."[103] Italian voters could logically be expected to choose the latter of each alternative.

La Tribuna Italiana Trans-Atlantica was not neutral, but overwhelmingly pro-Smith, whom it repeatedly characterized as a "Roman Catholic and anti-Prohibitionist." The message was clear. This paper ran a long and enthusiastic Smith campaign, concentrating on the candidate's personality and on the issues of Prohibition and religion.[104] Front-page space was given to a guest editor who argued that Smith was being opposed for "social and religious" reasons and also because he was the "son of immigrants"; were it not for these factors, he would easily be elected, and Italian voters should support him unanimously.[105]

The *Abendpost,* while more sophisticated, was no less enthusiastic. It

[101] *Dziennik Zjednoczenia,* Oct. 5, 1927, WPA.

[102] Chicago *Tribune,* Sept. 16, 1928, p. 2, Sept. 17, 1928, p. 15; *Osadne Hlasy,* Oct. 27, 1928, WPA; *Belorusskaya Tribune,* Oct. 20, 1928, WPA; *Radnik,* Oct. 31, 1928, WPA.

[103] *La Tribuna Italiana Trans-Atlantica,* Nov. 3, 1928, p. 7; Mrs. Oscar Durante, personal interview; *L'Italia,* July 15, 1928, p. 2, Oct. 14, 1928, p. 1, Oct. 21, 1928, p. 1, Oct. 27, 1928, p. 1, Nov. 4, 1928, p. 1.

[104] *La Tribuna Italiana Trans-Atlantica,* July 7, 1928, p. 1, and July 14, 21, 28, 1928, p. 3; Sept. 22, 1928, p. 1; Oct. 16, 1928, p. 1; Oct. 20, 1928, p. 3; Nov. 3, 1928, p. 1.

[105] Ibid., Nov. 3, 1928, p. 1. The writer was Luigi Barzini, editor of the *Corriere d'America* of New York.

covered the campaign fully, ran a full-page Smith campaign biography, and gave prominent notice to famous German-Americans and others who endorsed his candidacy and to various Smith-for-President organizations in which German-Americans participated. It insisted that Smith had nothing to do with the despised Wilson; indeed, Hoover was anti-German and had called Germany "a nation without honor" during the War. Smith's stand on all the issues, especially Prohibition, was frank and good, whereas Hoover was "a tool of the Anti-Saloon League," and "on every issue of importance he has gone around like a cat in hot porridge."[106] The paper's involvement and commitment were unprecedentedly great, as was the number of German-American organizations working in Smith's behalf.[107]

The Swedish press, like Swedish voters, remained Republican. Nonetheless, as with all other newspapers, foreign language and American, Smith received more publicity than Hoover.[108] And there was more support for Smith from Swedish organizations and leaders than for any other national political figure of the period.[109]

The Yiddish press and Jewish influentials were involved to an amazing extent in Smith's candidacy. The *Jewish Courier* was simply saturated with coverage of and enthusiasm for his campaign, and it reached unparalleled levels of linguistic ecstasy. The paper understood pretty well what Smith represented for the ethnic voter: "We are, it is true, developing in this country a new type [of individual], urban in background and different from the old. Governor Smith is one of its finest representatives. . . . The people love him for they know that their cause is his cause and that he speaks their mind and expresses their feelings and sentiments."[110] On every issue, and in every consideration, Smith was the ideal candidate:

---

[106] *Abendpost/Sonntagpost,* Oct. 24, 1928, p. 1; Oct. 25, 1928, p. 1; Oct. 29, 1928, pp. 4, 7; Oct. 31, 1928, p. 3; Nov. 1, 1928, p. 4; Nov. 3, 1928, p. 9; Nov. 4, 1928, p. 1ff.; Nov. 5, 1928, p. 1ff.

[107] Chicago *Tribune,* Aug. 17, 1928, p. 10, Sept. 10, 1928, p. 18; *Sonntagpost,* Oct. 21, 1928, p. 1, Nov. 4, 1928, p. 1; *Abendpost,* Oct. 27, 1928, p. 1.

[108] Johnson, "The Swedes of Chicago," pp. 53–54; *Svenska-Tribunen-Nyheter,* Oct. 3, 1928, p. 1, Oct. 31, 1928, p. 4.

[109] Johnson, "The Swedes of Chicago," pp. 53–54; Chicago *Tribune,* Sept. 23, 1928, p. 6.

[110] *Jewish Courier,* Oct. 1, 18, 19, 24, 1928, p. 8. Smith, like Cermak, became a member of the ethnic reference group and in this lay a good part of his strength.

"A Political Socrates," "the incarnation of genuine political wisdom."[111]

The popular Yiddish Socialist newspaper, the *Forward,* remained convinced of the unworthiness of capitalist political parties, but was nonetheless attracted to Smith. He was an attractive candidate, it said, who spoke on some issues "as if he were a Socialist."[112]

The number of Jewish Al Smith organizations in Chicago was countless—for women, for businessmen, for virtually everyone. And an equivalent number of Jewish leaders spoke on his behalf. Rabbi Stephen S. Wise of New York, for example, came to Chicago on a speaking tour for Smith and called him "the greatest political educator in half a century of American life."[113]

Even the Negroes demonstrated empathy with Smith. The *Defender* supported a Democratic presidential candidate for the first time in its history. It saw the contest as between the Republican party, on the one hand, and Smith, personally, on the other, and found the former ungrateful for long years of Negro support, while the latter was a fair and wise man who "stands for ALL the citizens of his dominion."[114] Other elements in the Chicago Negro community felt similarly. The three presiding elders of the influential African Methodist Episcopal Church, the leaders of several secular Negro organizations, and even Marcus Garvey, endorsed the Smith candidacy.[115] Oscar De Priest, campaigning successfully for the United States Congress, was curiously silent on the presidential race. And Louis B. Anderson, Republican alderman and ward committeeman of the Second Ward, went further and supported Smith openly: "The Republican Party has shown us the gate. Now let all the colored people walk out of this gate."[116]

This was the campaign among the ethnics that led to the great Democratic upsurge of 1928. The campaign was important in itself, and

[111] Ibid., see also issues of Oct. 1, 1928–Nov. 5, 1928, passim.

[112] *Jewish Forward,* Oct. 29, 1928; see also issues of Nov. 2, 3, 4, 6, 1928. The paper nonetheless endorsed Norman Thomas.

[113] Chicago *Tribune,* Oct. 26, 1928, p. 8; *Jewish Courier,* Oct. 28, 1928, p. 7.

[114] Chicago *Defender,* Nov. 3, 1928, Pt. 2, p. 2. There were also charges of racial bigotry leveled against Hoover and his organization. (See Chicago *Tribune,* Oct. 8, 1928, p. 1; Chicago *Defender,* Aug. 4, 1928, p. 4, Oct. 20, 1928, pp. 1, 8; Chicago *Eagle,* Oct. 13, 1928, p. 1.)

[115] Chicago *Defender,* Oct. 27, 1928, pp. 6, 9; Nov. 3, 1928, p. 1; Chicago *Tribune,* Aug. 21, 1928, p. 8.

[116] Chicago *Tribune,* Oct. 31, 1928, p. 3.

for two other reasons. First, ethnic political allegiance to the Democratic party continued to grow in succeeding elections—1930, 1932, and beyond. Thus the switch of 1928 was more than just personal or temporary: it helped precipitate a major party shift. And second, most large American cities were similarly affected, some even more so than Chicago; and they would share the same future development.[117]

[117] See Samuel Lubell, *The Future of American Politics* (Garden City, N.Y., 1952), ch. 3; Gustave R. Serino, "Italians in the Political Life of Boston: A Study of the Role of an Immigrant and Ethnic Group in the Political Life of an Urban Community" (Ph.D. diss., Harvard University, 1950), pp. 45–47; J. Joseph Huthmacher, *Massachusetts People and Politics, 1919–1933* (Cambridge, Mass., 1959), ch. 6; Robert A. Dahl, *Who Governs? Democracy and Power in an American City* (New Haven, Conn., 1961), pp. 45, 49–50. For a major exception, see John L. Shover, "Was 1928 a Critical Election in California?" *Pacific Northwest Quarterly* 58 (Oct. 1967).

IX. *Crime & Reform*

Reform sentiment in Chicago in the 1920s concentrated on the relationship between crime and politics. As such, reform played a role in the political behavior of Chicagoans. This is important because reform sentiment, perhaps contrary to tradition, ultimately aligned itself with the Democratic party.

Reform affected the ethnics of Chicago somewhat differently than did other forces, since interest in reform varied considerably with socioeconomic class. It was confined to middle- and upper-class Chicagoans, generally, and tended more to motivate them than the majority of the ethnics, who were lower in socioeconomic position. Nonetheless, reform was important, because it brought the voting of solidly middle-class ethnics into conjunction with that of the lower-middle and lower-class ethnics who were moving into the Democratic party for other reasons. The extent of the Democratic consensus by 1932 would have been less fully developed had it not been for the reform impetus affecting middle- and upper-class ethnics, and Native-Americans as well.

The term *reform,* as used here, is construed broadly, to include whatever Chicagoans of the time considered as "reform." Particularly, reform comprised an effort to seek honesty in government and to rid government of criminal influence. By the late 1920s, reform generally meant the ousting of Big Bill Thompson and his allies from political office, and of Al Capone and other gangsters from their position of influence in city affairs. That Thompson and Capone seemed to be working together made things that much clearer to the reformers.

The rise of organized crime in Chicago during the Prohibition Era is well known, even legendary, and little of the legend exaggerates the truth. Lawlessness was rife, and life was extremely cheap, especially among the gangsters themselves in their war for control of the spoils of Prohibition (in 1924, a typical year, the *Tribune's* "Hands of Death" clock showed 293 deaths by gun on election eve). Al Capone was not the only successful gangster in Chicago at this time—he had strong competition from "Bugs" Moran and others—but he was the most successful one, and the most powerful. The *Unione-Sicilione,* for example, which was just one organization under his control, was making about ten million dollars per year from distilling in 1928, when it translated its name to "The Italo-American Union" during the campaign preceding the primary election.[1]

This rampant criminality becomes important, for our purposes, through its connection with politics. Indications of this connection are endless. A good example was the funeral, in the spring of 1920, of "Big Jim" Colosimo, who was succeeded by Johnny Torrio, who was, in turn, succeeded by Al Capone. An editorial in a Norwegian newspaper noted that: "Following the body of "big Jim" Colosimo to the grave today will move a cortege which should interrupt the complacent thoughts of Chicago. Three judges, eight aldermen, an assistant state's attorney, a congressman, a state representative, and leading artists of the Chicago Opera Co. are listed as honorary pallbearers, along with gamblers, ex-gamblers, divekeepers and ex-divekeepers."[2] This turnout honoring a notorious criminal was indicative of the attitudes of the politicians involved. Judge Bernard P. Barasa and soon-to-be judge Francis Borreli were, respectively, leading Republican and Democratic Italian politicians in the city during the 1920s; both were honorary pallbearers (thus demonstrating the particularly close interconnection between Italian politics and crime). Michael Igoe, Democratic leader in the Illinois legislature and George Brennan's heir apparent, was also a pallbearer. The Democratic bailiff of the Municipal Court, Dennis J. Egan, and at least one Democratic Municipal Court judge, John K. Prindiville, were similarly honored. Most of the attendants were Democrats, since Colosimo was a First Ward figure (Aldermen "Bathhouse John" Coughlin and "Hinky Dink" Kenna were pallbearers, and Coughlin delivered a moving eulogy), but there were enough Republicans, especially among the Italians, to make it a nonpartisan affair. The funeral was a major event, and the curious list of

---

[1] See Fred D. Pasley, *Al Capone: The Biography of a Self-Made Man* (New York, 1930), pp. 228–29, and passim. This is another of the many vague indicators of the interrelationship between politics and crime.

[2] *Skandinaven,* May 15, 1920, WPA.

pallbearers gave it national publicity.[3] It was also something to give the citizenry pause.

The leading gangsters tended to create small fiefdoms for themselves within the city. That of Dean O'Bannion (and his successor, "Bugs" Moran, after the Capone mob killed O'Bannion) was the Near North Side, particularly the Italian areas. At the 1924 presidential election, O'Bannion's men patroled the polling places to make sure the electorate voted "right."[4] The overall effect of this kind of activity is difficult to determine, since the gangsters were not necessarily loyal to one party or another; rather, like individuals, they would deliver the votes under their control to the candidate or organization which offered the most in return at a given point in time. O'Bannion, like Capone, worked mainly for the Republicans. He would boast later that he personally turned the Forty-second Ward from Democratic to Republican, ensuring the victory of Robert E. Crowe, Thompson's sometime ally, over Michael Igoe, for state's attorney.[5]

Al Capone was far and away the most powerful gang leader in Chicago by the last half of the decade, in both criminal activities and political influence. He was one of the most powerful men in the entire county, for any purpose, and neither peace nor war could be easily had without his consent. When the dry-cleaning industry suffered great labor unrest, only those companies protected by the gangsters managed to stay open.[6] One operator, who hired the Capone organization for protection, later explained why: "Our stores were bombed forty times. The police, the State's Attorney, and the U.S. District Attorney refused to act. That is why we appealed to a man who was able to protect us—Al Capone."[7] This was forceful testimony to the breakdown of law and order, and it is

[3] Chicago *Herald & Examiner,* May 15, 1920, p. 1, May 16, 1920, p. 2; Chicago *Tribune,* May 16, 1920, p. 5; New York *Times,* May 16, 1920, p. 10.

[4] Harvey W. Zorbaugh, *The Gold Coast and the Slum* (Chicago, 1929), pp. 193–94, 193n.

[5] Illinois Association for Criminal Justice, *Illinois Crime Survey* (Chicago, 1929), pp. 1013–14; Herbert Asbury, *Gem of the Prairie* (New York, 1940), pp. 341–42.

[6] *Abendpost,* Nov. 1, 1929, WPA.

[7] The speaker was Morris Becker, testifying at the trial of certain others who were accused of conspiracy to obtain control of the dry cleaning industry by violence. *Abendpost,* Feb. 2, 1934, WPA.

important to remember that this occurred during Thompson's third term as mayor, 1927–1931.

Businessmen were not the only people who despaired of the traditional sources of law and order and turned to Capone. After the bloody climax of the "Pineapple Primary" of April 1928, Frank J. Loesch was called in as president of the Chicago Crime Commission, to see what could be done about the situation. Ultimately, it appears, Loesch could find no better means than to go to Capone himself and ask for his aid in keeping the hoodlums out of the November election. Capone magnanimously acceded and promised to pressure the hoodlums, and the police, to keep things on the up and up. As a result, November saw "the first really honest election in the city of Chicago in forty-five years." The cost, however, was great.[8]

The relationship between Capone and Thompson is clouded by the lack of reliable and firsthand information. By 1927, however, the two men seem to have reached at least an informal understanding. On the bullet-proof walls of his private office Capone allegedly had the portraits of Washington, Lincoln, and Big Bill Thompson.[9] More to the point, Capone probably contributed to Thompson's reelection campaign in 1927, perhaps in excess of one hundred thousand dollars, and he probably induced other gangsters to do the same.[10]

This was not really surprising, since the Dever administration had staged a number of raids against vice dens, endeavored to enforce Prohibition, and generally made things "hot" for the gangsters. Respite could be

---

[8] The story of Loesch going to Capone is frequently told, but I was not able to find anywhere an admission by Loesch that this was true or untrue. The comment quoted, however, is by Loesch, in an address called "The Criminal and His Allies," which he gave to the Nebraska State Bar Association in 1929 (*Nebraska Law Bulletin* 9 [July 1930]: 88–96). Verification of the visit is found in some reliable sources, especially Judge John H. Lyle, a reform Republican politician and prime enemy of Capone and Thompson (and also the man who allegedly invented the "Public Enemy" list) (*The Dry and Lawless Years* [Englewood Cliffs, N.J., 1960], pp. 185–87). See also V. O. Key, Jr., "The Unholy Alliance," *Survey Graphic* 23 (Oct. 1934): 473.

[9] See Lloyd Wendt and Herman Kogan, *Big Bill of Chicago* (Indianapolis, Ind., 1953), p. 250.

[10] Ibid., pp. 268–69. The Illinois Association of Criminal Justice also concluded that Capone had contributed to the Thompson campaign. (Pasley, *Al Capone*, p. 181.)

expected under another Thompson administration, and Thompson's "wide-open town" campaign made it clear that such respite would come.

The closeness of the Thompson-Capone relationship can be overemphasized. Indeed, 1928 saw the beginning of an organized hounding of Capone by the police force under a new chief, William Russell. Capone's biographer suggests that this resulted from the enormous publicity given Capone's every action at that time: Thompson could do nothing except fight him, because the public was aroused. Other factors were the disastrous primary election and court judgment against him, both in the spring of 1928, which left Thompson weak and afraid to refuse the reformers' demand for replacement of his old police chief, Michael ("Go-Get-'Em") Hughes.[11] But even during the 1928–1930 period when Thompson was hardly functioning as mayor, Capone continued to have a voice in his cabinet, through Daniel Serritella, the city sealer. During the 1931 campaign another outcry against Capone control in the city government broke out, when Serritella was indicted for conspiring with merchants to cheat the city out of fifty-four million dollars through short weights.[12]

The 1928 Republican "Pineapple Primary" was characterized not only by the bombing of the homes of candidates Charles Deneen and John A. Swanson. It was violent in a number of other ways as well. Five days before the bombings, "Diamond Joe" Esposito was gunned down. He was a kind of gangster-politician allied to the Deneen organization, and his murder opened the war between the two factions. The primary itself was indeed cause for Loesch's activity; it was characterized by "sluggings, vote thievery, intimidation and stuffing of ballot boxes." Even this, however, did not save the Thompson organization.[13]

The great part of the political-criminal interrelationship in the 1920s, then, appears to have been through the Thompson organization, particularly in its connection with Capone. A number of Thompson's on-again-off-again allies were equally culpable. Governor Len Small (1921–

[11] Pasley, *Al Capone,* pp. 181–82; William H. Stuart, *The Twenty Incredible Years* (Chicago, 1935), pp. 385–87.

[12] Chicago *Tribune,* Mar. 27, 1931, p. 1ff.; Harold F. Gosnell, *Machine Politics: Chicago Model* (Chicago, 1937), pp. 11–12; Alex Gottfried, *Boss Cermak of Chicago: A Study of Political Leadership* (Seattle, Wash., 1962), p. 235; V. O. Key, Jr., "The Unholy Alliance," p. 475.

[13] Wendt and Kogan, *Big Bill of Chicago,* pp. 303–308; Stuart, *The Twenty Incredible Years,* pp. 360–63; Loesch, "The Criminal and His Allies."

1929), who provided the downstate support for the Small-Thompson-Crowe combine, was accused of countless wrongdoings and much corruption, most of which was probably true.[14] And it was the Thompson-Small organization, along with Samuel Insull, which secured the Republican nomination of Frank Smith for the Senate in 1926. In 1928, the Thompson-Crowe-Small forces drafted Smith as their senatorial candidate, and this added to the disrepute of the ticket and the extent of its defeat in the primary.[15]

Certainly the Democrats were also involved with criminals in the 1920s, but the evidence indicates that this was to a lesser degree. They held the mayoralty for only four years, 1923–1927, and Mayor Dever was honest. Thus it was only logical for Capone and others to look to the Thompson Republicans, for two reasons: Thompson was popular and successful, and the alliance would be beneficial to the gangsters only if their man became mayor; and Thompson was apparently willing to make such an alliance, whereas Dever, and probably Cermak, were not.

Crime in politics did affect Chicago voting behavior. Lower socioeconomic groups were considerably less affected by the issue than higher ones, but all were affected to some degree. In the long run, Thompson's connection with the hoodlums worked to his own disadvantage, and to that of his party as well, particularly in that those socioeconomic groups which were most prone to vote Republican turned to the Democrats in desperation and helped to make Tony Cermak mayor of Chicago.

Two groups of people were actively involved in reform in Chicago politics. First, there were the middle-class political activists: people to whom involvement in the political or moral life of the city was almost a vocation. This group included people such as Harold Ickes, Jane Addams, and Donald Richberg. Second, there were the upper-class "gentlemen-in-politics," to whom political activities were secondary and ad hoc, and who entered political reform as a result, often, of participation in various commissions and "betterment" organizations of one kind and another. Julius Rosenwald of Sears, Roebuck and Co. was a leading representative

[14] See Carroll H. Wooddy, *The Case of Frank L. Smith* (Chicago, 1931), p. 159.
[15] See Wooddy, *The Case of Frank L. Smith* and *The Chicago Primary of 1926: A Study in Election Methods* (Chicago, 1926), passim.

of this group; others came from the cream of Chicago "society." Both groups were basically Republican in national politics, but the former were considerably to the Left of the latter; they, for example, were strong supporters of Robert La Follette in 1924, while the upper-class reformers were not. Most important, by the end of the period the two groups cooperated in local and state politics, supporting the Democrats.

Since susceptibility to reform influence in voting behavior seems to commence only with the middle class, it was often ethnic group leaders, rather than the masses, who were motivated for this reason. Leaders, however, are often the source of influence. Moreover, a universal interest in reform existed among those groups which tended to be middle class: the Scandinavians, Germans, and, to a lesser extent, the Jews.

As early as 1919 and 1920, Thompson was under fire for being too close to the gangsters. Julius Rosenwald and other leaders of the Chicago Jewish community opposed his reelection in 1919 and after that battled against his organization.[16] The Dovre Club, Chicago's leading Norwegian-American organization, endorsed Thompson in 1919 as a Republican duty, but began to fight him ferociously in 1920.[17] In 1924 this club endorsed all Republican candidates except those who were members of the Thompson-Small organization; even Democrats were preferable to the latter.[18] The Republican party was clearly split from 1920 on; to the reformers Thompson was the leader of the "bad guys."

In 1923, when Thompson did not run, the mayoralty campaign was between two "respectables"—Lueder and Dever. And the upper-class reformers were inactive. The professional, middle-class reformers, however, were involved and supported Democrat William Dever, although they continued to consider themselves Republicans. Harold Ickes organized an Independent Republican Dever Committee. Graham Taylor of Chicago Commons and Professor Charles Merriam were typical members.[19]

The upper-class reformers were active in the meantime in trying to

[16] Chicago *Tribune,* Mar. 5, 1919, p. 12; M. R. Werner, *Julius Rosenwald: The Life of a Practical Humanitarian* (New York, 1939), pp. 315–16.

[17] *Scandia,* Mar. 8, 1919, WPA; *Skandinaven,* Sept. 12, 1920, WPA.

[18] Chicago *Tribune,* Oct. 21, 1924, p. 6.

[19] Harold L. Ickes, *The Autobiography of a Curmudgeon* (New York, 1943), p. 248; *Jewish Courier,* April 2, 1923, p. 9; G. C. Sikes, "Thompson Rule in Chicago Ended," *Outlook* 133 (Mar. 14, 1923): 481.

purify Illinois Republican politics at the state level. Professor Carroll H. Wooddy's exposé of the 1926 primary nomination of Frank Smith was financed by Julius Rosenwald.[20] Moreover, Rosenwald, and apparently others, decided that Smith, though nominated, should resign before the November election and allow a reform candidate (Hugh S. Magill, suggested by Ickes) to run as an independent. Rosenwald, in the interest of good government, allegedly offered Smith 10,000 shares of Sears, Roebuck common stock if he would withdraw, but Smith turned him down.[21]

In 1927, when Thompson ran for mayor once again, all the forces of reform strived to defeat him. As always, the clergy was active. From pulpits all over the city on the Sunday before the election, the faithful were exhorted to reelect Mayor Dever and save the city from ruin. Upper-class preachers, from the Protestant Preston Bradley to the Reform Jewish Louis L. Mann, spoke and wrote to defeat Big Bill.[22] An Independent Republican Dever Committee showed many of the same names— Bradley, Mann, and representatives of both groups of reformers: the leaders of the German-Jewish community and Graham Taylor; Potter Palmer, carrying Chicago society's foremost name, and Agnes Nestor of the Glove Workers' Union; Walter Dill Scott of Northwestern University and Birger Osland of the Norwegian community.[23] They all apparently agreed with Rosenwald that Republicanism in national politics was irrelevant in the quest for good government locally.[24] Thompson took cognizance of his opposition, but dismissed them as the "university highbrows."[25] This was oversimplification, but it also showed that he knew where his real strength lay.

Middle-class ethnic organizations also participated in this political

---

[20] Werner, *Julius Rosenwald,* pp. 314–15. The book was *The Case of Frank L. Smith.*

[21] Ibid., pp. 295–310. These shares were worth about $500,000 at the time, and within two years would be worth about two million dollars. In his own way Mr. Smith was a dedicated man. Interestingly, Wooddy did not mention, in either of his two books on the subject, that he had been financed by Rosenwald, nor that Rosenwald had tried to bribe Smith.

[22] Chicago *Tribune,* April 4, 1927, p. 5.

[23] Ibid., Mar. 17, 1927, p. 28. See also Merriam-Dever correspondence of 1923–1927, in Merriam Papers, University of Chicago.

[24] Chicago *Tribune,* Mar. 17, 1927, p. 4; Werner, *Julius Rosenwald,* p. 316.

[25] Chicago *Tribune,* April 1, 1927, p. 1ff.

reform activity of 1927. The Chicago Chapter of the Sons and Daughters of Sweden endorsed Mayor Dever, as did the Dovre Club and the Danish Republican Club—all of them solid Republican, middle-class organizations. And each stressed the danger to good government of a Thompson return.[26] Voting for or against Thompson in 1927 was in good part a socioeconomic phenomenon.

The 1931 campaign was similar to that of 1927, except that the anti-Thompson furor among the reformers was even greater after another four years of his rule. Anton Cermak was not quite as "clean" as Dever, but the reformers nonetheless preferred him to Thompson. As Harold Ickes put it, "he had made his pile, and we believed him when he told us that he would give a straight administration."[27] Cermak himself had left little to chance, and, at the same time that he had been building his ethnic base, he had also endeavored to endear himself to the "better element." In the late 1920s, for example, he had become a vice president of the Chicago Regional Planning Association, working with Daniel Burnham, Mrs. Ickes, Lorado Taft, Charles E. Merriam, and other leaders of both reform groups.[28]

Cermak also benefited with the reformers from the long-range effects of Thompson's 1927–1928 interference with the Board of Education. The superintendent of schools whom Thompson had forced out of office had been supported most strongly by such groups as the Chicago Association of Commerce and Industry and the Illinois Manufacturers Association, while he had been opposed by the Chicago Federation of Labor. The former organizations tended to support Cermak in 1931; however, this is another reason for the continuing lower-class support of Thompson in the 1928 primary and, to a lesser degree, in 1931.[29]

Virtually every civic organization (as well as the ethnic ones) which took a stand in 1931 supported Cermak; the same was true of influential individuals. The Municipal Voters' League gave him its endorsement, as did most other organizations representing one or another of the two

[26] Ibid., Mar. 21, 1927, p. 4; Mar. 31, 1927, p. 9. See also Dever Papers, Chicago Historical Society.

[27] Ickes, *Autobiography,* pp. 254–55.

[28] See list of officers on letterhead of letter in Merriam Papers, University of Chicago.

[29] George S. Counts, *School and Society in Chicago* (New York, 1928), passim.

groups of reformers. As one leader put it, "even a yellow dog would be better than Thompson."[30]

Many Republican groups also worked for Cermak; the desire for reform was clearly more powerful than party regularity (which Thompson had already weakened). Emily Dean, a prominent social worker and longtime president of the Illinois Republican Women's Clubs, was very active in organizing women for Cermak. She insisted that "Thompsonism" must be defeated.[31] The Greek-American Republican Club of Chicago, in a widely publicized announcement, endorsed Cermak, so that Chicago could "regain its stature."[32] The Independent Republican Club of the Fifth Ward (upper-middle and upper class, Leopold-Loeb, University of Chicago area) announced likewise.[33] Many other Republican organizations and individuals did the same after Thompson defeated reformer Judge John H. Lyle in the primary.[34]

Emily Dean was not the only woman who opposed Thompson in 1931. The Swedish women, as one might expect, did the same.[35] The Saturday before the election a woman's parade for Cermak was held in downtown Chicago; 2,000 women marched, and sang:

> Glory, glory to Chicago,
> Glory, glory to Chicago,
> Glory, glory to Chicago,
> With Cermak marching on.[36]

Julius Rosenwald, who generally contributed little money or time to local politics, gave $2,500 and considerable time to the Cermak cam-

[30] M. A. Hallgren, "Chicago Goes Tammany," *The Nation* 132 (April 22, 1931): 446–48; *The New Republic* 66 (April 22, 1931): 261; Chicago *Tribune*, Mar. 19, 1931, p. 4; Mar. 20, 1931, p. 11. An exception was the Better Government Association, which supported Thompson. Cermak's biographer sees this as a result of the organization's "fundamentalist, Puritan, quasi-Know Nothing animus." Ethnic considerations could apparently outweigh others. (Gottfried, *Boss Cermak*, pp. 205, 216.)

[31] See 1931 correspondence in Dean Papers, Chicago Historical Society.

[32] *Greek Star*, Mar. 13, 1931, WPA; *Greek Press*, Mar. 12, 1931, WPA; *Saloniki*, Mar. 21, 1931, WPA.

[33] Chicago *Tribune*, April 6, 1931, p. 4.

[34] E.g., ibid., Mar. 12, 1931, p. 6.

[35] Ibid., April 1, 1931, pp. 3–4.

[36] Ibid., April 4, 1931, p. 3; April 5, 1931, p. 3.

paign and tried to persuade his peers to do likewise.[37] Rabbi Stephen S. Wise, who had spoken in Chicago for Al Smith, did the same for Tony Cermak, stressing the corruption of the Thompson regime and its ties with gangdom.[38] And not least important with Chicago's middle-class Jews, Judge Henry Horner actively supported his fellow Democrat.[39]

The ethnic press reflected these reform sentiments. The *Danish Times* criticized Thompson's primary campaign against Judge Lyle for making a laughingstock of Chicago.[40] The German press prominently mentioned all the "respectables" who endorsed Cermak and all the "disreputables" who endorsed Thompson. Thompson represented Al Capone and other evils, and Cermak was the only possible choice.[41] The newspapers of some lower socioeconomic groups reasoned similarly. The leading Hungarian paper argued that Thompson's administration was marked by too much "gangsterism" and therefore should be repudiated.[42] A Spanish paper felt the same.[43]

The rising Democratic vote among the ethnics of Chicago was definitely increased by this quest for reform, although its degree of effect cannot be measured. The Germans and Swedes, for example, voted Democratic for mayor for the first time in 1931. And the Native-Americans, who were higher in socioeconomic status than any ethnic group, and more Republican than any except the Negroes, voted Democratic for mayor in 1927 and 1931. It is clear that the socioeconomic variations played an important role in determining whether or not one voted for reform. Certainly some ethnics in lower socioeconomic groups were affected by reform, but this was to a decidedly lesser extent. Certainly, also, changing patterns in national voting, and issues other than reform, contributed to Cermak's rise and Thompson's fall. But the twin issues of crime and reform were clearly important, at least with an influential minority of Chicago's ethnics, and of Chicagoans generally.

[37] Werner, *Julius Rosenwald*, pp. 317–19; Chicago *Tribune*, Mar. 11, 1931, p. 4; Gottfried, *Boss Cermak*, p. 214.

[38] Chicago *Tribune*, Mar. 21, 1931, p. 5.

[39] *Jewish Courier*, Mar. 25, 1931, p. 6.

[40] *Danske Tidende*, Mar. 6, 1931, WPA.

[41] *Sonntagpost*, April 5, 1931, pp. 4, 6–7; *Abendpost*, April 6, 1931, pp. 1, 4.

[42] *Magyar Tribune*, April 3, 1931, WPA.

[43] *El Nacional*, April 11, 1931, WPA.

The reform impetus contributed to the growth and success of the Democratic party locally. This did not necessarily carry over to voting in national elections, but some effect was felt in that area as well. By and large there was a divergence here between the two groups of reformers. The professional, middle-class reformers (Ickes, Jane Addams, Richberg, Merriam) did tend to leave the Republican party at all levels. They deserted to La Follette in 1924 and did not return, since they were attracted by Smith in 1928 and Roosevelt and Horner in 1932. Thus, however much Harold Ickes might call himself a Republican in 1932, the fact was that he had been voting for the Democrats, locally, statewide, and nationally, since 1927. The same was true for many of his fellows.[44] The upper-class reformers, on the other hand, remained Republican in national politics. They were not attracted to La Follette in 1924, nor were they particularly attracted to Smith or Roosevelt later.

The case of the upper-class Jews is a good example. Julius Rosenwald, who played an important role in the continuing upper-class battle against Thompson, was one of Hoover's strongest supporters and gave him in 1928 the largest political contribution of his life ($50,000). Smith, he said, was not "the type I would like to see in the White House."[45] Rosenwald's rabbi was even more explicit. Reform Jews, he said, were offended by Smith's "commonness" and lack of gentility, and by his wife's appearance as an "humble Irish scrubwoman." "Reform Jews didn't want their president or his wife to speak with bad grammar."[46] Voting for Cermak over Thompson made sense to the socioeconomically highest among Chicago's ethnics and citizens generally, but this did not automatically translate into national Democratic voting.

This translation was partially accomplished, however, by the association of reform with statewide as well as citywide politics. Reform animosity to Thompson's ally, Governor Len Small, was almost as great as that to Thompson himself.[47] When Small managed to get the gubernatorial

[44] Richberg and Ickes, for example, were active in the National Progressive League of 1932, which was a nonpartisan Roosevelt organization. See *Chicago Tribune*, Sept. 26, 1932, p. 4; Oct. 19, 1932, p. 6.

[45] Werner, *Julius Rosenwald*, pp. 292–93.

[46] Dr. Louis L. Mann, personal interview.

[47] A good example: When the Dovre Club endorsed Democrat Jones for governor in 1924, rather than Small, it was the first time in the club's existence

nomination in 1932, after being out of the governor's office for four years, he faced a very "respectable" Democratic opponent; thus reform served the Democrats, vigorously, in a statewide election in 1932.

Henry Horner was a good representative of a particular type of American politician, seen often in Illinois politics: the professional honest man.[48] Both parties, but especially the Democrats, have nominated such men for office, particularly at times when the pressure was felt, or when there seemed little chance of winning anyway.[49] Such candidates serve a purgative purpose when they lose and can sometimes win when a regular party man cannot. At the same time they sometimes become sticks in the party wheel, if elected (as was eventually the case with Horner).

Horner was a longtime judge of the Probate Court and had been famously honest throughout his career. He had received reform support from the beginning. In 1918, for example, 1,400 lawyers formed a nonpartisan Horner organization to support his reelection to the Probate Court. There was more publicity, of more kinds, in his behalf, than for any other candidate in the election.[50]

Horner's candidacy for the governorship in 1932 was greeted with tremendous support from the same groups and individuals which had supported Cermak against Thompson the year before. If anything, the reform outpouring was greater, since Cermak, unlike Horner, was not a professional honest man. Professional groups of all kinds—physicians, lawyers, restaurant owners, grocers—established Horner organizations in a manner and to an extent not seen elsewhere in the period.[51] A "Horner Minute Men" organization of business and professional people was created and obtained about 100,000 pledges for him.[52] Two hundred mem-

that it supported a Democrat for this office. And this was due to the scandals of the Small administration. (Chicago *Tribune,* Oct. 8, 1924, p. 4.)

[48] His career and character were very similar to those of a later governor of Illinois, Otto Kerner (the son of one of Cermak's closest allies, and Cermak's son-in-law as well).

[49] The latter applied, for example, when Adlai Stevenson and Paul Douglas were given the nominations for governor and United States senator, respectively, in 1948, which looked to boss Jacob Arvey to be a bad year anyway.

[50] Chicago *Daily News,* Nov. 4, 1918, p. 19; Chicago *Tribune,* Nov. 4, 1918, p. 13.

[51] See Chicago *Tribune,* Oct. 1–Nov. 6, 1932, passim.

[52] Ibid., Nov. 4, 1932, p. 4.

bers of the University of Chicago faculty and Chancellor Robert M. Hutchins endorsed his candidacy, as did the Women's Republican Club of suburban (and conservative and prohibitionist) Evanston, Illinois.[53]

There was a great outpouring of Jewish support, since Horner was the first Jewish gubernatorial nominee in Illinois in over a generation. Since he represented the upper class, Reform Jewish group (he was a member of the same congregation as Julius Rosenwald), the Reform elements were as enthusiastic as the mass of Chicago Jews.[54] Other ethnic groups also showed considerable interest in Horner's candidacy, despite the fact that in presidential years attention was generally focused on the highest contest. Not surprisingly, this support emanated primarily from middle- and upper-class representatives of the ethnic groups. The Polish-American Chamber of Commerce, and other Polish influentials, for example, publicly endorsed his candidacy, as did an independent German-American organization of business and professional people.[55]

The Horner candidacy aided the Democrats considerably in pulling Republican voters into the Democratic column. He ran ahead of Roosevelt among Jews, Swedes, and Native-Americans (63 percent to FDR's 43 percent). Many who had voted Democratic only at the local level before now voted Democratic in a national election also. This did not mean that these voters were now Democrats, but it was another occasion when they were voting Democratic, and every such occasion contributed to the establishment of a tradition. The Democratic consensus was bolstered at another level, and the association of Democratic voting with reform was extended.

The question of political reform was an active one in Chicago politics during the 1920s. And as with most other questions already considered, it worked in the Democrats' favor. It was not nearly as important with the mass of ethnics as an issue like Prohibition, but it did affect some of them and thus contributed to the rise of the Democratic consensus.

[53] Ibid., Oct. 10, 1932, p. 6; Oct. 26, 1932, p. 4.

[54] Louis L. Mann, personal interview; *Jewish Courier*, Oct. 25, 1932, p. 8, Nov. 6, 1932, p. 6.

[55] Chicago *Tribune*, Oct. 19, 1932, p. 6, Oct. 22, 1932, p. 2; *Dziennik Zwiazkowy*, Nov. 7, 1932, p. 5.

X. *Socioeconomic Class*

To understand ethnic group political behavior generally, it has been necessary up to this point to ignore socioeconomic variations within and between groups. With this general behavioral pattern now clear, it will be advantageous to add the socioeconomic factor. Indeed, arguments have been made that socioeconomic position is a more important behavioral determinant than ethnicity.[1] This is not true for Chicago ethnic groups between 1890 and 1936, but class position did have some political effects.

With the use of census data and other criteria, our ethnic political units were placed into one of four socioeconomic classes. These are labeled lower-lower, upper-lower, lower-middle, and middle-middle. Additionally, one of the Native-American units has been labeled upper-middle. Not all the ethnic groups are represented in every class; the need to use areas of high ethnic concentration precluded this. Table X:1 gives the distribution of ethnic units among the several socioeconomic classes. It also indicates that the Jewish, Czech, and Polish middle-middle units became usable, for methodological reasons, only after the middle of the 1920s.

The vote of each of the four classes in the major elections of the period is summarized in Table X:2. Because of the unequal representation of the various ethnic groups within each class, these data are not definitive. But from them emerge some tentative conclusions which will help in understanding the more intensive data which follow.

Perhaps the most striking thing about these data is the lack of any clear pattern. Certainly nothing jumps out and proclaims itself a major voting change on socioeconomic grounds. The clearest differentials are between the middle-middle class, on the one hand, and the other three, on the other. While one might expect more variation between lower-lower, upper-lower, and lower-middle class ethnics, the fact is that all three were essentially working class and have this socioeconomic characteristic in common. It is interesting that upper-lower and lower-middle ethnics tended to be more Democratic throughout than were lower-lower ethnics. This was a function of several forces.

One might reasonably expect that the greatest socioeconomic variations in voting (within classes between elections, and between classes) would come in elections where there were economic questions at stake, particularly in the Depression-time elections of 1930 and 1932. In 1932, for example, there was an unprecedented mobilization of the forces of organized labor on one side, and of organized business on the other, with each force supporting a rival presidential candidate more strongly than ever before.[2] But the difference in voting between middle-middle units and the others was not unusually great in 1932, and in some cases was less than in 1928 (a significant exception here being the Jews and Germans—see Table X:3). And for all classes, the change in vote from the previous election was considerably less for both 1928–1930 and 1928–1932 than it was for 1920–1928 or 1924–1928.

Socioeconomic questions were simply not as important, or as effective, as purely ethnic ones. The fact that the Germans and Jews were different and did show more interclass variation in 1932 than in 1928 is indicative. They were the two groups relatively most issue-oriented, and as such they were apparently more concerned with economic issues. The others, particularly the highly ethnocentric newer immigrants, simply do not show significant variations on a socioeconomic basis.

There is more of a socioeconomic breakdown, then, in 1928 than in the Depression-time elections of 1930 and 1932. When the ethnics were politically aroused—and this came for essentially ethnic reasons—their voting was more distinguished on all bases. And it appears that Smith's appeal had socioeconomic as well as simply ethnic strength.

---

[1] A recent participant-observation study of a second-generation Italian community tends to stress socioeconomic class above ethnicity as a determinant of behavior generally. But, at the same time, the reader can see the ethnic determinant constantly present; indeed, ethnicity is a major determinant of their class position. The ethnic factor did prevail; the ethnic reference group was far and away the most important. (See Herbert J. Gans, *The Urban Villagers: Group and Class in the Life of Italian-Americans* [New York, 1962], ch. 2, and passim.)

[2] See, e.g., Chicago *Tribune*, Oct. 8, 1932, p. 5; Oct. 20, 1932, p. 2; Oct. 21, 1932, p. 4; Oct. 22, 1932, p. 2; Oct. 30, 1932, p. 8.

TABLE X:1   *Distribution of Ethnic Political Units in Four*
Socioeconomic Classes * (Number of units in each*
class)

Group	Lower-Lower class	Upper-Lower class	Lower-Middle class	Middle-Middle class
Czechoslovaks	none	2	3	1[†]
Poles	2	3	1	1[§]
Lithuanians	none	2	2	none
Yugoslavs	none	3	none	none
Italians	4	2	none	none
Germans	none	none	2	2
Swedes	none	none	2	3
Jews	none	none	3	1[†]
Negroes	2	2	1	none
Native-Americans	none	none	none	1[Δ]
TOTAL	8 units	14 units	14 units	9 units (8 ethnic)

*See Appendix for the method of selecting units and their character-
istics.

[†]Usable starting with the election of 1923.

[§]Usable starting with the primary of 1927.

[Δ]There was also a Native-American unit in upper-middle class.

TABLE X:2　*Vote of Nine Ethnic Groups Subsumed into Four*
Socioeconomic Classes, 1918-1932 (Percentage
*Democratic)**

Election	Lower-Lower class	Upper-Lower class	Lower-Middle class	Middle-Middle class
1918: Senator	62	64	67	43
1920: President	24	35	28	17
1924: President	26	33	26	14
1928: President	56	62	64	42
1930: Senator	60	73	82	77
1932: President	59	68	75	57
1919: Mayor	51	55	56	34
1923: Mayor	78	67	66	38
1927: Mayor	33	44	47	38
1931: Mayor	44	58	66	55

*Percentage Democratic of the two-party vote except 1924—percentage Democratic of the three-party vote.

All of this can be rendered clearer and more definitive by considering socioeconomic variations in voting within the individual ethnic groups. Table X:3 summarizes these patterns for the relevant national elections.

The several newer immigrant groups demonstrated similar patterns in national voting, with upper-lower and lower-middle class units being the most Democratic throughout. Among the Czechs, for example, there were no significant differences between upper-lower and lower-middle units, but the middle-middle unit remained consistently twenty to thirty points less Democratic. Thus there was a relationship between higher class position and Republican voting. This did not vary much over time —as the lower-class units became more Democratic, so too did the

TABLE X:3   Ethnic Group Vote in Selected National Elections, 1918-1932, by Socioeconomic Class (Percentage Democratic)*

Group and class (no. of political units in each class)		1918 Senator	1920 President	1924 President	1928 President	1930 Senator	1932 President
Czechoslovaks:							
Upper-Lower	(2)	80	46	48	79	88	86
Lower-Middle	(3)	86	42	41	77	90	87
Middle-Middle	(1)	—	—	24	51	86	66
Poles:							
Lower-Lower	(2)	75	31	37	77	82	85
Upper-Lower	(3)	70	47	35	73	86	80
Lower-Middle	(1)	68	29	30	70	91	85
Middle-Middle	(1)	—	—	—	55	85	67
Lithuanians:							
Upper-Lower	(2)	77	53	61	75	82	82
Lower-Middle	(2)	77	53	35	80	87	87
Yugoslavs:							
Upper-Lower	(3)	61	22	20	54	74	67
Italians:							
Lower-Lower	(4)	74	29	30	59	63	62
Upper-Lower	(2)	65	34	32	70	76	69
Germans:							
Lower-Middle	(2)	67	22	19	76	89	80
Middle-Middle	(2)	41	14	8	39	81	58

Swedes:						
Lower-Middle	(2)	43	14	11	36	81	53
Middle-Middle	(3)	44	19	21	33	69	48
Jews:						
Lower-Middle	(3)	60	15	22	63	85	80
Middle-Middle	(1)	—	—	10	55	80	66
Negroes:						
Lower-Lower	(2)	27	6	6	28	31	27
Upper-Lower	(2)	32	11	10	21	21	17
Lower-Middle	(1)	55	21	14	17	15	15
Native-Americans:						
Middle-Middle	(1)	48	22	18	41	68	39
Upper-Middle	(1)	44	19	15	39	69	47
Lower-Lower *TOTAL*		62	24	26	56	60	59
Upper-Lower *TOTAL*		64	35	33	62	73	68
Lower-Middle *TOTAL*		67	28	26	64	82	75
Middle-Middle *TOTAL*[†]		43	17	14	42	77	57

*Percentage Democratic of two-party vote except for 1924—percentage Democratic of three-party vote (see Table X:4 for socioeconomic breakdown of La Follette 1924 vote).

[†]Ethnic vote only: Middle-Middle Native-American unit excluded.

middle-middle unit, maintaining the same relative position from 1923 to 1932. This indicates that higher socioeconomic Czechs were subject to the same ethnopolitical pressures as those lower on the socioeconomic scale; were it otherwise, the spread would have enlarged with time.

Virtually the same thing was true among the Poles. The lower-lower, upper-lower, and lower-middle units voted quite similarly in national elections, and the middle-middle unit remained more Republican though closer to the others than among the Czechs (and reasonably so, since it was socioeconomically slightly lower than the Czech middle-middle unit —see Appendix).[3] The limited spread among Lithuanian and Yugoslavian units again demonstrates the lack of any considerable difference in voting behavior between upper-lower and lower-middle units: both classes were essentially working class, and entrance into the economically middle-class lower-middle did not seem automatically to entail an adoption of middle-class political values.

Among the Italians, who were all lower class, there was considerable variation that is not explicable in socioeconomic terms. But upper-lower units were somewhat more Democratic than lower-lower, and this became more pronounced as time passed; this was consistent with the intra-lower-class behavior of other newer immigrant groups.

The more middle-class older immigrants demonstrated clearer and more predictable socioeconomic voting patterns. The German lower-middle units, for example, were clearly more Democratic than the middle-middle units throughout, and the difference became greater toward the end of the period. The same was true of the Jews. But the highly Republican Swedes varied from this pattern before 1928. Until that time the lower-middle units rivaled the middle-middle units in Republicanism. But in 1928 and after, the lower-middle units were more Democratic. Thus the Smith campaign and the Depression created division in Swedish voting behavior, with working-class Swedes moving more readily into the

---

[3] An interesting exception here was an upper-lower class Polish unit (Polish area F on the map in the Appendix), which was the most Republican Polish unit for almost the entire period. This is a good example of the role of geography, since this unit was in the far south side steel mill area, far removed from the mainstream of Polish residence and Polish organizational activity. Thus geographical isolation is another determinant of political behavior and one which is not necessarily socioeconomic in nature; it is, however, potentially antiethnic in its effect.

Democracy than their white-collar countrymen; and Swedish voting behavior was henceforth more like that of socioeconomically similar groups.

Socioeconomic forces in Negro voting are not clear. Early in the period the one lower-middle unit was more Democratic than the others, but later it was more Republican. Similarly, the lower-lower units changed from being more Republican than the upper-lower, to less Republican as time passed. Since all Negro areas were overwhelmingly Republican anyway, socioeconomic variations do not seem very meaningful.

Generally, then, in national politics, ethnic voting behavior was affected only moderately, and in certain situations, by socioeconomic class. Predictably, ethnics who were solidly entrenched in the middle class, both economically and, one supposes, in terms of values (i.e., middle-middle units), tended to be Republican, while among the three lower classes there was little consistent variation, except that lower-lower units were not quite so Democratic as upper-lower and lower-middle. The Republicanism of middle-middle ethnics reflected general American middle-class feelings, both for the protection of an assumed economic position and in upwardly mobile emulation of the leaders of society, who were, in Chicago as elsewhere, strongly Republican.[4] This is logical, since middle-middle ethnics tended to be more assimilated; middle-middle areas, for example, had higher proportions of second-generation group members than did socioeconomically lower areas.

The relatively high Democratic voting of lower-middle class ethnics, relative to their groups, is intriguing. These people were more middle class economically than socially and in many respects would still consider themselves lower, or at least working class. The fact that so many of them were first-generation Americans served to reinforce this. Thus their political behavior resembled that of their upper-lower class countrymen. This class also probably included the highest proportion of union members—they filled the ranks of those skilled and semiskilled blue-collar occupations which were pretty well organized by the 1920s (as opposed to the nonskilled factory jobs, held by lower-class ethnics, which were not well organized until the New Deal). As such they were affected by

[4] On the virtually innate Republicanism of Chicago's upper class, see Arthur Meeker, *Chicago, with Love: A Polite and Personal History* (New York, 1955), p. 76.

growing organized labor support of the Democratic party. This had started in the Wilson era and continued during the 1920s; labor was moving toward the Democrats in Chicago at this time and strongly supported Smith and Roosevelt.[5] Thus lower-middle ethnics had a strong socioeconomic reason for staying within or joining the Democratic party over the period. (That lower-middle ethnics were the most pro-La Follette in 1924 reinforces this conclusion; see below.)

The data in Table X:3 provide some other insights into the effect of socioeconomic status on voting. Those elections which resulted in the greatest socioeconomic variations in the voting of a given ethnic group would appear to be the elections wherein socioeconomic considerations were most important. I have found no clear pattern here encompassing all the ethnic groups and have seen that the 1928 election resulted in a more general socioeconomic voting breakdown than did either of the more "logical" Depression-time elections of 1930 and 1932. Thus I am led to conclude that most ethnic group members did not vote as members of a given socioeconomic class, that class was not a major reference group, especially for lower-class ethnics.

But the Smith candidacy does seem to have a socioeconomic as well as purely ethnic explanation. This conclusion is reinforced by the comparative increases in Democratic voting. All lower-lower units (Polish, Italian, and Negro) showed their largest gains in Democratic percentage strength in the 1928 election. And among the Poles and Negroes the lower-lower Democratic gains were clearly greater than those among the socioeconomically higher units of the same ethnic group. Smith's appeal to the ethnics was basically ethnic in nature, but he was also attractive to lower-class ethnics to an unprecedented degree. Whether the attraction was for socioeconomic or purely ethnic reasons is not clear, but it did change the socioeconomic bases of Democratic support. And this helps explain the Democratic resurgence of 1928.

On the whole, socioeconomic variations in national voting were not

[5] With the exception of 1924, when labor supported La Follette, most national, state, and local labor organizations supported the Democrats at all levels during the 1920s. This became more pronounced from 1928 on. (For Chicago, see John Fitzpatrick Papers, Chicago Historical Society; Chicago *Tribune*, April 30, 1920, p. 3; Sept. 7, 1920, p. 2; Nov. 1, 1920, p. 12; Sept. 4, 1924, p. 6; Mar. 28, 1927, p. 15; Mar. 31, 1927, p. 9; Mar. 14, 1931, p. 8; Oct. 21, 1932, p. 4; Oct. 30, 1932, p. 8.)

surprising. Those ethnics who had entered the substantial middle class (middle-middle) tended to be the most Republican of their groups. By and large, however, all socioeconomic levels of a given ethnic group were on the same side of the political balance by 1932 (except the Swedes, with lower-middle units just above 50 percent Democratic, and middle-middle units just below). And all socioeconomic levels of a given group were affected by the same political forces. The Democratic party throughout the decade, and particularly after 1928, was the party of the majority of lower-class ethnics; and most Chicago ethnic voters were lower class.

The 1930 election is interesting in that a woman led the Republican ticket. This probably explains the unusually high Democratic vote for senator in 1930; all ethnic groups (except Negroes) at all socioeconomic levels delivered landslide Democratic votes. What is somewhat surprising is that lower-lower and upper-lower ethnics were no more strongly affected by this factor than were lower-middle and middle-middle ethnics. Indeed, the latter, having been less affected by the forces of 1928, show a considerably higher 1928–1930 Democratic switch. Repulsion from a female candidate for major office, then, seems to have been a general immigrant phenomenon, irrespective of socioeconomic class.

Finally, in national politics, socioeconomic class does contribute to our understanding of La Follette's strengths and weaknesses in 1924 and of his role in pulling voters out of the Republican party, facilitating a shift to the Democrats four years later. La Follette received only 11 percent of the lower-lower vote, 18 percent of the upper-lower, 24 percent of the lower-middle, and 22 percent of the middle-middle. Within the individual ethnic groups, too, his support was greatest among lower-middle units (see Table X:4). With ethnic groups whose units fell mainly into the lower-lower to lower-middle range, it was the units in lower-middle and, to a lesser extent, upper-lower classes which were most attracted to La Follette. And among those groups mainly in lower-middle and middle-middle classes, lower-middle units were again the most pro-La Follette.

Thus again the working class and trade union influence was operating on ethnics in the lower-middle class. La Follette was strongly supported by organized labor at all levels; he was also supported by the Socialist party, which likewise had the allegiance of many class-oriented ethnics. Many of these lower-middle voters had been Republican, but the La

TABLE X:4 *Ethnic Response to La Follete Candidacy, 1924, and Rise in Democratic Vote, 1924-1928, by Socioeconomic Class*

Group and class (no. of political units in each class)		Percentage for La Follette, 1924	Increase in Democratic percentage strength, 1924-1928
Czechoslovaks:			
Upper-Lower	(2)	15	32
Lower-Middle	(3)	21	36
Middle-Middle	(1)	29	27
Poles:			
Lower-Lower	(2)	11	40
Upper-Lower	(3)	25	38
Lower-Middle	(1)	26	40
Middle-Middle	(1)	—	—
Lithuanians:			
Upper-Lower	(2)	13	14
Lower-Middle	(2)	17	45
Yugoslavs:			
Upper-Lower	(3)	16	34
Italians:			
Lower-Lower	(4)	14	29
Upper-Lower	(2)	25	38
Germans:			
Lower-Middle	(2)	34	57
Middle-Middle	(2)	31	31
Swedes:			
Lower-Middle	(2)	22	25
Middle-Middle	(3)	16	16
Jews:			
Lower-Middle	(3)	30	41
Middle-Middle	(1)	17	39
Negroes:			
Lower-Lower	(2)	6	22
Upper-Lower	(2)	15	11
Lower-Middle	(1)	15	3
Native-Americans:			
Middle-Middle	(1)	15	23
Upper-Middle	(1)	8	24
Lower-Lower *TOTAL*		11	30
Upper-Lower *TOTAL*		18	29
Lower-Middle *TOTAL*		24	38
Middle-Middle *TOTAL*[*]		22	28

[*]Ethnic vote only—Middle-Middle Native-American unit excluded.

Follette candidacy served to bring them out of that party. Thus upper-lower ethnics had been slightly more Democratic than lower-middle in 1920 and 1924, but starting with 1928 these positions reversed, as ethnics who had voted Republican in 1920 and La Follette in 1924 entered the Democratic party. La Follette first pulled these workers out of the Republican party; then in 1928, when there was no Progressive party and labor supported Smith, many of them opted for the Democrats. Then with the Depression, and organized labor's animosity to the Hoover administration, they followed the path of least resistance and remained Democratic. It is indicative that the Germans and the Jews, the two groups most attracted to La Follette in 1924 (and two groups with relatively high proportions of union members), were also the two groups which made the greatest pro-Democratic shift in 1928. Finally, the strong middle-middle support for LaFollette resulted from the fact that well-established middle class ethnics were more likely to be blue collar than Native-Americans of the same socioeconomic position. They were thus subject to many of the same forces as lower-middle ethnics, and their political behavior was similarly affected.

All of this is not to deny the purely ethnic forces operating in 1928 and other elections as well. Nor is it to deny that, for the Germans at least, there were strong ethnic reasons behind support for La Follette in 1924. But these socioeconomic considerations do provide our best indicator of the strengths and weaknesses of the La Follette movement and its contribution among selected ethnics to the rise of the Democratic majority.

Socioeconomic factors operated somewhat differently in local voting and offer some insight into the interrelationship between ethnicity, class, and reform. The relevant data are presented in Table X:5.

Socioeconomic patterns in mayoral voting were even less predictable than at the national level. For example, lower-lower units were the most Republican in 1927 and 1931, after having been the most Democratic in 1923. Within individual ethnic groups similar incongruities also emerge. But most of these apparent problems can be explained through considering the twin questions of Big Bill Thompson and reform.

The pattern of ethnic Democratic voting at the national level (upper-lower and lower-middle units most Democratic, followed by lower-

TABLE X:5 Ethnic Group Vote in Local Elections, 1919-1931, by Socioeconomic Class

Group and class (no. of political units in each class)	Percentage Democratic 1919 Mayor	1923 Mayor	1927 Mayor	1931 Mayor	Percentage Pro-Thompson* 1928 Republican Primary
Czechoslovaks:					
Upper-Lower (2)	68	92	63	82	77
Lower-Middle (3)	77	74	62	92	50
Middle-Middle (1)	—	49	79	61	43
Poles:					
Lower-Lower (2)	55	85	57	65	80
Upper-Lower (3)	55	71	52	70	42
Lower-Middle (1)	51	69	52	82	30
Middle-Middle (1)	—	—	58	67	41
Lithuanians:					
Upper-Lower (2)	76	80	51	59	76
Lower-Middle (2)	76	84	64	65	49
Yugoslavs:					
Upper-Lower (3)	52	52	36	64	42
Italians:					
Lower-Lower (4)	65	84	35	44	80
Upper-Lower (2)	54	72	58	52	77
Germans:					
Lower-Middle (2)	65	60	54	66	39
Middle-Middle (2)	34	29	20	49	31

Swedes:						
Lower-Middle	(2)	37	41	28	46	37
Middle-Middle	(3)	33	43	45	57	21
Jews:						
Lower-Middle	(3)	40	66	40	66	41
Middle-Middle	(1)	—	31	35	46	25
Negroes:						
Lower-Lower	(2)	16	60	7	21	77
Upper-Lower	(2)	22	40	6	13	64
Lower-Middle	(1)	33	65	10	11	59
Native-Americans:						
Middle-Middle	(1)	39	42	53	58	22
Upper-Middle	(1)	45	45	58	64	21
Lower-Lower TOTAL		51	78	33	44	79
Upper-Lower TOTAL		55	67	44	58	58
Lower-Middle TOTAL		56	66	47	66	40
Middle-Middle TOTAL†		34	38	38	55	29

*Equals mean of vote for Crowe for States Attorney and Small for Governor.
†Ethnic vote only: Middle-Middle Native-American unit excluded.

lower and then middle-middle) breaks down locally, particularly in the last two Thompson elections of 1927 and 1931. Here, and in the Republican primary of 1928, there are strong suggestions of socioeconomic effect on voting. In his first reelection campaign, in 1919, Thompson did not break traditional voting patterns. But in 1927 and 1931 he did: the pro-Thompson vote increased as one went down the class scale.

The same tendency prevailed within most ethnic groups, even where there were no lower-lower units. The Lithuanian upper-lower units, for example, were more Republican in 1927 and 1931 than the Lithuanian lower-middle units, while this had not been the case in 1919, and had prevailed to a lesser degree in 1923. The Italian lower-lower units were clearly more Democratic than the upper-lower units in 1919 and 1923, and then clearly more Republican in 1927 and 1931. Similarly, the Czech upper-lower and lower-middle units were much more Republican than the middle-middle in 1927 (but this broke down in 1931, when a Czech opposed Thompson; again, the ethnic factor overwhelmed the socioeconomic). An important key to Thompson's strength thus emerges—a socioeconomic, or class, rather than ethnic attraction to the socioeconomically lowest among virtually all ethnic groups.

This phenomenon is even clearer in the Republican primary of 1928, where the issue of reform predominated. This "Pineapple Primary" witnessed a new high in corruption and violence, as the Thompson-Crowe-Small organization fought for its life and lost. All the forces of "respectability" were organized against the Thompson candidates, and the vote for Governor Small and State's Attorney Crowe, or their opponents, provides an excellent indicator of pro-Thompson versus pro-reform sentiment. The issue was never clearer.

The results are striking: an obvious relationship between lower socioeconomic class and pro-Thompson voting. The lower-lower units voted 79 percent pro-Thompson (i.e., average of vote for Crowe and Small); the upper-lower units 58 percent; the lower-middle 40 percent; and the middle-middle 29 percent.

This use of a primary election eliminates one of the major problems in dealing with the question of socioeconomic reaction to reform: the most pro-reform voters were in the middle-middle class and above, and were largely Republican. But in Chicago in the 1920s "reform" generally meant being anti-Thompson and thus voting Democratic. This created a real ambivalence within the middle-class electorate, which wanted to reform the city and eliminate Thompson, but which was nonetheless reluctant to vote Democratic. The 1928 Republican primary afforded an opportunity around this dilemma, and they used it to repudiate overwhelmingly the Thompson organization within the Republican context. This feeling was clearly middle class rather than ethnic: the Native-Americans, also strongly Republican, gave Thompson's candidates only 21 percent.

Lower-class ethnics, on the other hand, were not positively motivated toward reform. Or, at least they did not allow questions of reform to dissuade them from voting in favor of politicians—in this case, Thompson and his organization—whom they otherwise preferred. For each of the ethnic groups which had a lower-lower unit, that unit was the most pro-Thompson in the primary. And within every single ethnic group, the socioeconomically lowest units were those most pro-Thompson.

The primary returns reflected a personal, Thompson appeal to lower-class ethnics (as was made clear by their voting in 1923, when Thompson did not run). If the mayor's appeal was not successfully ethnic, it was successfully class. He was an effective demagogue, not like a Cermak or a LaGuardia, who built on an ethnic base, but rather like a Huey Long, who built on an essentially socioeconomic base. His demagoguery, however, was constructed on a rather fragile foundation, since ethnic motivation was considerably stronger than socioeconomic. And when Cermak confronted Thompson in 1931 this was proved conclusively. Upper-lower and lower-middle Czechs, for example, were influenced by ethnic rather than socioeconomic forces in their strong support of Cermak. And among the Poles, the middle-middle unit moved from least Republican in 1927 to second most Republican in 1931—a more predictable stance and one which reflected the ethnic factor operating among lower-class Poles once again. Among the most middle-class ethnic groups, lower-middle and middle-middle units drew closer together in 1931, to Cermak's advantage. Cermak profited from the ethnic attraction among socioeconomically lower ethnics and the quest for reform among socioeconomically higher. Thompson retained popularity in 1931 with lower-class units generally, but to a definitely lesser degree than in 1927, and thus he could not win. The lower-lower units were the most opposed to Prohibition (89 percent "Anti" in the 1919 referendum, to 83 percent for upper-lower,

85 percent for lower-middle, and 71 percent for middle-middle), and, while there might be much to hold them to Thompson in 1931, Tony Cermak was *the* Wet in Chicago, and they knew it. His strength on the basis of ethnicity and ethnic issues simply outweighed Thompson's non-ethnic socioeconomic appeal.

When Thompson was reelected in 1927, one commentator offered a word of optimism: "Remember, however, that the same people who vote enthusiastically for a Thompson or a Hylan at one election may vote with even more rejoicing for Al Smith at the next. They are not so much opposed to good government as they are to the exclusive gentlemen who conspicuously favor it, and to the repressive objects which puritannical government often proposes."[6]

Thus "reform" did not always make much sense to the lower-class ethnic, while Thompson, who flouted the reformers, could seem attractive indeed. But Anton Cermak was similar to Al Smith in his appeal to the ethnics, promising clean government that was also highly attuned to ethnic sentiments and desires. This made Thompson considerably less attractive in 1931 than he had been four years earlier.

Reform sentiment tended to favor the Democrats, particularly in local politics. The socioeconomic breakdowns I have made qualitatively in Chapter 9 and quantitatively here establish that this was a reason for rising middle- and upper-class ethnic Democratic voting. Lower- and working-class ethnic Democratic voting increased more for ethnic than for reform or socioeconomic reasons, and in ethnic rather than socioeconomic patterns; but even here Cermak and Smith undermined the socioeconomic attraction of the Thompson organization. This combination of Democratic forces, appealing at once to ethnics of all socioeconomic classes, was really unbeatable, and the Democracy had it made.

Because socioeconomic class divisions comprise categorical and not interval variables, I am unable here to use Pearson's r correlations. But I can substitute another correlation measure, known as Goodman and Kruskal's lambda-b (L-b), whose computation is a good deal less forbidding than its name. This is a measure of strength of association for categorical variables, used here for association between our four socioeco-

---

[6] "Why Chicago Did It," *The New Republic* 50 (April 20, 1927): 234–36.

nomic categories and voting in selected elections (with voting made categorical by dividing percentages into equal quartiles). As distinct from Pearson's *r*, *L-b* is not a measure of linear relationship, but only of monotonicity; and it ranges only from zero to one, since negative relationships are not possible. I shall actually be using the square root of *L-b* in all the values given here, to make it statistically comparable to the values expressed by Pearson's *r;* the nature of this measure will preclude values of as high an order as occur with Pearson's *r*, however.[7]

Table X:6 gives *L-b* for selected elections in our period of major concern. When using two-party vote, *L-b* will be the same for either candidate, since it is a symmetrical measure; moreover, it does not show the direction of association. For example, *L-b* computed for either the Smith or Hoover vote of 1928 comes out .39, indicating some relationship between socioeconomic class and voting, but not from which classes

---

[7] Lambda-b is based on quite simple calculations, made from modal categories in a contingency table, as illustrated below:

$$X = \text{Socioeconomic class}$$

		1	2	3	4	Σ
	1	2	5	4	0	11
	2	3	6	7	2	18
Y = Voting	3	3	2	2	6	13
	4	0	1	1	0	2
	Σ	8	14	14	8	44

Here, the X variable is socioeconomic class (1 = lower-lower, 2 = upper-lower, 3 = lower-middle, 4 = middle-middle), and the Y variable is voting for the candidate concerned (1 = 76–100 percent, 2 = 51–75 percent, 3 = 26–50 percent, 4 = 0–25 percent). To compute Lambda-b, add the modal figure for each X variable (*viz.,* 3 + 6 + 7 + 6), and subtract from it the modal total voting figure (*viz.,* 18). This is divided by the value derived when the modal total voting figure (*viz.,* again, 18) is subtracted from the corner total (*viz.,* 44). Thus:

$$\frac{(3 + 6 + 7 + 6) - 18}{44 - 18} = \frac{4}{26} = .154 = \text{Lambda-b}$$

Then take the square root of .154 and arrive at the correlation of .39 for socioeconomic class and Smith voting in 1928. For further explanation and examples, see Jensen, "Methods of Statistical Association for Historical Research," mimeo. (St. Louis, Mo., 1968), pp. 37–40.

each candidate benefited (whereas there was a difference: Smith carried five of eight lower-lower units, eleven of fourteen upper-lower and lower-middle, and two of eight middle-middle).

The table, first of all, strongly supports the assertion that socioeconomic class was not as important an overall determinant of voting behavior as was ethnicity; there are no very strong correlations. It also supports the idea that there was some socioeconomic effect in 1928 voting, especially when compared to 1920 and 1924, and that this increased in 1932. The 1920 presidential election seems to have elicited no reaction in socioeconomic terms. This is largely true of 1924 as well; note that if the La Follette vote is added to that of Coolidge, the election as a whole has a L-b of zero, as did 1920.

In local elections there is a striking effect in 1931, just as was indicated by the voting returns by class. While each preceding Thompson election had to some degree been associated with socioeconomic class, and this reached its highest point in the 1928 primary where Thompson's organization fought for its life, the L-b of zero in 1931 shows the purely ethnic nature of that election, to Cermak's profit. Thompson's socioeconomic as well as ethnic appeal had been broken; L-b points to the source of this defeat.

In Table X:7 I again use the standard deviation (s) as a measure of dispersion to see the effect of major elections on dispersion of the vote between classes and between the units comprising the sample for each class. In national elections there is a hint that 1928 had socioeconomic overtones, since s between classes is highest of all there. On the other hand, s within classes shows no very clear pattern, except an overall increase over time. Were the relationship between socioeconomic class and Smith voting really great, for example, we should expect intraclass s to be low, and this does not obtain. The figures are not entirely satisfactory.

This is even truer of the s values for the La Follette vote, where s both between and within classes is extremely low. This is best explained by questioning the measure, since La Follette was a third-party candidate, whose vote nowhere exceeded about 40 percent; thus the range (and s) is bound to be narrow, when compared to major-party candidates. There is still a hint of support for the earlier suggestions about the socioeco-

TABLE X:6   *Lambda-b Correlations of Socioeconomic Class and Selected National and Local Elections, 1919-1932*[*]

Year, office, candidates	Square root of Lambda-b
1920: President: Cox–Harding	0.00
1924: President:[†] Davis Coolidge	0.00 .37
1928: President: Smith–Hoover	.39
1932: President: Roosevelt–Hoover	.57
1919: Mayor: Sweitzer–Thompson	.31
1923: Mayor: Dever–Lueder	.52
1927: Mayor: Dever–Thompson	.40
1928: Republican Primary[§]	.57
1931: Mayor: Cermak–Thompson	0.00

[*]For explanation of this statistic, see text.

[†]Figure is not the same for Davis and Coolidge because percentage computed on basis of three-party vote; if La Follette vote is added to that of Coolidge, L-b for the election = 0.00.

[§]Based on mean percentage of two-candidate vote received by two leading Thompson candidates in the primary: Small for governor and Crowe for states attorney.

TABLE X:7   *Standard Deviations for Socioeconomic Class Breakdowns of Vote of*
Nine Ethnic Groups in Selected National and Local Elections, 1919-
*1932**

Year and election	s between four classes	s within classes			
		Lower-Lower	Upper-Lower	Lower-Middle	Middle-Middle
1920: President	7.5	17.1	18.4	15.8	9.5
1924: President	7.9	15.8	20.3	12.8	8.8
1928: President	9.9	19.7	21.0	20.8	10.1
1932: President	8.3	23.3	23.1	20.8	9.5
1924: La Follette	5.7	6.6	7.6	5.6	5.7
1919: Mayor	10.2	22.2	22.0	19.4	11.3
1923: Mayor	17.0	14.4	21.5	18.9	9.4
1927: Mayor	6.2	19.1	19.7	19.4	14.7
1931: Mayor	9.1	17.5	21.7	22.8	7.9

*Standard deviation computed for range between classes or between areas
comprising sample for each class, based on Democratic percentage of two-party
vote, except for 1924—Democratic percentage of three-party vote. Figures for
La Follette based on La Follette percentage of the three-party vote.

nomic effect of the La Follette candidacy, in the somewhat lower *s* among middle- as opposed to lower-class ethnics.

In local elections, the highest interclass *s* by far occurs in the least controversial mayoralty of the period. The reason for this is unclear, as is that for the low *s* of 1927, which is rather the opposite from what we would expect, given our suggestions about the socioeconomic strength of Thompson's appeal prior to 1931.

Our *L-b* correlations pretty generally agree with the other quantitative and qualitative measures of this chapter; this is at best partially true for the standard deviations, which are unsatisfactory at the local level.

Regarding the role of socioeconomic class in the political behavior of Chicago's ethnic groups, it appears to be a rather selective force, operating only in certain situations and in various ways. In national politics, the clearest socioeconomic breakdown in voting was that of relatively stronger Republicanism among ethnics firmly established in the middle class. This is as one should expect. Ethnics of other classes seem to have behaved more in terms of the ethnic rather than the socioeconomic reference group, and thus socioeconomic factors do not tell us very much about them. The major exception to this generalization would seem to be that union member ethnics—and particularly those in the lower-middle class—did sometimes operate in terms of a class reference group. We learn this more by inference than anything else, but it does seem to explain some otherwise inexplicable developments and is particularly useful in understanding the effects of the La Follette candidacy of 1924.

Locally, socioeconomic class operated differently, because it was intimately associated with the question of reform and in this period reform involved support of the Democrats. Involvement in reform was very much a class phenomenon, with higher class correlating with greater support of reform. Class, then, was a factor in bringing middle-class ethnics into the Democratic party in the local context. And as a corollary to this, class operated among lower-class ethnics to reinforce local Republicanism until nonclass forces persuaded them to switch.

In some ways, then, socioeconomic class had antithetical effects at the national and local levels. But in the long run the Democrats profited in both. Class either ultimately worked to the Democrats' advantage or else ceased to be an effective causative factor. Locally, class served to bring the otherwise Republican ethnic middle class into the Democracy; and lower-class ethnic voters were brought into the Democracy for other than class reasons. Nationally, class did produce in the solid middle class a certain reluctance to vote Democratic, but it also seems to have supported Democratic voting among the much larger ethnic working class.

Socioeconomic class did not have the political force of ethnicity among any except perhaps the highest class ethnics. But it was somewhat effective in the situations noted—situations which, on the whole, served to make it another servant of the Democratic consensus.

XI. Conclusion:
A House for all Peoples

Ethnic political behavior and the politics of Chicago underwent considerable change and development between 1890 and 1936. As the ethnic groups increased in number and became larger and more acculturated to American political mores, their role in the city's politics changed. They became not only more important generally, and more hearkened to, but they came to affect the style of Chicago politics, the kind of people and the kind of issues that would characterize the city's political life. Perhaps the most important change of this half-century is just that—Chicago's politics became a house for all peoples, wherein each could find at least something it was looking for. In the 1890s Chicago had many immigrants, most of whom could not vote and almost all of whom were concerned primarily with surviving in a hostile environment; as such they were a rather passive force and one which politicians tended to take for granted—the ethnics, after all, had no alternatives. In the 1930s, on the other hand, the ethnics were well organized, largely naturalized and thus able to vote, and by then accustomed to being recognized as specific groups, with individual interests of their own and the power to reciprocate if those interests were not met. It is this general change, built up slowly, over time and with much trial-and-error, that had the greatest effect on Chicago and American politics.

It is difficult to generalize about newer immigrant voting behavior prior to the First World War, since small proportions of these groups were naturalized and voting. The ethnics as a whole voted as Chicago and Illinois voted, although frequently more Democratic in this era of Republican hegemony. The older immigrant groups—Germans and Swedes—as the nation at large, were generally Republican in their voting for national and state offices. Most of the newer immigrants, however, were living in areas that generally delivered national and state Democratic majorities through the coming of the war. Negroes remained overwhelmingly Republican. Local voting tradition in this early period was also mixed, although the Democrats did better than at state and national levels. Thus many of the immigrants did have their first political experience in Democratic neighborhoods.

It was not until the end of the First World War, however, that the newer immigrants began to become naturalized in large numbers, and it is here that I have sought major indications of ethnic political behavior. There were heavy Republican majorities of almost all ethnic groups for national and state office in the first half of the 1920s, followed by rapidly increasing Democratic majorities starting with 1928. By 1931 most groups were voting locally much the same as they were for national office. However, in the 1920s there is less change in traditional voting patterns than the establishment of the first real long-term political commitments that many of these groups ever had. The late 1920s to early 1930s, then, witnessed not so much changes in coalitions as the formation of the first ethnic voting coalition; not so much realignment as a first alignment, for most of these groups. There was, of course, some real change, particularly for the older immigrant groups, and most especially the Germans and Jews, who clearly surrendered long-term Republican loyalties for new Democratic ones in this critical period (as the Negroes would do in the mid-1930s). But this was a period for the settling down of the percolating forces of rapidly naturalizing new groups, creating in the process a political coalition with some older groups that would last for a generation and replacing in power the really preethnic or preurban coalition which had maintained the Republicans since the 1890s.

A variety of quantitative and qualitative measures have been employed in this study to view changes in ethnic political behavior and Chicago politics after 1918. Democratic voting and Democratic party membership grew at all levels, and for really all groups, after 1928. Political heterogeneity among the ethnics was slowly replaced by political homogeneity. Seven of the nine groups voted Democratic for mayor in 1931, and eight for president in 1932. Only the Negroes could be rightly labeled Republican in 1932, and even that would not last too much longer. When Edward Kelly, Cermak's successor, was reelected with a record majority in 1935, his opponent said, "There is no local Republican

Party."[1] This was true. The Republican party in Chicago, as a viable political opposition, was dead and would largely remain so. Without the rising consensus of Chicago's ethnic groups this Democratic strength could not have come about. There was a complex of factors leading to this consensus: ethnically attractive and attentive national and local Democratic politicians; the Democratic versus Republican stand on issues of ethnic concern; ethnic representation on party tickets and in patronage jobs; the entanglement of the Republicans locally with crime; superior Democratic party organization and solidarity. The ethnics entered the Democracy because their support was sufficiently reciprocated to make it reasonable for them to do so; or, negatively, because the Republicans offered no reason for them not to vote Democratic. Because the Democrats came to represent a politics that was a house for all peoples, while the Republicans did not, the Democrats became the majority party for the second third of the twentieth century.

This change was created by no one election or issue, nor by any single variable. But there were crucial elections, issues, and other phenomena. According to my ethnic variant of the theory of critical elections, as defined by V. O. Key, and further developed by others, I have found that what was true in other cities emerges as true for Chicago also: the 1928 election was certainly the most critical of the period.[2]

But although 1928 was the single election contributing most to changes, or permanent developments in ethnic voting behavior, it did not exist in a vacuum. Both our qualitative information and our quantitative

[1] *News-Week* 5 (April 13, 1935): 7.

[2] V. O. Key, Jr., "A Theory of Critical Elections," *Journal of Politics* 17 (Feb. 1955); Duncan MacRae, Jr., and J. A. Meldrum, "Critical Elections in Illinois, 1888–1958," *American Political Science Review* 54 (Sept. 1960); Jerome M. Clubb and Howard W. Allen, "The Cities and the Election of 1928: Partisan Realignment?" *American Historical Review* 74 (April 1969); John L. Shover, "Was 1928 a Critical Election in California?" *Pacific Northwest Quarterly* 58 (Oct. 1967). See also J. Joseph Huthmacher, *Massachusetts People and Politics, 1919–1933* (Cambridge, Mass., 1959); Samuel Lubell, *The Future of American Politics* (Garden City, N.Y., 1952); M. J. Bluestein, "Voting Tradition and Socioeconomic Factors in the 1936 Presidential Election in Illinois" (M.A. thesis, University of Chicago, 1950), p. 5; Harold F. Gosnell and N. N. Gill, "An Analysis of the 1932 Presidential Vote in Chicago," *American Political Science Review* 29 (Dec. 1935); William F. Ogburn and Nell S. Talbot, "A Measurement of the Factors in the Presidential Election of 1928," *Social Forces* 8 (Dec. 1929).

measures (voting, party identification, etc.) have pointed to the importance of 1930 and 1932 in building into a tradition ethnic national and
state Democratic voting, and of 1931 in bringing local voting behavior
into line with national. It is better, therefore, to speak of a critical period
of voting change than of a critical election. One Illinois voting study so
labeled the period 1924–1936.[3] But in terms of our data this seems
unnecessarily long; 1924 really had little effect on overall voter loyalties,
and all the changes that obtained in 1936 had really been well developed
by 1932 (Negro Democratic voting majorities at the national level are
really a post-1936 phenomenon). There is a temptation to stop in 1931
and exclude the Roosevelt election because of the overwhelming importance of voting tradition as a determinant of voting behavior and the fact
that there was already an ethnic Democratic tradition by 1932.[4] Roosevelt's strength certainly built on the Democratic impetus created during
1928–1931.[5] But Roosevelt also contributed to the firmness of this tradition (e.g., our party identification measure), adding more ethnics and
regaining voters who had left the party in reaction against Smith (Protestants, southerners).[6]

Thus 1928–1932 comprises an ideal critical period in the politics of
Chicago's ethnic groups, as well as for the city as a whole, and indeed for
the nation. This is supported by almost all our measures of political
behavior, in addition to those built on voting alone. This was the first
such period since the 1890s and was even larger in its scope and more
permanent in its effects.

[3] MacRae and Meldrum, "Critical Elections in Illinois," pp. 669–83.

[4] On the importance of party tradition as a force of political behavior, see
Angus Campbell and others, *The Voter Decides* (Evanston, Ill., 1954), pp.
88–90. Gosnell and Gill found Democratic party tradition the strongest factor in
Roosevelt's 1932 victory, which indicates his indebtedness to Smith ("An Analy-
sis of the 1932 Presidential Vote in Chicago," p. 983). See also Bluestein,
"Voting Tradition," p. 28.

[5] Gosnell and Gill, "An Analysis of the 1932 Presidential Vote in Chicago."
Nationally the "simple coefficient of correlation" between Roosevelt and Smith
voting was .94 (ibid., p. 976), while that between Smith and Cox or Davis was
not significant (Ogburn and Talbot, "A Measurement of the Factors," p. 178).
We have seen for Chicago a Roosevelt-Smith Pearson *r* correlation of .95, even
higher than the national. See also Harold F. Gosnell, *Machine Politics: Chicago
Model* (Chicago, 1937), p. 102.

[6] This was true in Illinois: MacRae and Meldrum, "Critical Elections in
Illinois, p. 678.

I have made little effort here to determine if any one issue created any given voting shift, since this determination cannot really be made. The Smith election is a good case in point, since it has been intensively studied in a variety of ways and at several points in time. Scholars differ strongly on what they see as the major variables of Smith voting, and their conclusions often differ partially from those of the quantitative and qualitative measures used in this study.[7] In dealing with political relationships one must be as catholic and inclusive as possible. No one quantitative tool or subjective insight will alone suffice. The political decision-making process of each individual is a complex phenomenon, innately multivariate, and at least partially irrational.[8] In 1928, for example, an ethnic voter supported Smith because of his Wetness, urbanness, Roman Catholicism, or apparent social familiarity; because he was paid or otherwise influenced to do so; or for any of a variety of other reasons. There is evidence—in correlation coefficients and in the ethnic press—to associate Smith voting with opposition to Prohibition, and good evidence about the lesser roles of empathy, prejudice, and general liberalism. It is quite clear that these were the major issues of 1928 since both quantitative measures and qualitative evidence point to them as the issues of utmost ethnic concern. Beyond this, however, there is an area of uncertainty. The voter chooses as an individual, within the framework of his reference groups, because and in spite of the many forces operative upon him; one underestimates the voter and the complexities of his decision process if he tries fully to isolate individual forces.

Were it possible to quantify other issues as has been done for Prohibition (e.g., had there been referenda on immigration restriction, etc.), partial analysis would have been possible and might have provided statistical insights into the relative weight of various issues. Multivariate analysis is another possibility, but one still needing considerable develop-

[7] E.g., Ruth C. Silva, *Rum, Religion and Votes: 1928 Re-Examined* (University Park, Pa., 1962), p. 43; Ogburn and Talbot, "A Measurement of the Factors," pp. 176–78. The former found Wetness and Catholic religion statistically insignificant correlates of Smith voting; the latter found a negative partial correlation between urban residence and Smith voting. This points not to weaknesses of statistics, but of statisticians; and to the need for qualitative research as a check on quantitative data, as well as vice versa.

[8] See, e.g., A. J. Brodbeck, "The Problem of Irrationality and Neuroticism Underlying Political Choice," in *American Voting Behavior,* ed. Eugene Burdick and A. J. Brodbeck (Glencoe, Ill., 1959), pp. 121–35.

ment for applicability to historical problems.[9] And even with the addition of these more sophisticated quantitative techniques, the elements of emotion and irrationality that accompany political decision-making would still remain.

To endeavor to differentiate between forces of party, issues, and candidates, or between different types of issues, can also be misleading. One leading voting study postulates three main variables (party, candidates, and issues), any one of which can predominate in any given election, with party generally the most important.[10] This is a useful distinction, but not always possible. Smith's 1928 strength was certainly not from party loyalty; it was, in fact, an antiparty vote: the voting change centered around Smith as an individual versus the Republicans as a party. But the candidate and the issues were really one package, inseparable. And Cermak's 1931 victory was a careful blend of all three variables. The evaluations of campaigns in the ethnic press show the difficulty of maintaining this type of distinction.

In terms of types of issues, a distinction has been made between "Position" (content) and "Style" (attitudinal) issues, with the latter having importance mainly when the former fail to occur.[11] But what was Prohibition in the 1920s? or the Ku Klux Klan? or religious prejudice? Clearly these issues involved both content and attitude, both rational and irrational factors, and cannot be so easily characterized. A distinction between ethnic issues and issues of ethnic interest makes more sense for this study, and generally, as a distinction between those issues which encompass social and cultural problems and those which do not. The former can be called more attitudinal or less substantive than the latter, but they tend also to be more determining.[12]

In short, an effort to isolate the variables of political behavior must not lead to oversimplification of the complexities of political relationships

---

[9] Note 7 above points to some of the problems that seem to emerge when partials and multivariate techniques are employed. The answer, of course, lies not in abandoning the techniques, but in further exploration by historical statisticians.

[10] Campbell and others, *The Voter Decides*, pp. 183–84.

[11] Bernard Berelson and others *Voting: A Study of Opinion Formation in a Presidential Campaign* (Chicago, 1954), pp. 184–85.

[12] Samuel P. Hays, "History as Human Behavior," *Iowa Journal of History* 58 (July 1960); Gosnell and Gill, "An Analysis of the 1932 Presidential Vote in Chicago."

and the element of irrationality in political decision-making by individuals and by groups. Political motivation is complex and involves a multiplicity of factors which often cannot be separated. Just as the study of political behavior which ignores quantitative tools cannot possibly be complete, so too is a study limited by an ignoring of the irrational and subjective forces which are always present. Some historians of this period have recognized this, at least implicitly.[13] And I have hopefully made it explicit in this study of ethnic political behavior in Chicago.

I have considered only one city and its ethnic groups. The characteristics and forces of ethnic political behavior, however, are general and applicable to all cities. There are very strong similarities in the responses of different ethnic groups to similar stimulii at the same or different times. This suggests that the forms of American ethnic group thought-patterns, behavior, and belief would be constant from city to city, even where the substance of political response might vary for local reasons.

The substance of Chicago's ethnic politics 1890–1936 does have some elements which make the city's experience unique. No other American city, for example, had a mayor quite like Big Bill Thompson, and Thompson certainly affected the configurations of ethnic political behavior in Chicago. But each city has its distinctive elements (James Curley in Boston was in several ways a Democratic Thompson), none of which are as powerful as the similarities which link all American cities. Where local Republican organization was more effective (Philadelphia, for example) the rise of the Democratic party came more slowly.[14] But the fact is that it came everywhere, and for essentially the same reasons. The political acculturation of the immigrant and other ethnic minority groups followed a pretty consistent path throughout the United States, and it was just this similarity of forces operating in most places at the same time that created the revival of the Democratic party.

Indeed, given the variations in the political and ethnic makeup of

[13] E.g., Huthmacher, *Massachusetts People and Politics;* Lubell, *The Future of American Politics;* Oscar Handlin, *Al Smith and His America* (Boston, 1958).

[14] See J. T. Salter, *Boss Rule: Portraits in City Politics* (New York, 1935), and David H. Kurtzman, "Methods of Controlling Votes in Philadelphia" (Ph.D. diss., University of Pennsylvania, 1935). The distinctiveness of California, which did have unique elements, is noted in Shover, "Was 1928 a Critical Election in California?" And a multi-city approach can be found in Clubb and Allen, "The Cities and the Election of 1928."

American cities, the similarities of their political development are a good deal more striking than the differences. This study, then, provides a microcosmic view of a general process taking place in American political life at this time. This half-century view has hopefully provided focus not only on the substantive question of the rise of the Democratic party but also on those problems of form mentioned above: the desires, complaints, and tensions of people in the process of acculturating and assimilating themselves into an essentially alien society. Ethnic political behavior, in the American democratic context, was a rather good measure of ethnic Americanization generally (and perhaps of the relation between any minority ethnic group and a larger society) and of the ethnic role in and effect on American life. The United States of the twentieth century has been overwhelmingly affected—in domestic affairs, relations with foreign nations, and myriad specific problems—by its ethnically pluralistic nature. Thus the forces dealt with in this study are not without their significance in understanding the unfolding of American history.

The ethnic groups of Chicago comprised a majority of its population long before they came to have any real force in the making of its political decisions. Partially this was because of their inability to work together; but far more so was it because the groups in power in Chicago sought to maintain their own positions and keep the ethnics out. Thus the process outlined in these pages was a rather dramatic one, as groups of Americans sought the powers that were essential to the realization of their version of the American dream.

As the Democratic party, and Chicago politics generally, became more of a house for all peoples by the early 1930s, this signified a considerable expansion of American democracy. Certainly it was a jerry-built house, whose elements had little more in common with one another than a mutual need for its shelter. But the house was now open to nearly everyone, and each could enter in company with his ethnic peers; if that was not the American dream of some older Americans, it fit very well indeed with that of the ethnic groups of Chicago, 1890–1936.

Appendix

There are two main reasons for my adoption of a different methodology for ethnic political behavior in the period 1890–1916 than for the years following. First, there is the fact that most of the immigrants were just entering Chicago during these years, and that, at least for the newer immigrant groups, majorities of each group were not naturalized and thus able to vote until about the time of the First World War. Thus a newer immigrant group's preponderance of the population in a given political unit did not necessarily mean a similar preponderance of the voters in that unit. Second, we are limited by the nature of census information for this period. The Bureau of the Census, for example, before 1920 reported data for cities on inconsistent bases, and never for units smaller than the ward. Wards are large units, often with tens of thousands of people (Chicago had thirty-five wards through 1921, for a population of just over a million in 1890 and 2.7 million in 1920); obviously, there would be few instances where one ethnic group would comprise the majority of a ward. School censuses are another important source of information, but since these use data from schoolchildren, they are bound to underrepresent newer immigrant groups and Negroes, who, because of poverty, kept their children in school less often and for shorter periods of time than did more established groups.

We must, therefore, use a more cursory approach to the prewar era and recognize that the data are less reliable than for the 1920s. It is for this reason that I speak of, for example, the "Italian area" vote rather than the "Italian vote" for these years. Moreover, the proportions which some of our groups comprise of the wards of their main concentration are often quite small, making any generalizations questionable (Table A:1). But I had the alternatives of using these imprecise data or simply ignoring voting behavior prior to 1918; and considering the alternatives, it was reasonable to proceed as I have, a glimmer of light being preferable to none at all.

There are a couple of subjective factors also arguing for this decision. First, the censuses tended to underrepresent the ethnics. Second, it can be argued that an ethnic group's dominance of an area stems not only from its proportion of the area's population but also from its being the largest ethnic group in the area regardless of its numbers. I chose the sample

TABLE A:1   Characteristics of Ethnic Areas Studied, 1890-1916

Group	1890-1901		1901-1910		1911-1917	
	Ward number(s)	% of ward population*	Ward number(s)	% of ward population*	Ward number(s)	% of ward population*
Germans	14, 20, 21, 22, 26	57	24, 26, 27	46	24, 26, 27	41
Swedes	23	38	22	17	23	14
Bohemians	8, 9	42	10, 12	39	10, 12	41
Poles	16	46	16, 17	43	16, 17	57
Italians	19	15	19	30	4, 19	41
Jews†	7	39	9	47	10, 20	40
Negroes§	2	15	2	23	2	39

*In multiple-ward units the figure is the mean of the group percentages for each of the wards included.

†Percentages given are those for Russians in these known Jewish areas; in fact the number of Jews would be higher, especially for the Twentieth Ward which was the ghetto and included Jews from many eastern European countries.

§Negro percentages probably considerably higher than indicated; they would probably be most underrepresented in school censuses.

areas not only on the basis of group proportion of total population but also when possible from areas where no other group existed in large numbers. Additionally, at all times the data is at most for the first and second generations (i.e., the immigrants and their children) and does not include the third generation (listed as native-born white of native-born white parentage by the census) who are often quite ethnic in every way; this factor is even more pertinent to the samples for 1918–1936. Finally, I have also followed the lead—where it did not conflict with the data—of contemporary students of the ethnic groups.

Table A:1 describes the sample used for 1890–1916. It is based primarily on the Chicago School Censuses of 1898, 1908, and 1914, and secondarily on the federal censuses of 1890, 1900, and 1910 (the eleventh, twelfth, and thirteenth). The changes in ward numbers reflect the decennial redistricting that took place in Chicago; the geographic areas remain pretty much the same, but the ward number(s) applicable to these areas changed over time.

Table A:2 gives the vote for each of the ethnic areas for the contests included 1890–1916. The vote is expressed in terms of the percentage Democratic of the major-party vote. For all except four years this is the two-party vote, and the Republican percentages can be computed by simple subtraction. For 1891, 1897, 1912, and 1914, however, I have included minor party voting; so for these elections the figures in Table A:2 indicate Democratic percentage of the three- or four-party vote. Table A:3 shows the percentages of the vote received by these minor party candidates. And the Republican vote in these cases can be computed by subtracting from 100 first the Democratic vote shown in Table A:2, and then the minor party vote shown in Table A:3.

Finally, in Table A:4 are listed the names of all the candidates in all the elections studied for the period 1890–1916. This may be of use to readers who wish to remanipulate my data, or for those who are interested in drawing substantive conclusions beyond the areas of concern in this study. It also makes the information for the first half of this inquiry as complete as possible.

For the period after 1918 I have been able to apply a more satisfactory methodology; it is, however, controlled to a degree by the nature of the quest. Since this is a study of ethnic political behavior, wherein the

TABLE A:2   Ethnic Area Voting, 1890–1916 (Percentage Democratic)*

Year, office	German	Swedish	Bohemian	Polish	Italian	Jewish	Negro
1890: State Treasurer	43	57	67	59	70	54	46
Sheriff	47	59	65	61	72	60	41
1891: Mayor	18	35	30	46	39	32	30
1892: President	60	57	74	72	71	63	47
Governor	60	57	74	72	71	64	46
1893: Mayor	51	58	73	71	75	62	54
1894: State Treasurer	39	48	55	49	58	46	39
Sheriff	42	52	57	52	59	47	43
1895: Mayor	47	42	59	49	53	43	36
1896: President	41	42	55	52	55	41	32
Governor	47	44	60	56	58	46	34
1897: Mayor	49	52	73	68	71	66	59
1898: State Treasurer	53	49	63	58	69	48	48
Sheriff	53	49	60	58	67	46	44
1899: Mayor	58	57	70	63	74	54	62
1900: President	52	45	66	63	64	54	40
Governor	56	47	69	65	68	65	44
1901: Mayor	56	57	60	72	68	56	44
1902: State Treasurer	45	48	56	60	65	51	36
Sheriff	54	54	56	62	67	52	43

1903: Mayor	51	54	59	57	67	63	43
1904: President	32	39	39	38	46	36	24
Governor	31	38	40	37	46	37	25
1905: Mayor	50	56	64	60	75	71	46
1906: State Treasurer	33	46	49	45	60	47	25
Sheriff	36	52	56	51	69	54	30
1907: Mayor	44	45	61	56	70	53	37
1908: President	40	47	53	50	57	52	31
Governor	50	54	65	54	67	70	42
1910: State Treasurer	53	57	74	63	73	85	43
Sheriff	53	53	76	62	70	85	44
1911: Mayor	51	57	70	69	69	63	51
1912: President	26	28	34	30	39	34	25
Governor	36	33	48	46	55	46	32
1914: Senator	43	37	61	63	67	68	31
Sheriff	49	39	64	64	71	70	34
1915: Mayor	34	31	40	55	59	44	29
1916: President	44	37	68	68	68	67	27
Governor	46	41	67	68	67	66	28

*Two-party vote except for 1891, 1897, 1912, and 1914; see Table A:3.

TABLE A:3   Minor-Party Vote in Four Elections (Percentage in each ethnic area)

Year, office	German	Swedish	Bohemian	Polish	Italian	Jewish	Negro
1891: Mayor*	42	31	45	31	41	39	26
1897: Mayor†	31	28	10	17	10	7	18
1912: President§	41/16	47/11	23/20	25/16	24/15	19/18	48/5
Governor	26/17	30/10	15/17	15/14	14/13	18/15	33/4
1914: SenatorΔ	26	30	14	11	13	11	18
Sheriff	15	17	6	5	6	5	12

*Independent Democratic party.

†Independent Republican party.

§Two minor parties: Progressive/Socialist.

ΔProgressive party.

TABLE A:4   *Candidates in Chicago Elections, 1890-1916*

Year, office	Republican	Democratic	Other*
1890: State Treasurer	W. Amberg	Wilson[†]	
Sheriff	Gilbert	Lawler	
1891: Mayor	H. Washburne	D. Cregier	C.H. Harrison I
1892: President	B. Harrison	G. Cleveland	
Governor	Fifer	J.P. Altgeld	
1893: Mayor	S. Allerton	C.H. Harrison I	
1894: State Treasurer	Wulff	Claggett	
Sheriff	Pease	Peabody	
1895: Mayor	G.B. Swift	F. Wenter	
1896: President	W. McKinley	W.J. Bryan	
Governor	J.R. Tanner	J.P. Altgeld	
1897: Mayor	N.C. Sears	C.H. Harrison II	J.M. Harlan
1898: State Treasurer	Whittemore	Dunlap	
Sheriff	Magerstadt	Kersten	
1899: Mayor	Z.R. Carter	C.H. Harrison II	
1900: President	W. McKinley	W.J. Bryan	
Governor	R. Yates	S. Alschuler	
1901: Mayor	E. Hanecy	C.H. Harrison II	
1902: State Treasurer	F.A. Busse	G. Duddleston	
Sheriff	D.D. Healy	T.E. Barrett	
1903: Mayor	G. Stewart	C.H. Harrison II	
1904: President	T. Roosevelt	A.B. Parker	
Governor	C.S. Deneen	L.T. Stringer	
1905: Mayor	J.M. Harlan	E.F. Dunne	
1906: State Treasurer	J.F. Smulski	N.L. Piotrowski	
Sheriff	C. Strassheim	H.R. Gibbons	
1907: Mayor	F.A. Busse	E.F. Dunne	
1908: President	W.H. Taft	W.J. Bryan	
Governor	C.S. Deneen	A.E. Stevenson	
1910: State Treasurer	E.F. Mitchell	A.K. Hartley	
Sheriff	F.A. Vogler	M. Zimmer	

TABLE A:4   *(continued)*:

Year, office	Republican	Democratic	Other*
1911: Mayor	C.E. Merriam	C.H. Harrison II	
1912: President	W.H. Taft	W. Wilson	T. Roosevelt/ E. Debs
Governor	C.S. Deneen	E.F. Dunne	F.H. Funk/ J.C. Kennedy
1914: Senator	L.Y. Sherman	R. Sullivan	R. Robins
Sheriff	G.K. Schmidt	J. Traeger	F.S. Oliver
1915: Mayor	W.H. Thompson	R.M. Sweitzer	
1916: President	C.E. Hughes	W. Wilson	
Governor	F.O. Lowden	E.F. Dunne	

*Parties of other candidates: 1891: Independent Democrat; 1897: Independent Republican; 1912: Progressive/Socialist; 1914: Progressive.

†For some of the earlier contests, only the last names of the candidates are recorded.

major quantitative measure is that of ethnic voting behavior, the basic methodological problem was that of isolating unchanging political units of high ethnic concentration for each of the ethnic groups under study. Therefore, the first criterion applied to any area was the degree to which it was dominated by a single group. This innately prejudiced the results in favor of those ethnic group members who lived among large numbers of their fellow ethnics. Obviously the socioeconomically higher members of any group are underrepresented in such a scheme, since they are less likely to live in such homogeneous areas. But successful quantitative conclusions precluded using nonhomogeneous areas; and since most ethnics in the 1920s were socioeconomically lower and lower-middle class, the problem is minimized. Once ethnic group members have moved out of the area of high ethnic concentration, their political and other behavior lose much of their previous ethnic reinforcement, and the ethnic group becomes a less important reference group to them anyway.

Census data for 1920 and 1930 were used to determine every area of high ethnic concentration in Chicago for each of the nine groups. This was facilitated by extensive compilations of otherwise unpublished 1920 and 1930 census data for Chicago done by social scientists at the University of Chicago in the early 1930s.[1] Areas whose ethnicity changed significantly between 1920 and 1930 were eliminated, leaving areas which were dominated by the same group throughout. These areas were then entered on a map of the city (Map A:1) and labeled for purposes of identification (e.g., Italian A, Italian B, *et seq.*).

The next step was to isolate political units in each of the ethnic areas. A number of problems arose at this point. Census data were collected from Census Bureau-created units: Community Areas and their constituent Census Tracts; while voting data were collected from wards and their constituent precincts.[2] Since the two systems did not correspond, it was necessary to correlate them in order to have political data for ethnic areas and vice versa. Moreover the boundaries of political units were changed repeatedly, making it difficult to discover and follow stable political units over the 1918 to 1932 or 1936 period. Until 1921 Chicago had thirty-five wards; in that year the number was changed to fifty, with few wards escaping major redrawing and renumbering. Subsequently, ward lines changed with each decennial census. Beyond this, however, for most of the ethnic groups considered, and for most of the ethnic areas being used, the ward was too large a political unit anyway. Thus precincts had to be used. There were over 3,000 precincts in Chicago, and their boundaries were redrawn after each election (they often were not changed, but could be changed this often); their numbers could be changed just as frequently. Thus I had to find precincts, or groups of precincts, lying within a selected ethnic area, whose boundaries remained essentially the same from 1918 to 1932.

With the map of ethnic areas in hand, I consulted the bound sets of Chicago ward and precinct maps for the period. Six of these sets had to be consulted to ascertain changing boundaries and numbers of the wards and

[1] Ernest W. Burgess and Charles Newcomb, *Census Data of the City of Chicago, 1920* (Chicago, 1931), and *Census Data of the City of Chicago, 1930* (Chicago, 1933); and Charles Newcomb and R. O. Lang, *Census Data of the City of Chicago, 1934* (Chicago, 1934).

[2] 1920 was the first year in which the Census Bureau began to use its own units rather than those of the cities themselves. Published 1920 census data (the Fourteenth Census) were still given for wards, but Burgess and Newcomb used Community Areas and Census Tracts in their published returns and correlated the Community Areas and Census Tracts of 1920 with those of 1930. I was therefore able to use Community Areas and Census Tracts for both 1920 and 1930.

precincts. Often, for example, a given precinct would retain its boundaries throughout the period, but change its number, or even the ward to which it belonged, several times. Each of these changes had to be noted. I started with the 1932 maps and picked a number of precincts in each ethnic area. Then the next earlier set of ward-precinct maps was studied to see if boundaries or numbers had changed, and any such changes were noted; then I went on to the maps next earlier in time, and so on, until I had reached 1918. This process was followed for each of the ethnic areas I had chosen (all those on Map A:1 and others). During this process many precincts became unusable. Often, as I went back in time, I found groups of precincts gradually becoming single ones, as I was dealing with population decrease; sometimes the reverse was true—what was one precinct in 1932 was four or five in 1918. But if the overall boundaries remained the same I simply grouped the precincts together as one political unit. Sometimes I found that no single precinct in an ethnic area retained its boundaries over the years, but that groups of four or five, or even more, did maintain their overall boundary and could be used in this way. For individual precincts the general rule adopted was that if they changed their boundaries more than two city blocks (in any direction and in either addition or subtraction) over the fourteen-year period, they would be eliminated; for groups of precincts slightly more latitude was allowed.[3] I thus was able to create a situation wherein I was dealing with the same ethnic group in the same political unit from 1918 to 1932 (and, generally, to 1936); and I could assume I was dealing with many of the same individuals throughout.

As I moved back in time, more and more precincts had to be eliminated, as were some whole ethnic areas for want of stable political units within them. It is for this reason that some of the middle-middle class ethnic political units used in this study become usable only in the middle of the decade—earlier than that the political unit was indeterminable, or the area was insufficiently homogeneous. Since I started in 1932 with large numbers of precincts for each ethnic area, I was generally able

[3] This rule was observed fairly religiously, but not without exception. Particularly early in the period, and in areas of low population density, a precinct might be very large (a square mile or more), and in situations like this more latitude was allowed. Conversely, in geographically tiny precincts (two to four blocks) in areas of high population density, I eliminated precincts that changed even less than our two block standard.

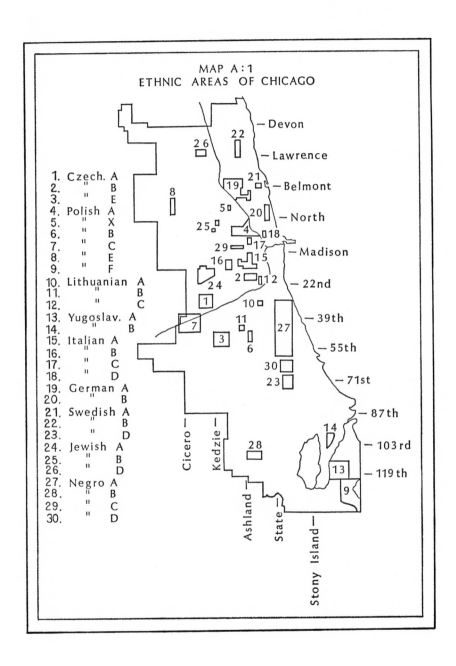

MAP A:1
ETHNIC AREAS OF CHICAGO

1. Czech. A
2.   "   B
3.   E
4. Polish A
5.   "   X
6.   "   B
7.   "   C
8.   "   E
9.   "   F
10. Lithuanian A
11.   "   B
12.   "   C
13. Yugoslav. A
14.   "   B
15. Italian A
16.   "   B
17.   "   C
18.   "   D
19. German A
20.   "   B
21. Swedish A
22.   "   B
23.   "   D
24. Jewish A
25.   "   B
26.   "   D
27. Negro A
28.   "   B
29.   "   C
30.   "   D

— Devon
— Lawrence
— Belmont
— North
— Madison
— 22nd
— 39th
— 55th
— 71st
— 87th
— 103rd
— 119th

Cicero
Kedzie
Ashland
State
Stony Island

TABLE A:5 Characteristics of Ethnic Areas Studied (See Map A:1)

Group and area	Census tracts or community areas included (1930 Census)	Total pop. of area	Group % of total pop. (1st & 2nd gen.)*	Other ethnic groups present if 10% or more of total pop.
Czechoslovak A	Tracts 478, 490, 491	16,441	68 (28)	None
Czechoslovak B	Tracts 496, 497, 499	15,488	55 (25)	Yugoslav – 20%
Czechoslovak E	Tracts 821, 823	10,795	44 (17)	Polish – 16%
Polish A	Tracts 293, 294, 311, 312, 313, 314, 315	44,804	78 (30)	None
Polish X	Tract 248	6,238	77 (27)	None
Polish B	Tract 799	6,287	73 (27)	None
Polish C	Tracts 734, 736	1,264	59 (23)	None
Polish E	Tracts 213, 218	10,356	60 (20)	None
Polish F	Tract 718	7,118	55 (20)	None
Lithuanian A	Tract 773	2,869	48 (26)	None
Lithuanian C	Tract 501	5,865	41 (22)	None
Yugoslavian A	Tract 710	483	36 (20)	None
Yugoslavian B	Tract 703	3,641	46 (18)	None

Italian A	Tracts 409, 421, 428, 429, 430, 435, 436	20,898	70 (29)	None
Italian B	Tracts 392, 393, 394, 396, 397	10,928	68 (27)	None
Italian C	Tract 318	5,329	56 (26)	Polish - 23%
Italian D	Tract 133	2,957	63 (25)	Negro - 21%
German A	Tracts 56, 57, 62, 63, 64, 65	13,234	42 (18)	None
German B	Tracts 115, 116	12,798	33 (18)	None
Swedish A	Tracts 84, 85	8,680	51 (30)	German - 10%
Swedish B	Tracts 30, 31	10,295	31 (18)	German - 14%
Swedish D	Tract 889	8,097	26 (16)	Irish - 11%
Jewish A	Tracts 446, 447, 450, 451, 452, 453, 461, 463	57,908	57† —	Polish - 13%
Jewish B	Tracts 285, 286	9,023	27† —	Polish - 26%
Jewish C	Tract 165	7,204	38† —	None
Negro A	Areas 35, 38§	117,913	87 —	None
Negro B	Tract 934	1,897	92 —	None
Negro C	Tracts 385, 386	1,261	92 —	None
Negro D	Tract 625	8,689	81 —	None

TABLE A:5 (continued):

Group and area	Census tracts or community areas included (1930 Census)	Total pop. of area	Group % of total pop. (1st & 2nd gen.)*	Other ethnic groups present if 10% or more of total pop.
Native-American A	Areas 1 & 3 minus Tracts 30, 31, 32, 33	162,184	48 —	German - 11%
Native-American B	Areas 71, 72, 73, 74, 75	105,096	42 —	Jewish - 12% German - 12%

*The figure in parentheses is the foreign born percentage. Thus Czechoslovak A is 28 percent Czech foreign-born and 40 percent native-born with one or both parents born in Czechoslovakia.

†Jewish percentage of total was much higher, especially for A and B. The number of Russians only was used for Jewish population, while most of the Poles and others here were also Jewish. A was probably 90 percent Jewish, and B 70-80 percent Jewish.

§This area includes Wards 2 and 3, which encompassed more than Community Areas 35 and 38. Most of the data used were taken on a ward basis rather than a community area basis, since this information was more readily available. Community Areas 35 and 38 are good percentage indicators for information about these two wards.

to find at least one precinct or group of precincts for each of the areas for the entire period.

Thus we have geographic areas of ethnic concentration throughout the city—areas which remained ethnically the same from 1918 to 1932. And we have political units—precincts, groups of precincts, or wards—within each of these geographic areas, whose boundaries likewise remained constant. The voting behavior of the political unit provides a quantitative measure of the political behavior of the members of the group in that area. This is by no means random sampling; it is a particular kind of sampling procedure dictated both by the questions I wanted to answer and by the data available. The conclusions are more meaningful with more precincts for each area and more areas for each ethnic group. Since we have in effect sampled the voting behavior of almost every ethnic area in the city, we are in a reasonably good position to generalize about the voting of each group and of the ethnics as a whole. And with this ethnic *voting* tool, the greater question of ethnic *political* behavior can be more confidently approached.

It should be remembered that these demographic data come from the census, on census-created units rather than political ones. Therefore all this data is for the ethnic area in its entirety, rather than for the political units which were taken from within the ethnic area. That is, it is impossible to determine, for example, the percentage of Italians, or the percentage of homeowners in any given precinct. But this determination can be made for the larger ethnic area in which the precinct is found. Since I chose the ethnic areas on the basis of homogeneity, this is not really a problem; we can reasonably infer conclusions about the political unit from data on the larger ethnic area in which it was found.

The following series of summary tables gives much of the basic ethnic and socioeconomic data used in this study for the period 1918–1932. Table A:5 summarizes characteristics of the ethnic areas described above and pictured in Map A:1. This includes, first of all, the numbers of the Census Tracts and/or Community Areas which comprise the ethnic area, based on the census of 1930. Also included are the total population of the area, its ethnicity (i.e., the percentage of its total population which is first or second generation of the ethnic group involved), and other ethnic groups present in the area if they comprise 10 percent or more of its total population.

TABLE A:6 *Measures of Socioeconomic Status for Ethnic Areas Considered in Table A:5*

Group and area	Region of city (Map A:2)	% area homes owned	Rental group	% in white-collar industries	% families with radio	Socioeconomic class*
Czechoslovak A	III	47	I to II	15	59	Lower-Middle
Czechoslovak B	II	19	I	18	34	Upper-Lower
Czechoslovak E	IV	61	II to III	18	61	Middle-Middle
Polish A	I	19	I	15	32	Lower-Lower
Polish X	II	28	I	14	42	Upper-Lower
Polish B	IV	35	I	12	35	Upper-Lower
Polish C	III	70	II to III	8	34	Lower-Middle
Polish E	IV	47	II to III	15	55	Middle-Middle
Polish F	IA	48	I	10	46	Upper-Lower
Lithuanian A	III	31	I	22	56	Lower-Middle
Lithuanian C	II	24	I	20	34	Upper-Lower
Yugoslavian A	IA	55	I	8	73	Upper-Lower
Yugoslavian B	IA	51	I	13	42	Upper-Lower
Italian A	I	19	I	15	27	Lower-Lower
Italian B	II	30	I to III	15	34	Upper-Lower
Italian C	I	10	I	15	29	Lower-Lower

Italian D	I	14	I	13	23	Lower-Lower
German A	III	35	I to III	23	67	Middle-Middle
German B	II	20	I	20	49	Lower-Middle
Swedish A	III	16	II to III	18	57	Lower-Middle
Swedish B	IV	24	IV	31	76	Middle-Middle
Swedish D	IV	38	III	26	74	Middle-Middle
Jewish A	III	22	III to IV	40	58	Lower-Middle
Jewish B	II	22	III	32	57	Lower-Middle
Jewish C	IV	30	IV	44	72	Middle-Middle
Negro A[†]						
Ward 2	II	10	I to II	15	30	Lower-Lower
Ward 3	III	9	I to IV	12	46	Upper-Lower
Negro B	IV	70	I	12	53	Upper-Lower
Negro C	II	8	I	9	20	Lower-Lower
Negro D	IV	26	III	18	65	Lower-Middle
Native-American A	IV	13	V	42	75	Upper-Middle
Native-American B	IV	57	III to V	29	80	Middle-Middle

*Based on all preceding measures.
†Subdivided to show differences between the two wards in this ethnic area.

Table A:6 provides further information on the same areas and explains how they were tagged with socioeconomic classifications. The following measures were employed:

1) Region of the city: This followed one standard practice of determining social class in part from the proximity of one's place of residence to the center of the city—with greater proximity correlating with lower class position. Map A:2 shows the regional divisions created, from Region I at the city core, proceeding outward to Regions II, III, and IV. Standardized progressions, census information, and my own knowledge of the city were used here—thus a far-south side steel mill area was tagged Region IA, rather than Region IV, because in all important respects it was similar to the center of the city.

2) Percentage of area homes owned by their occupants: from census data.

3) Median rental group: based on the median rent paid by renters in the area; from census data. Where there was variation in median rental among Census Tracts in the same ethnic area, the general range is given. (I = $14–33;   II = $33–45;   III = $45–58;   IV = $58–67; V = $67–172.)

4) Percent of area population in white-collar industries: The 1930 Census did not list occupations, but rather the industry in which one was employed. Thus a bank president and a bank janitor were both listed under "banking." I therefore isolated four categories wherein the great majority of members would be white collar and middle class in employment (banking and brokerage; insurance and real estate; wholesale and retail trade, except automobiles; other professional and semi-professional service). Obviously this is not an ideal measure, but it was decided that it could safely be used in conjunction with the other measures in our socioeconomic index.

5) Percentage of families in the area owning a radio: from census data. This is a good indicator not only of economic position but also of social attitude. The purchase of a radio by an immigrant was in some respects a sign of a desire to achieve acculturation.

These five measures were the basic determinants of the socioeconomic class into which each ethnic area—and so the political units within them —was placed. But other criteria, both objective and subjective, were also used, for example the relative proportion of first- to second-generation

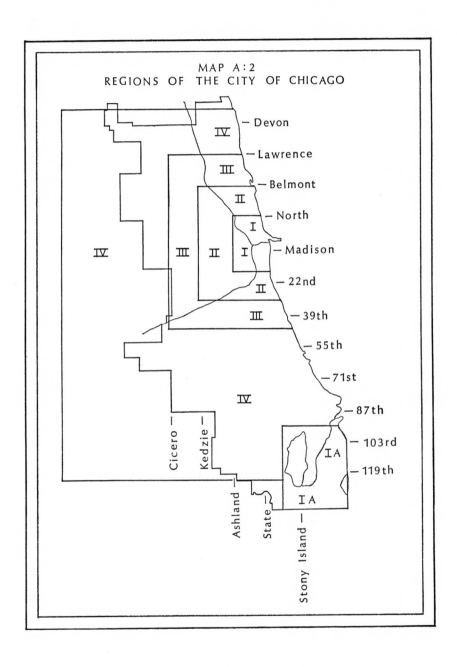

MAP A:2
REGIONS OF THE CITY OF CHICAGO

TABLE A:7   Ethnic Area Location and Ward and Precinct Numbers of Political Units Studied

Ethnic area of which unit a part	Ward (W) and precinct (P) number of the political unit				
	1918-1921	1921-1926	1926-June 1928	July 1928-1931	1932
Czechoslovak A	W12-P2	W22-P2	W22-P2	W22-P2	W22-P41
Czechoslovak A	W12-P1	W22-P1	W22-P1	W22-P1	W22-P40
Czechoslovak A	W34-P71	W23-P35	W23-P35	W23-P35	W23-P38
Czechoslovak B	W10-P24	W26-P24	W26-P24	W26-P34	W21-P38
Czechoslovak B	W10-P25	W26-P25	W26-P25	W26-P35	W21-P39
Czechoslovak E	—	W15-P17	W15-P18	W15-P18	W15-P15
Polish A	W17-Ps13,14	W31-P18	W31-P6	W31-P6	W26-P23
Polish A	W17-P4	W31-P4	W31-Ps4,5	W31-Ps4,5	W26-Ps21,22
Polish X	W16-P1	W33-P1	W33-P1	W33-P1	W33-P51
Polish B	W30-P20	W14-P16	W14-P16	W14-P16	W14-P22
Polish C	W5-P29 & W29-P12	W12-Ps32,34	W12-P42	W12-Ps58,61*	W13-Ps1,2,3
Polish E	—	—	W39-P23	W39-Ps23,28, 84,86,103†	W35-Ps39,40,41, 42 & W38-Ps52, 53,54,55
Polish F	W8-P55	W10-P25	W10-P31	W10-Ps31,33	W10-Ps41,44

Lithuanian A	W4-P20	W11-P16	W11-P16	W11-P18	W11-P38
Lithuanian A	W4-P27	W11-P19	W11-P19	W11-P33	W11-P19
Lithuanian C	W20-P17	W20-P17	W20-P17	W20-P17	W21-P47
Lithuanian C	W20-P18	W20-P15	W20-P15	W20-P15	W21-P46
Yugoslavian A	W8-52	W10-P22	W10-P30	W10-P30	W10-P39
Yugoslavian B	W8-P39	W10-P7	W10-P11	W10-P11	W10-P30
Yugoslavian B	W8-Ps40,37	W10-P6	W10-P8	W10-P8	W10-P28
Italian A	W10-P8	W26-P10	W26-P10	W26-P12	W20-P8
Italian A	W19-Ps22,23	W26-Ps4,5	W26-Ps4,5	W26-Ps5,6	W20-Ps2,3
Italian B	W11-P3	W25-P30	W25-P30	W25-P30	W25-P26
Italian B	W13-P6	W25-P15	W25-P15	W25-P15	W25-P24
Italian C	W17-P14	W31-P10	W31-P10	W31-P26	W26-P43
Italian D	W22-P31	W42-P20	W42-Ps20,37	W42-Ps20,37	W42-Ps38,39
German A	W24-P13	W45-P11	W45-P11	W45-P11	W45-P37
German A	W24-P17	W45-P15	W45-P15	W45-P15	W45-P42
German B	W22-P13	W43-P12	W43-P12	W43-P12	W43-P16
German B	W22-P10	W43-P9	W43-P9	W43-P9	W43-P11
Swedish A	W23-P7	W46-P29	W46-P29	W46-P29	W46-P36

TABLE A:7 *(continued):*

Ethnic area of which unit a part	Ward (W) and precinct (P) number of the political unit				
	1918-1921	1921-1926	1926-June 1928	July 1928-1931	1932
Swedish A	W23-P15	W46-P33	W46-P33	W46-P33	W46-P39
Swedish B	W26-P70	W50-P12	W50-P12	W50-P32	W50-P42
Swedish D	W7-P68	W8-P25	W8-P25	W8-P25	W6-P34
Swedish D	W7-P71	W8-P24	W8-P24	W8-P24	W8-P3
Jewish A	W34-Ps9,10, 11,13,20, 21,22,23, 24,25	W24-Ps4,5, 14,15,16, 18,19,20	W24-Ps4,5, 14,15,16, 18,19,20, 30	W24-Ps4,5, 12,15,16,18, 19,20,36,37, 38,39	W24-Ps 3 thru 8 and 15 thru 28
Jewish B	W15-Ps13, 14,15	W35-Ps25, 26,27	W35-Ps25, 26,27	W35-Ps27,39 40	W31-Ps33,34,35
Jewish B	W15-Ps29, 30,31	W35-Ps37,38	W35-Ps37,38	W35-Ps37,38	W31-Ps29,32
Jewish C	———	W40-Ps8,9	W40-Ps8,9, 56	W40-Ps56,71, 72	W39-Ps10,12,13, 14
Negro A	Ward 2	Ward 2	Ward 2	Ward 2	Ward 2
Negro A	Ward 3	Ward 3	Ward 3	Ward 3	Ward 3
Negro B	W32-P106	W19-P46	W19-P52,59	W19-Ps52,59, 96	W19-Ps44,45,46

Negro C	W14-P51	W28-P28	W28-P28	W28-P32	W28-P38
Negro D	W7-P53	W6-P56	W6-P56	W6-Ps56,57	W6-Ps21,22
Native-American A	Ward 25	Ward 49	Ward 49	Ward 49	Ward 49
Native-American B	Ward 32	Ward 19	Ward 19	Ward 19	Ward 19

*For 1930 and 1931 elections, P62 of W12 should also be added.
†For 1930 and 1931 elections, Ps110 and 111 of W39 should also be added.

TABLE A:8 *Size of Samples Employed in the Study (First and second generation)*

Group	(1) Population in city	(2) Population in areas studied	(2÷1) Sample percentage of group city population
Czechoslovaks	122,089	24,882	20
Poles	401,316	56,075	14
Lithuanians	63,828	3,870	6
Yugoslavs	32,291	1,897	6
Italians	181,861	27,501	15
Germans	377,975	9,976	3
Swedes	141,913	9,951	7
Jews	325,000*	39,253†	12
Negroes	233,903	112,630	48
Native-Americans	945,403	122,697	13

Source: *Fifteenth Census*, 1930.
*Source: *Census of Religious Bodies*, 1926.
†The figures for Jews are not accurate because only Russians were counted; the actual Jewish sample was probably over 50,000, making the sample percentage at least 15 percent.

TABLE A:9   *Candidates in Chicago Elections, 1918-1936*

Year, office	Republican	Democrat
1918: Senator	M. McCormick	J.H. Lewis
Congressman*	R. Yates	W.E. Williams
Sheriff	C.W. Peters	A.J. Cermak
1919: Mayor	W.H. Thompson	R.M. Sweitzer
1920: President	W.G. Harding	J.M. Cox
Senator	W.B. McKinley	R.A. Waller
Governor	L. Small	J.H. Lewis
1922: State Treas.	O. Nelson	P. Bartzen
1923: Mayor	A.C. Lueder	W.E. Dever
1924: President†	C. Coolidge	J.W. Davis
Senator	C.S. Deneen	A.A. Sprague
Governor	L. Small	N.L. Jones
1926: Senator	F.L. Smith	G. Brennan
1927: Mayor	W.H. Thompson	W.E. Dever
1928: President	H. Hoover	A.E. Smith
Senator	O.F. Glenn	A.J. Cermak
Governor	L.L. Emmerson	F.E. Thompson
1930: Senator	R.H. McCormick	J.H. Lewis
Congressman§	R. Yates	W.A. Dieterich
	F.L. Smith	W. Nesbit
Pres.—Cook County Board	O.F. Reich	A.J. Cermak
1931: Mayor	W.H. Thompson	A.J. Cermak
1932: President	H. Hoover	F.D. Roosevelt
Senator	O.F. Glenn	W. Dieterich
Governor	L. Small	H. Horner
1934: State Treas.	W.J. Stratton	J. Stelle
1936: President	A. Landon	F.D. Roosevelt

*Congressman-at-Large, elected statewide.

†Minor party significant vote for president: Robert M. La Follette, Progressive party.

§Two Congressmen-at-Large elected.

ethnics in the area, whether it was an older or newer immigrant group, the general social position of the group in the city, and so on.

Table A:7 provides information, by political unit, for every political unit studied. The ethnic area in which it was located is first noted (thus allowing the reader to check back to Tables A:5 and A:6 for demographic data on the political unit), and then its ward and precinct number(s) at every point in time from 1918 to 1932.

Table A:8 gives the size of the samples used: the percentage which the ethnic areas studied comprised of the total membership of each ethnic group (first and second generation) in the city.

Data on the voting of each group for each election 1918–1936 can be found in Chapter 3 (especially Table III:3 and Chart III:3), and so are not repeated here.[4]

Table A:9 gives the names of the candidates in each of the elections studied for this period.

---

[4] Data on the voting of each individual political unit are not included here, since it would be extensive, while being of interest only to those scholars who wanted to reanalyze the data. Readers who have use for this data may feel free to correspond with me.

Bibliographical Essay

The basic quantitative materials for the study were data on ethnicity and residential and socioeconomic characteristics of the ethnic groups, and data on precinct voting patterns over time. For the former I relied on the Eleventh through Fifteenth censuses, 1890–1930, and the census of *Religious Bodies, 1926* (Washington, D.C., 1892–1932, 1930). Very valuable for Chicago are several compilations of census data prepared by social scientists at the University of Chicago, with 1920 and 1930 areas collated: Ernest W. Burgess and Charles Newcomb, eds., *Census Data of the City of Chicago, 1920* (Chicago, 1931) and *Census Data of the City of Chicago, 1930* (Chicago, 1933); and Charles Newcomb and R. O. Lang, eds., *Census Data of the City of Chicago, 1934* (Chicago, 1934).

Some voting returns, even at the precinct level, can be found in the *Chicago Daily News Almanac* (published annually from 1890 to 1937), but for my needs it was necessary also to employ the official returns of the Chicago Board of Election Commissioners, bound in large, heavy, dusty volumes. The same agency also had bound volumes of ward and precinct maps which I needed to follow changes over time in ward and precinct numbers and boundaries.

As important as the availability of the data itself were the means for utilizing them. While my methodology is explained in detail in the Appendix, I might mention here a couple of my major guides. Hubert M. Blalock, *Social Statistics* (New York, 1960) is a valuable text. Richard Jensen, "Methods of Statistical Association for Historical Research," Mimeo. (St. Louis, Mo., 1968) is very useful for the historian.

For the conceptual, rather than the manipulative framework, I learned much from a variety of social scientists. Robert K. Merton, *Social Theory and Social Structure*, rev. and enl. ed. (Glencoe, Ill., 1957) is a very important work. Lee Benson's article on "Voting Behavior" in *American History and the Social Sciences*, ed. Edward N. Saveth (New York, 1964) was also helpful, especially on reference group theory. Seymour M. Lipset's *Political Man: The Social Bases of Politics* (New York, 1963) is another seminal work, as are these basic voting studies: Paul F. Lazarsfeld, Bernard Berelson, and Helen Gaudet, *The People's Choice*, 2d. ed. (New York, 1948); Angus Campbell, Gerald Gurin, and Warren E. Miller, *The Voter Decides* (Evanston, Ill., 1954); and

Bernard Berelson, Paul F. Lazarsfeld, and William N. McPhee, *Voting: A Study of Opinion Formation in a Presidential Campaign* (Chicago, 1954). There are also a number of good articles in Eugene Burdick and A. J. Brodbeck, eds., *American Voting Behavior* (Glencoe, Ill., 1959), and in Heinz Eulau, Samuel J. Eldersveld, and Morris Janowitz, eds., *Political Behavior: A Reader in Theory and Research* (Glencoe, Ill., 1956), among other such collections. Samuel P. Hays, "History as Human Behavior," *Iowa Journal of History* 58:3 (July 1960) makes clear the relationship of these and other social science concepts to the study of history. Elihu Katz and Paul F. Lazarsfeld, *Personal Influence: The Part Played by People in the Flow of Mass Communications* (Glencoe, Ill., 1955) guided my analysis of this central problem in political decision-making. James A. Davis, "A Formal Interpretation of the Theory of Relative Deprivation," *Sociometry* 22:4 (Dec. 1959), is a good guide to this underused concept. And William L. Warner and Leo Srole, *The Social Systems of American Ethnic Groups* (New Haven, Conn., 1945) remains worthwhile.

I have also benefited from other studies of urban and ethnic voting. The seminal work is V. O. Key, Jr., "A Theory of Critical Elections," *Journal of Politics* 17:1 (Feb. 1955). Others that have followed are: Duncan MacRae, Jr., and J. A. Meldrum, "Critical Elections in Illinois, 1888–1958," *American Political Science Review* 54:3 (Sept. 1960); John L. Shover, "Was 1928 a Critical Election in California?" *Pacific Northwest Quarterly* 58 (Oct. 1967), which points to that state's atypicality; and Jerome M. Clubb and Howard W. Allen, "The Cities and the Election of 1928: Partisan Realignment?" *American Historical Review* 84:4 (April 1969), which adds little to this intriguing question. Two older studies retain value: Harold F. Gosnell and N. N. Gill, "An Analysis of the 1932 Presidential Vote in Chicago," *American Political Science Review* 29:6 (Dec. 1935); and William F. Ogburn and Nell S. Talbot, "A Measurement of the Factors in the Presidential Election of 1928," *Social Forces* 8:2 (Dec. 1929). A more recent study, Ruth C. Silva, *Rum, Religion and Votes: 1928 Re-Examined* (University Park, Pa., 1962) comes up with answers incompatible to my own. And Bruce M. Stave, "The 'La Follette Revolution' and the Pittsburgh Vote, 1932," *Mid-America* 49:4 (Oct. 1967), sees effects from the La Follette candidacy in Pittsburgh that do not seem to have been present in Chicago.

I benefited only moderately from manuscript collections, since few urban political or ethnic leaders have left such materials behind. The William E. Dever papers at the Chicago Historical Society contain little beyond clippings, but the Carter H. Harrison II papers at the Newberry library do offer some interesting insights into the politics of his time. The Adolph J. Sabath papers at the American Jewish Archives were somewhat helpful, but had little material relative to Chicago. The papers of John Fitzpatrick, Chicago union leader, in the Chicago Historical Society had little of ethnic interest. Unfortunately the papers of Negro political leader Arthur Mitchell were not available at the Chicago Historical Society when I was doing my research; they may be useful to future students.

The Emily Dean, Mary McDowell, and Agnes Nestor papers in the Chicago Historical Society are quite useful, since each of these individuals was involved in a variety of Chicago problems, not excluding work among the ethnics and in politics. Finally, the Charles E. Merriam papers in the University of Chicago are full of a variety of relevant materials left behind by this scholar. And interspersed and unclassified among the Merriam papers are some papers of Harold F. Gosnell, the first and one of the finest students of American ethnic politics.

Personal interviews played a very small part in my research. Most of the people who would have been helpful were dead, a number were more or less senile, and others simply refused to talk. I am grateful to Mrs. Oscar Durante, loyal wife of the late publisher of *L'Italia,* for her information on the ethnic press; and to Victor Arrigo, Virgil P. Puzzo, and George J. Spatuzza for conversations on the Italians in Chicago. The late Dr. Louis L. Mann offered some interesting comments on the politics of the 1920s, and especially the place of Chicago's Reform Jews therein.

Along with the quantifiable data, my most important source of information was the press, both metropolitan and ethnic. The latter is a real mine of information on American history which has been sadly underused. I carefully read the Chicago *Tribune* for the whole period, which gave good political coverage. I also used the Chicago *Herald and Examiner* and Chicago *Daily News.*

For the ethnic press, the German-language *Abendpost/Sonntagpost* was very useful, as were *L'Italia* and *La Tribuna Italiana Trans-Atlantica* for the Italians. Less useful for the latter were the smaller *La Parola del Popolo* and *Avanti*. For the Poles, I was able to use two of their three leading newspapers: *Dziennik Zwiazkowy* and *Dziennik Chicagoski;* the third, unfortunately, was unavailable. For the Jews, their great national newspaper, *Yiddisher Vorwarts* (*Jewish Forward*) was useful, but limited by its still-doctrinaire socialism. I got considerably more from its local Chicago competitor, *Teglicher Yiddisher Kuryer* (*Daily Jewish Courier*).

For the Swedes I relied primarily on the *Svenska-Tribunen-Nyheter,* and for the Danes on *Danske Tidende. Hellenikos Aster* (*Greek Star*) was a good source concerning the Greeks. I regret that I was incapable of reading any of the Czech papers. For the Negroes, in Chicago and anywhere, the *Defender* is very valuable. The *Broad-Ax* was also informative, until it went out of business in the late 1920s.

The official publication of the Foreign Language Information Service, originally titled *The Interpreter* and later *The Bulletin,* had several useful articles and statistics. And I mined a good deal of information, especially for those groups whose languages I could not read, from: Works Projects Administration, *Chicago Foreign Language Press Survey* (Chicago, 1942). This is a collection of over 70 reels of microfilm of translations from Chicago foreign language newspapers from the 1880s to the 1930s. While it is not as complete as one would like, especially on politics, it is a well-organized sampling of writings on many subjects from the ethnic press during this long period. In this context I might also mention some studies of the foreign language press, the most important still being the first: Robert E. Park, *The Immigrant Press and Its Control* (New York, 1922). Also useful were: Mordecai Soltes, *The Yiddish Press: An Americanizing Agency* (New York, 1924); Carl Wittke, *The German-Language Press in America* (Lexington, Ky., 1957); and Edmund G. Olszyk, *The Polish Press in America* (Milwaukee, Wis., 1940).

On the history of Chicago and its politics, Bessie L. Pierce, *A History of Chicago,* 3 vols. (New York, 1937–1957), is very good, but thus far ends in the 1890s. The work of early University of Chicago social scientists, especially Harold F. Gosnell and Charles E. Merriam, is very valuable. Gosnell, *Machine Politics: Chicago Model* (Chicago, 1937);

Grass Roots Politics (Washington, D.C., 1942); "The Chicago Black Belt as a Political Battleground," *American Journal of Sociology* 39 (Nov. 1933); Merriam, *Chicago: A More Intimate View of Urban Politics* (New York, 1929); "Recollections" (Manuscript autobiography, filed in Merriam papers, University of Chicago). Merriam and Gosnell, *Non-Voting: Causes and Methods of Control* (Chicago, 1924).

Equally valuable were a number of journalistic accounts, written by perceptive newspaper reporters who often knew the people and events about which they wrote: John Bright, *Hizzoner Big Bill Thompson* (New York, 1930); Lloyd Lewis and Henry J. Smith, *Chicago: The History of Its Reputation* (New York, 1929); William H. Stuart, *The Twenty Incredible Years* (Chicago, 1935), valuable for the author's apparent closeness to Mayor Thompson; and Lloyd Wendt and Herman Kogan, *Big Bill of Chicago* (Indianapolis, Ind., 1953), and *Lords of the Levee: The Story of Bathhouse John and Hinky Dink* (Indianapolis, Ind., 1943).

Among many biographies and autobiographies I used to advantage was Alex Gottfried, *Boss Cermak of Chicago: A Study of Political Leadership* (Seattle, Wash., 1962), which is best if one ignores its psychoanalytic appendix. The two volumes of autobiography by Carter H. Harrison II provide some useful insights into Chicago politics: *Stormy Years: The Autobiography of Carter H. Harrison, Five Times Mayor of Chicago* (Indianapolis, Ind., 1935) and *Growing Up with Chicago* (Chicago, 1944). Harold F. Gosnell, *Negro Politicians* (Chicago, 1935), has some good short biographies. Roi Ottley, *The Lonely Warrior: Life and Times of Robert S. Abbot* (Chicago, 1955), is good on the founder of the Chicago *Defender*. And Fred D. Pasley, *Al Capone: The Biography of a Self-Made Man* (New York, 1930), has some information on this important but elusive national figure. M. R. Werner, *Julius Rosenwald: The Life of a Practical Humanitarian* (New York, 1939), is a reasonably objective study of this interesting man.

A great deal has been written on ethnic groups, individually and collectively, much of it of doubtful value. But many of these books served me well. J. Joseph Huthmacher, *Massachusetts People and Politics, 1919–1933,* is good overall, but wants a more intensive look into the ethnic groups; as a state-level study it is valuable. Samuel Lubell, *The Future of American Politics* (Garden City, N.Y., 1952), remains a model combination of quantitative analysis and qualitative insight. Paul F. Cressey, "The Succession of Cultural Groups in the City of Chicago" (Ph.D. diss., University of Chicago, 1930), helped to reinforce my own conclusions about ethnic residential dispersion.

There are several good works on the Scandinavians: Reuel G. Hemdahl, "The Swedes in Illinois Politics: An Immigrant Group in an American Political Setting" (Ph.D. diss., Northwestern University, 1932), and Gustave E. Johnson, "The Swedes of Chicago" (Ph.D. diss., University of Chicago, 1940), are both informative. Adolph B. Benson and Naboth Hedin, *Americans from Sweden* (Philadelphia, 1950); Adolph B. Benson, ed., *Swedes in America* (New Haven, Conn., 1938); and Birger Osland, *A Long Pull from Stavanger* (Northfield, Minn., 1945), are all useful.

For the Poles, the classic work remains William I. Thomas and Florian Znaniecki, *The Polish Peasant in Europe and America,* 2d ed., 2 vols. (New York, 1927). And for the Czechs there is considerable useful information in Gottfried, *Boss Cermak,* mentioned above. For the Germans I profited from Andrew J. Townsend, *The Germans of Chicago* (Chicago, 1927). Among the vast literature on the Jews in America, I might single out here Lawrence J. Fuchs, *The Political Behavior of American Jews* (Glencoe, Ill., 1956), which is very well done. I also used the Louis Wirth classic, *The Ghetto* (Chicago, 1928), and Philip P. Bregstone, *Chicago and Its Jews* (Chicago, 1933).

Much has been written on the Italians, little of it very good. Virgil P. Puzzo, "The Italians in Chicago, 1890–1930" (M.A. thesis, University of Chicago, 1937), was helpful, and Herbert J. Gans, *The Urban Villagers: Group and Class in the Life of Italian-Americans* (New York, 1962), is quite good, although I disagree with the extent of his emphasis on class.

Literature on the Negro in America is happily growing rapidly. I benefited from the works of Harold F. Gosnell cited above, as well as his "How Negroes Vote in Chicago," *National Municipal Review* 22 (1933). St. Clair Drake and Horace R. Cayton, *Black Metropolis* (New York, 1945), remains outstanding.

These are but some of the many sources to which I am indebted. For more comprehensiveness I refer readers to the footnotes.

Index